THE USE OF MICROCOMPUTERS IN ACCOUNTING

Sam A. Hicks
and Donald V. Saftner

Department of Accounting
Virginia Polytechnic Institute
and State University

WEST PUBLISHING COMPANY
ST. PAUL • NEW YORK • LOS ANGELES • SAN FRANCISCO

COPYRIGHT (c) 1985 By WEST PUBLISHING COMPANY
                    50 West Kellogg Boulevard
                    P.O. Box 64526
                    St. Paul, MN   55164-1003

Printed in the United States of America

Library of Congress Cataloging in Publication Data

Hicks, Sam A.
   Microcomputers in Accounting

   1. Accounting--Data processing. 2. Microcomputers--
Programming. I. Saftner, Donald V. II. Title.
HF5679.H535 1985   657'.028'54   85-8950
ISBN 0-314-87064-4
1st Reprint—1985

DEDICATION

This book is dedicated to . . .

. . . my wife Ruthann Hicks

. . . my parents Victor and Thelma Saftner

PREFACE

The purpose of this text is to introduce accountants to microcomputers. The major types of software covered are spreadsheets (Lotus 1-2-3 and SuperCalc3), database management (dBase), and word processing (Wordstar). It is written with an orientation toward the problems that the typical accounting graduate encounters early in his career. It is written by accountants for accountants.

The student is encouraged to experiment with the software to become comfortable and competent in its use. Due to the interactive nature of this book, it is assumed that the software is available to the student. A practice diskette, which may be copied by each student purchasing the book, is supplied to the teacher. This diskette contains data files and partial solutions to problems. These reduce the time spent in noninstructive, laborious data entry. Humor has been added to the presentation in order to make studying an even more enjoyable experience.

The IBM PC is explicitly covered because it has gained a widespread acceptance in both the business and academic communities. The text has a software emphasis, however, and can easily be used with any computer that supports the popular software packages considered herein.

The text is divided into four parts. The first part introduces the student to important computer concepts involving hardware and software. This part is required reading for the computer novice and should at least be skimmed by the experienced user because it provides the background necessary to understand the subsequent parts. Parts two, three and four are independent modules. They may be covered in any order and any one part may be considered optional.

The second part of the text covers the electronic spreadsheets Lotus 1-2-3 and SuperCalc3. Electronic spreadsheets made the microcomputer, which was originally a hobbyest's toy, an important tool of the business world. Familiarity with electronic spreadsheets is rapidly becoming a prerequisite to entrance into the managerial ranks of business and has already become required knowledge for today's accountant. This part of the text begins with chapter 3, which introduces the basic concepts of electronic spreadsheets. It is followed by three chapters on Lotus 1-2-3 (chapters 4, 5, and 6) and three chapters on

SuperCalc3 (chapters 7, 8, and 9). This part of the text was written with the assumption that either Lotus 1-2-3 or SuperCalc3 would be covered. Upon completing either set of chapters, the problems in chapter 10 allow the student to gain additional hands on experience.

Part three covers dBase, the best selling database management package. dBase II and III are covered simultaneously. Coverage of both chapters 11 and 12 is required to understand the fundamentals of dBase. Chapter 13, dBase Programming, unlocks the full potential of dBase but could be considered optional for the occasional user. Part four provides an introduction to the word processing package Wordstar.

We, the authors, express our appreciation to our fellow teachers and to the hundreds of students who have used preliminary versions of these materials. The students include practicing professionals who have taken continuing education courses and resident undergraduate and graduate students. Their reactions have been a valuable input. We especially thank Professors Jack Maher, Cherie O'Neil, and Fred Richardson for their critiques of drafts of the manuscript. We also thank Professor G.K. Nelson who collected the humorous names of part three from his students. Our graduate assistants and the secretarial staff, particularly Kihyun Do, Phyllis Neece, Tane McPeak, and Barbara Mitchell, have been very helpful and their efforts are much appreciated. Last, but certainly not least, we express our appreciation for the support we received from our families while we completed this text.

Comments and suggestions are solicited from our readers. Those comments and suggestions that deal with the entire book should be addressed to either or both authors c/o Department of Accounting, Virginia Tech, Blacksburg, Virginia 24061. Those that are specific to parts one or three should be sent to Dr. Don Saftner and those that are specific to parts two or four should be sent to Dr. Sam Hicks.

The following trademarks are used in this text:

IBM PC and PC/XT:
    International Business Machines Corporation
    (see the yellow pages of your phone book)

Lotus 1-2-3:
    Lotus Development Corporation
    161 First Street
    Cambridge, MA 02142

SuperCalc3:
    Sorcim
    2310 Lundy Avenue
    San Jose, CA 95131

dBase:
    Ashton-Tate
    10150 West Jefferson Blvd.
    Culver City, CA 90230

Wordstar:
    MicroPro International
    1299 4th Street
    San Rafael, CA 94901

Some of these firms offer discounts to educational users. Contact them to determine their current policy.

CONTENTS

PART I: INTRODUCTION TO COMPUTER CONCEPTS

COMPUTER HARDWARE

CHAPTER 1

INTRODUCTION

"If the aircraft industry had evolved as spectacularly as the computer industry over the past 25 years, a Boeing 767 would cost $500 today, and it would circle the globe in 20 minutes on five gallons of fuel".[1] This is an indication of the remarkable progress that has been made in the computer industry. These trends are likely to continue for the foreseeable future.

BENEFITS OF COMPUTER USAGE

The reduced cost and improved performance of computers has allowed a fundamental shift in emphasis within the computer industry. No longer must the human speak to the computer in its language. There is a definite trend toward a more natural human-computer interface. The computer is now cheap enough and powerful enough to make truly user friendly programs possible.

----

[1] Toong, Hoo-min D. and Amar Gupta, Scientific American (Dec. 1982) pp. 87-107.

These changes are drastically affecting the lives of those who manipulate information (i.e. knowledge workers.) Their effect on the accountant represents a good example of this. Not many years ago it was quite possible for an auditor to complete his career without ever encountering a computer. Today that same auditor is likely to see computers being used by even his smallest clients. Not only must he audit computerized systems, the auditor must also use the computer himself to remain competitive. The computer can assist in many areas including analytical review, confirmations, and statistical sampling.

The management accountant is also finding the computer to be an indispensable tool in evaluating accounting information. By using database packages, it is possible to extract just the information needed from vast bodies of data. Using spreadsheet packages, it is possible to analyze the extracted information and acquire answers to "what-if" type questions. This permits the accountant to explore the consequences of alternative decisions.

COSTS OF COMPUTER USAGE

These advances do not come without a price however. It is easy to be mesmerized by the computer. Some people think that if the computer generates a report, then the report is accurate without a doubt. Actually the computer's output is only as good as its input. This idea is captured quite well by the expression "garbage in, garbage out" (GIGO). Computerized information systems must be designed to screen out bad input. Extensive testing should be done to assure that no errors are introduced during processing.

To obtain the maximum benefit from the computer, you must make an investment of time as well as money. Although the computer is becoming easier to work with, it is still necessary to spend time learning to use a computer system. A combination of formal education and "playing" with the system leads to a comfortable working knowledge of the computer.

MICROCOMPUTER EMPHASIS

The previous discussion dealt with computers in a generic sense. In fact, whether you are working with a large mainframe or a personal computer on a desktop, many of the concepts remain the same. This book concentrates on the personal computer. The small size of the personal computer makes it less mysterious and frightening and therefore easier to approach for the first time. The one-to-one nature of the communication also helps in this aspect. Because you may very well be the owner, operator, programmer, and user of the computer, it is easier to see the total picture. Later as you specialize, you will hopefully retain an appreciation for the problems faced by the other computer specialists.

Although the IBM PC is featured in the rest of this book, most of what is said is equally applicable to those machines that are compatible with the IBM PC. Because this chapter deals with computer hardware (i.e. the tangible computer equipment) the information is specific to the IBM PC. The chapters that deal with the software are not specific to one type of hardware. If the particular piece of software runs on a non-IBM compatible machine, it will usually run in the manner described herein. Lotus 1-2-3, for instance, operates in much the same way on all personal computers.

HARDWARE CATEGORIES

Hardware may be divided into four categories: processor, input, output, and storage (See Figure 1-1). The processor performs the arithmetic and control functions normally associated with a computer. The input devices are responsible for the initial receipt of data from the user and the output devices are responsible for the presentation of processed data in an understandable format. Storage represents the memory of the computer, and serves to hold intermediate results.

Figure 1-2 shows a typical configuration of the IBM PC. Some devices, such as the keyboard, fit into one category alone (i.e. input). Other devices, such as the disk drive, can be used for both input or output, thus allowing them to be used as storage areas for intermediate results. In the following discussion a device such as a diskette drive is classified as a storage device although it should be recognized that it can also be used for input and output.

FIGURE 1-1   SCHEMATIC OF COMPUTER SYSTEM

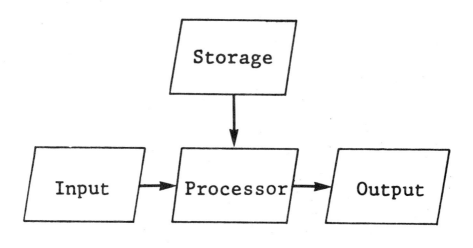

FIGURE 1-2   IBM PC

SYSTEM UNIT

Figure 1-3 shows the IBM PC system unit. The system unit contains the processor and some, but not necessarily all, of the storage of the computer. The most prominent features of the system unit are the diskette drives on the front. These and the other storage components are discussed in the next section.

FIGURE 1-3   IBM PC SYSTEM UNIT

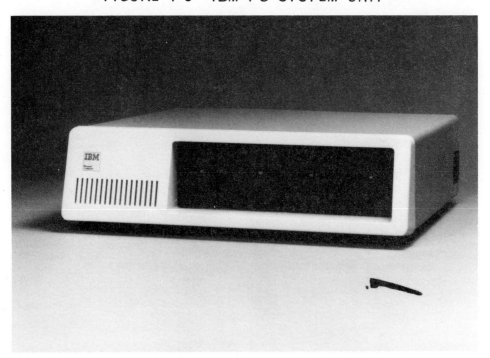

The processor is the computer's equivalent of a brain. It is here that arithmetic functions such as addition and multiplication are performed. The processor is also responsible for logical decision making and coordination of the activities of the other components of the computer system. Evidence of this latter function may be obtained by examining the back of the housing (see Figure 1-4). Various peripheral devices are connected to the system by plugging them into the back of the system unit. The back of your machine may appear slightly different than Figure 1-4, depending upon which options have been selected. The connectors are shaped in such a manner that they can only be plugged into the machine in one way (see Figure 1-5), eliminating the possibility of potentially costly misconnections.

FIGURE 1-4   BACK OF SYSTEM UNIT

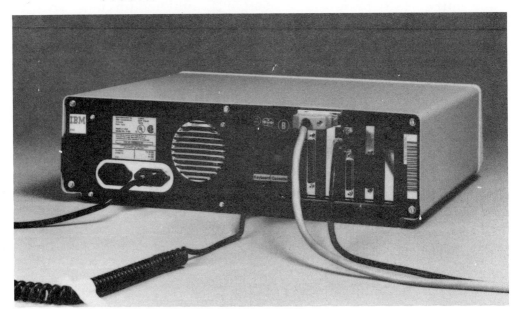

FIGURE 1-5   PLUG CONNECTOR

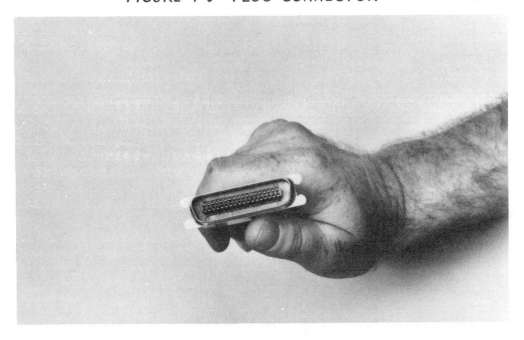

EXPANSION MODULES

Figure 1-6 shows the inside of the IBM PC. Along the back left side (as viewed from the front) are various circuit boards, labeled expansion modules. Typically these expansion modules have a plug at one end that extends back through the computer housing. These plugs are the same ones that are visible when looking at the back of the machine. As noted above, these expansion modules are often used as interfaces between the computer and the various devices attached to it. They allow the computer to communicate with the devices. When buying a printer, modem or similar device be sure to purchase the appropriate expansion module if it is not already present in your machine. Simple hand tools are all that are required to install the circuit boards.

FIGURE 1-6   SYSTEM UNIT WITH COVER REMOVED

Expansion modules may also be used to enhance the inner workings of the PC. For instance, an expansion module may be purchased that allows adding additional memory chips (see discussion that follows for a discussion of memory chips). These chips increase the storage capacity of the machine allowing larger programs and data files to be held. The IBM PC has a limit of five expansion slots. You must be selective in picking which circuit boards you buy due to the

7

limit. One of the main advantages of using an IBM PC is that a large number of third party (i.e. non-IBM) vendors sell expansion boards compatible with the IBM PC.

MICROPROCESSOR

The microprocessor is just to the right of the expansion modules (see Figure 1-6). The microprocessor is responsible for arithmetic operations, logical comparisons, and control of the other components of the computer. It is called a chip because a small piece (i.e. chip) of silicon has the various circuits inscribed on its surface.

STORAGE

RANDOM ACCESS MEMORY

Random access memory (RAM) is located in the front left corner of the system unit (see Figure 1-6). Programs and data are stored on these RAM chips. Unfortunately, RAM is a volatile form of storage. When the power is turned off the information stored in RAM is lost. RAM does have the advantage, however, that when the power is on it is possible to both read and write information to it at high speed.

READ ONLY MEMORY

Read Only Memory (ROM), as the name implies, may be read from but not written to. It does have the advantage, however, that it is nonvolatile. Because it does not lose the information stored on it when the power is turned off, it is used to store programs and data needed when the machine is first turned on. Realize that after the power has been turned off, RAM contains no programs. The computer cannot function without a program in it to tell it what to do. Therefore, a program in ROM is necessary when the machine is first turned on to direct its activities until programs from a disk or other storage device can be loaded into RAM. Another use for ROM is to store frequently used programs. These programs can be loaded into the computer at the time of manufacture and left there without any fear that they will be overwritten because they are in Read Only Memory.

RAM and ROM together form a part of the computer's memory known as primary storage. Primary storage may be accessed at electronic speeds. Secondary storage must be accessed through physical motion. Examples of secondary storage include diskettes and cassettes. Since physical movement is slow in comparison to the flow of electricity in a circuit, secondary storage has much slower access speeds than primary storage. In general, however, secondary storage is cheaper per byte than primary storage so secondary storage is typically much larger than primary storage.

MEMORY VOCABULARY

When working with computers, the term "K" (e.g. 256K or 512K) describes the memory capacity of a machine. To fully understand this term, you must understand how data is stored in the computer. The most elementary piece of data in the computer is the bit. A bit can take on only one of two possible values: 0 or 1. A bit by itself is not very useful. When several bits are linked together, however, more useful pieces of data may be stored. If two bits are placed together, it is possible to store one of four different combinations (i.e. 00, 01, 10, 11). With three bits, there are eight combinations (i.e. 000, 001, 010, 011, 100, 101, 110, 111). In general there are two-to-the-nth power combinations possible where n is the number of bits.

A byte typically consists of eight bits. A little bit of arithmetic shows that it is possible to store one of 256 (i.e. $2^8 = 256$) different possible combinations in such a byte. Each combination could represent a different letter (either upper or lower case), digit, or special character such as a period, comma, quote, etc. For example 11000001 might represent the letter A and 11000010 might represent the letter B.

The storage capacity of a machine may be measured in terms of bytes. A kilobyte or K consists of 1024 bytes. It is convenient to think of a K as approximately 1,000 bytes so a 512K computer would have a memory capacity of approximately 512,000 bytes. Larger computers may have their memory capacity measured in terms of megabytes (or M), where M = 1024K. One megabyte is equal to approximately one million bytes.

Stringing bits together to form a byte is the first step in a series known as the data hierarchy. The data hierarchy consists of bits, bytes, fields, records and files. Just as bits are linked together to form a byte, bytes may be placed together to form a field or item of data. Using a personnel system as an example, a data field is used to hold a name, address, phone number, age, or other characteristic of a person.

Related fields may be linked together to form a record. Continuing with the personnel example, a personnel record would consist of all the fields concerning a single individual. All related records may be placed together to form a file. A personnel file would consist of a collection of personnel records, one for each employee of an organization.

DISKETTES

A diskette (also known as a disk or floppy disk) is a circular piece of plastic with a magnetic coating contained in a stiff jacket. (see Figure 1-7).

FIGURE 1-7   DISKETTE

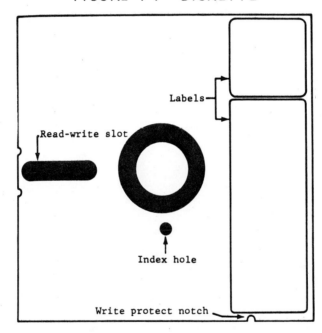

The hole in the middle of the diskette allows a drive mechanism to rotate the circular piece of plastic within its lubricated protective cover. The read-write slot is an elongated oval opening in the jacket. This slot allows the read-write heads of the disk drive to come into contact with the magnetic coating of the diskette. A photoelectric device senses the rotational position of the diskette by measuring the light that comes through the index hole. This allows the reading and writing of data to be synchronized with the rotation of the diskette.

The write-protect notch is an opening in the edge of the jacket. When it is open (as in Figure 1-7) writing on the diskette is possible. If a piece of tape supplied with the diskette is placed over this opening, then a device senses the presence of the tape and prohibits the writing of data on the diskette. This is a control mechanism used to protect important data from being overwritten. If you have written important data on a diskette, place one of the pieces of tape supplied with the diskette over the opening. When you again want to write on the diskette, the tape must be removed, but in the meantime the sensitive data has been protected from accidental erasure during operation.

DISKETTE DRIVE

A typical configuration of the IBM PC includes two diskette drives mounted in the front of the system unit (see Figure 1-8). Each of these has a latch that must be opened before inserting a diskette. Holding the diskette with the right thumb on the diskette label area assures that the diskette is inserted with the read-write slot forward and the label side up. Closing the latch engages the drive mechanism allowing the diskette to be rotated. A small red light comes on when the drive is reading or writing information on the diskette.

FIGURE 1-8   INSERTING DISKETTE INTO DRIVE

Diskettes can continue to operate properly after small amounts of mistreatment. To be on the safe side, however, the precautionary steps listed in Table 1-1 should be followed. Failure to follow those steps can result in the loss of data and perhaps even the destruction of the entire diskette.

TABLE 1-1 CARE AND HANDLING OF DISKETTES

<u>Do</u>

- Make frequent backups
- Store diskette in paper envelope
- Store diskettes in vertical position
- Use felt tip pen to write on labels
- Keep in envelope when not in use
- Gently insert diskette into drive
- Cover write protect notch of diskettes that contain important information

<u>Don't</u>

- Touch read-write slot with fingers
- Attempt to clean diskette with alcohol or other solvents
- Use pencils, ball point pens, or erasers on labels
- Fold or bend diskettes
- Expose to temperature extremes
- Expose to humidity extremes
- Expose to magnetic fields that may exist near transformers, motors, and other electrical equipment
- Use paper clips or rubber bands on diskettes

HARD DISK

The IBM PC/XT typically comes equipped with a single floppy disk drive and a single hard disk drive. It is also possible to add a hard disk drive to the regular IBM PC. The superficial appearance of the hard disk drive resembles a diskette drive without a diskette opening and latch. The hard disk can store many times more data than a diskette and also allows faster access to data. This permits relatively large data files to be processed quickly and efficiently. Frequently used programs can also be stored on the hard disk. This reduces the aggravation of inserting and removing diskettes.

The hard disk does have a number of disadvantages, however. It is expensive to purchase and to backup. Because the capacity of one hard disk is so great, it takes many diskettes to backup a single hard disk. This can be a long and tedious process. Alternatively, a relatively expensive tape or removable hard disk system may be acquired.

Because a hard disk is typically mounted permanently in the drive, a single drive has a large but finite amount of storage space available. Because diskettes are removable, a single diskette drive could theoretically have access to an infinite number of diskettes. Similarly a permanently mounted hard disk cannot be used to pass data to another machine. Finally, access to data on the hard disk can be hard to control. Anyone who has access to the machine has access to all the files on the hard disk. Coding the data so only those who know the decoding procedure can use the data is possible but is seldom done. Although the hard disk has some disadvantages, most people who have used a hard disk find it difficult to go back to using a microcomputer that does not have the speed and large capacity of a hard disk.

CASSETTE TAPE

Cassettes are an inexpensive form of storage. They are, however, a sequential storage media which means that in order to read the one thousandth record one must first read the 999 records that precede it in the file. Diskettes and hard disks are direct access storage devices (DASD's). This means that a record may be read directly without reading the records that precede it in the file. Because cassettes are sequential storage media, data access is very slow. Even writing data onto the tape is time consuming.

INPUT

The keyboard is the most common input device for a microcomputer. Other devices such as a mouse, light pen, and touch sensitive screen are used solely for input, but none of these rival the keyboard for a rich and varied range of input without typically requiring that a new skill be acquired.

MOUSE

A mouse is a small hand held box typically connected to the computer by a wire. When the mouse is moved on the desktop the cursor moves in a corresponding direction on the screen. The mouse typically comes equipped with one or more buttons or keys. These buttons permit more than just cursor movement, but in general the mouse is used in conjunction with a conventional keyboard.

LIGHT PEN AND TOUCH SENSITIVE SCREEN

The light pen and touch sensitive screen are typically used as a means to select options from a menu or list of options on a screen. In the case of a light pen, a small rod is held in the hand and moved around the screen. When using a touch sensitive screen, a simple touching of the screen with your finger is all that is necessary to pick an option.

KEYBOARD

Since the keyboard is so important, at least some typing skill is a prerequisite to fully productive use of a microcomputer. If you do not know how to type, it is advisable to take a class or use one of the many self training aids that are available.

The IBM PC has an 84 key keyboard (see Figures 1-9 and 1-10). The lighter colored keys in the middle of the keyboard are similar to a standard typewriter keyboard. There are some differences, however.

Return or enter key: The return or enter key is perhaps the most important key on the keyboard. It is a gray elongated key located on the right side of the keyboard and it has a left pointing bent arrow on it. This key is used to tell the computer that you are finished entering a command or line of input.

FIGURE 1-9 IBM PC KEYBOARD

FIGURE 1-10 LABELED IBM PC KEYBOARD

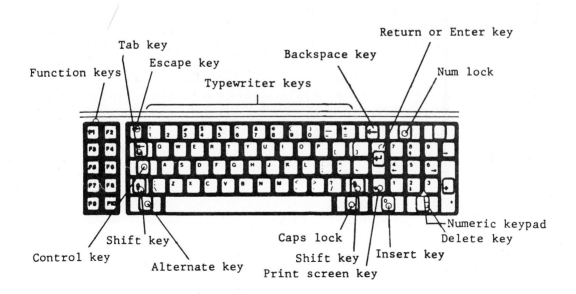

Shift keys: As on a typewriter keyboard, the IBM PC has two shift keys each designated with a hollow, upward pointing arrow. They are located on the left and right sides of the typewriter-like section of the keyboard. They are used in conjunction with the letter keys for upper case letters. Holding down the shift key while depressing a key with two symbols on it causes the upper symbol to be used.

Caps lock key: The caps lock key is located just to the right of space bar. When it is depressed once, all the letters on the keyboard are capitalized. The number keys across the top remain in their original "lower case" setting. Upper case letters are easier to read on the screen and for most computer work it is convenient to use only capital letters. For these reasons the caps lock key is very useful. Depressing the caps lock key again returns it to lower case mode.

Backspace key: The backspace key is just above the return key and has a left pointing straight arrow on it. Each time it is depressed the cursor is moved left one position and the character that was located in the final position of the cursor is erased.

Tab key: The tab key is the second key above the left shift key. It has two arrows on it, the upper one pointing to the left and the lower one pointing to the right. The tab key functions in a manner similar to a typewriter tab key, moving the cursor right to the next tab stop. If the shift key is depressed when using the tab key, the cursor moves to the left one tab stop.

Editing keys: On the far right side of the keyboard there are several keys that are useful in editing (i.e. modifying) text. The arrow keys (located on the numeric pad keys 2, 4, 6, and 8) move the cursor in the direction the arrow points. When the "Ins" or insert key is pressed once, the keyboard is placed into insert mode. While in insert mode, text may be inserted at the current cursor position. The preexisting character at that current cursor position and all text to the right is moved right one character position. Pressing the insert key again places the keyboard into overwrite mode in which characters may be overwritten with no movement of other characters.

The "Del" or delete key operates in a manner just the reverse of the insert key. Each time the delete key is depressed a character is removed from the current cursor position and all characters to the right are moved left one position.

Numeric pad: The numeric pad uses the same keys as the editing keys plus some additional keys. The numeric pad consists of the 0 through 9 keys, decimal point (same as delete key), plus sign, minus sign and Num Lock (i.e. numeric lock). The Num Lock key does for the numeric pad what the Caps Lock key does for the alphabetic portion of the keyboard. Depressing the Num Lock key once puts the upper symbol (usually a number) in effect. Depressing the Num Lock again puts the editing keys back in effect. Note that the numbers along the top of the keyboard may also be used for numeric input. They have an advantage over the numeric pad in that they do not require the use of the shift key or the Num Lock. It is possible to buy keyboards for the IBM PC that have separate keys for editing and numeric pads.

Function keys: On the far left side of the keyboard there are ten gray keys labeled F1 through F10. These are the function keys. Various software packages define the function keys differently. In general, each function key is used for a common command within the software package. Depressing a single function key is easier than keying in an entire command. This saves time and effort, and makes learning the use of the function keys worthwhile.

Escape key: The escape key is just to the right of the function keys and is labeled "Esc". It also is used in different ways by different software packages but in general it removes the computer from the current mode of operation and returns the computer to the previous mode. This essentially allows you to escape an unwanted condition.

Control and alternate keys: The control (Ctrl) and alternate (Alt) keys are located just to the right of the function keys. They are physically used in a manner similar to the shift key. The control or alternate key is first depressed and held down while another key is depressed. This allows each key on the keyboard to have several different possible meanings depending upon whether the control, alternate or shift key is also depressed at the same time. The meaning of a key with the shift key depressed is normally placed on the key itself whereas the meanings with the control or alternate key depressed must be memorized or looked up in a table. Although most of the combination keystrokes are defined uniquely by each software package, some combinations work with many packages and are discussed below.

Alt-Ctrl-Del (depress Alt and Ctrl and while holding them down depress Del) causes the system to start up as if the machine was just turned on. This is very useful if the system locks up and does not accept any other input. It is also useful if you become lost and wish to start over. This key combination does cause RAM to be erased, however, so you lose everything in RAM and must reload it.

The Ctrl-Num Lock key combination suspends the current operation of the computer until another key such as the space bar or return key is pressed. This is particularly useful when the computer is displaying information on the screen faster than it can be read.

The Ctrl-PrtSc (read "control - print screen") causes anything that is displayed on the screen to be simultaneously printed. This process of printing as it is displayed on the screen continues until the Ctrl-PrtSc is entered again. Note that pressing PrtSc while holding the shift key down causes just the current screen to be printed.

OUTPUT

MONITOR

The monitor, also known as the screen or CRT (short for cathode ray tube), is the most common microcomputer output device (see Figure 1-2). There are three basic types of screens for the IBM PC: monochrome, color graphics, and television.

The monochrome screen displays the clearest characters. They have good resolution, making them easy to read, and as a result they do not tire the eyes as quickly as the color graphics or television screen. The screen is able to display 80 characters across by 25 rows down. The monochrome display cannot display color graphics.

The color monitor is designed for color graphics. The color monitor does not produce characters with high resolution. This makes the color monitor less desirable than a monochrome monitor for the typical textual nature of much computer work. When a forceful presentation of summarized data is required, however, it is difficult to beat color graphics.

The television is one of the cheapest computer output devices available for a microcomputer. The TV monitor typically displays a screen with 40 characters across by 25 rows down. It also uses a lower resolution character display similar to the color monitor.

PRINTER

The monitor produces a transitory image on the screen. To obtain a more permanent "hard copy" of the computer's output on paper, a printer is used (see Figure 1-2). There are two basic types of printers typically associated with a microcomputer. A dot matrix printer prints a character as a matrix of dots similar to the way a monitor displays a character. Dot matrix printers are characterized by high speed. Letter quality printers are typically slower but produce a higher quality output. Instead of using a dot matrix to form a character, the characters are printed in their entirety. For instance, on a daisy wheel letter quality printer, a disk-like object made up of many metal fingers has the individual characters already formed at the ends of the fingers.

MODEM

Modem is a shortened form of modulator / demodulator. The function of the modem is to translate (modulate) the digital signal of the computer into the analog signal typically carried on a telephone line and to retranslate (demodulate) the analog signal back into a digital signal. A digital signal may be thought of as a series of on/off flows of electricity whereas an analog signal has the electricity varying in more of a wave like pattern. The modem sends and receives computer data over an ordinary telephone wire.

POSTSCRIPT

The price of hardware has been dropping dramatically. This trend is expected to continue for the foreseeable future. Not only are prices dropping, but the performance is increasing. A typical new microcomputer is now sold with twice the memory that it had just a year or two earlier. Floppy disks are being released that have capacities that only hard disks had a couple of years ago. This is an interesting and exciting area in which to be involved.

1. What is meant by the expression "garbage in, garbage out" (GIGO)?

2. Discuss how the recent developments in the computer industry affect the accounting profession.

3. What are the advantages of using the personal computer?

4. Hardware may be divided into four categories. Identify them and describe the functions of each category.

5. What is the computer's equivalent of a brain?

6. List the functions of the processor.

7. Describe the functions of the expansion modules.

8. Compare the advantages of random access memory (RAM) and read only memory (ROM).

9. What is meant by "volatile" storage?

10. Distinguish between a bit and a byte.

11. How many different combinations can be stored in a typical byte?

12. Explain the data hierarchy using an inventory system.

13. Discuss the advantages and disadvantages of primary storage and secondary storage.

14. How can you protect important data on a diskette from accidental erasure?

15. Take a blank diskette and practice inserting it in the left drive. Remove the diskette from the drive.

16. List the Do's and Don't's in handling a diskette.

17. What are the advantages and disadvantages of a hard disk?

18. What is the major difference between cassettes and diskettes as a storage media?

19. Outline the types of input devices for a microcomputer.

20. What is the function of the following keys on the IBM PC:
    (a) Return key
    (b) Shift keys
    (c) Caps Lock key
    (d) Backspace key
    (e) Tab key
    (f) Editing keys
    (g) Numeric pad
    (h) Function keys
    (i) Escape key
    (j) Control key
    (k) Alternate key

21. Suppose the system locks up and does not accept any input. What can you do other than turning off the computer and turning it on again?

22. How can you suspend the current operation of the computer? How can you resume operation?

23. How can you cause any information displayed on the screen to be printed? How can you cause only the current screen to be printed?

24. Describe three basic types of monitors for the IBM PC.

25. Distinguish between dot matrix printers and letter quality printers.

26. Describe the functions of a modem.

COMPUTER SOFTWARE

CHAPTER 2

INTRODUCTION

WHAT IS SOFTWARE?

Software is the set of instructions that tells the computer hardware what to do. Without software, the IBM PC would merely be a curious collection of wires and electrical components of little practical value. With well written software, this small computer is capable of many and varied data processing tasks.

TYPES OF SOFTWARE

There are basically two types of software: systems software and application software. Systems and application software complement each other. Systems software makes the computer easier to use. Application software is written to solve a particular problem or a particular class of problems.

Systems software is usually designed to be used on a particular machine. It provides a buffer between the user or application programs and the hardware. With good systems software, it is unnecessary to change the user's habits or modify the application programs when moving from one model of brand X computer to another model of brand X. The systems software smooths out the differences between models and allows the user to interact with what appears to be the same machine. Examples of system software that are discussed in this chapter include operating systems and programming languages.

While systems software is designed to run on a particular machine, application software is often designed to be run on many different computers. It takes advantage of the buffer that systems software provides. The major focus of application software is getting a particular job or type of job done. There is a large variety of application software. The payroll programs that write checks and maintain tax information are application programs. The word processing package used to write this book is application software.

OPERATING SYSTEM

WHAT IS AN OPERATING SYSTEM?

The operating system is a program or set of programs that provides a foundation upon which the user and application programs may work. It is the operating system that is in most immediate contact with the hardware. It must "understand" the peculiarities of the various hardware devices and protect the user and application programmer from the need to know all of the details.

Suppose you want to store some information on a diskette. You do not have to know all the steps required to be taken by the hardware. A single command to the operating system is sufficient. Imagine how little useful work would be accomplished if you had to keep track of the physical location of the data on the diskette or keep track of how the on and off bits must be strung together to form the characters. The operating system is the first of perhaps several layers of software that allows you to step back from the details and work on the big picture.

There are two basic ways in which the operating system may be used: directly and indirectly. In the direct use of the operating system the user issues commands to the operating system itself. Some of the commands that may be used are discussed in this chapter. The indirect use of the operating system is more important but much less visible.

In the indirect use of the operating system the user issues commands to a particular application program. In completing the assigned task, the application program relies on the operating system to provide an interface with the hardware. Whenever the computer is turned on, the operating system is providing you with service, either directly or indirectly.

TURNING THE COMPUTER ON

The IBM PC uses an operating system called DOS (disk operating system). When the machine is turned on, some of the operating system is already present in the machine in the nonvolatile ROM. The entire operating system is too large to fit in the ROM of most machines. Some of the operating system must be loaded into the machine when it is turned on. This process is known as booting the system.

It might be nice to have the entire operating system already in the machine when it is turned on, but this would also have a distinct disadvantage. As improvements to the operating system are made under the current way of doing things, it is possible to acquire the improved operating system by buying a new systems diskette. If the entire operating system was in ROM, the machine would have to be opened and ROM chips replaced. Since this changing of ROM chips would be expensive, the operating system would not be improved very often, making the entire system less flexible.

To boot the system, put the DOS diskette into the left drive. It may be necessary to first flip up the load lever on the drive. Make sure the diskette is all the way into the drive and then push the load lever down. Turn the machine on by flipping up the orange power switch located on the right rear side of the system unit. Do not expect an immediate response from the system. The portion of the operating system that resides in ROM has a number of housekeeping functions to perform. It checks the circuits to make sure they are functioning properly and loads the rest of the operating system from the DOS diskette.

ENTERING DATE AND TIME

After the system is booted from the diskette, it asks for the current date. The small blinking light on the screen is called the cursor. It indicates where the characters you are keying will appear. Only the number of the month, day, and year separated by dashes should be entered. Remember to press the return key when you are finished with any line of input. Next the system asks you to enter the time. Only the hours and minutes separated by a colon need to be entered. Note that in order to key a colon the shift key must be depressed. The time should be entered in military fashion which means that the hours are numbered from 0 (i.e. midnight) through 23 (i.e. 11 p.m.).

If the machine fails to ask for a date and time, you are in cassette BASIC. In order to load DOS, make sure the system disk is in the left drive and then hold the Alternate and Control keys down while depressing the Delete key. This will force the machine to boot the operating system.

It is not absolutely necessary to enter a date and time. When asked for the date or time press the return key to skip giving an answer. If you do that, however, the machine defaults to midnight of January 1, 1980. Whenever the machine uses the date, for instance when saving a file to a diskette, it will use January 1, 1980 rather than the current date.

DEFAULT DRIVE

After you enter the date and time, the system places the cursor on the next line beside the characters "A>". The letter A followed by a greater than sign (>) is known as the A prompt. It indicates that the A or left drive is the default disk drive. Unless a different drive is specified, all commands entered assume that the default drive is to be used. To change the default drive, the new default drive's letter should be entered along with a colon. For instance to make the right or B drive the default drive, enter:

B:

After changing the default drive to B change it back to A with the following command:

A:

DIRECTORY AND FILE SPECIFICATIONS

Each diskette and hard disk used by DOS contains a directory. The directory lists the names and other information about each file found on that disk. To see some of this information enter the directory command:

DIR

Assuming the DOS diskette is in the A drive, a five column listing of all the files on that disk similar to the following appears:

```
        Volume in drive A has no label
        Directory of  A:

    COMMAND  COM     17792   10-20-83   12:00p
    ANSI     SYS      1664   10-20-83   12:00p
    FORMAT   COM      6912   10-20-83   12:00p
    CHKDSK   COM      6400   10-20-83   12:00p
    SYS      COM      1680   10-20-83   12:00p
    DISKCOPY COM      2576   10-20-83   12:00p
    DISKCOMP COM      2188   10-20-83   12:00p
    COMP     COM      2534   10-20-83   12:00p
    EDLIN    COM      4608   10-20-83   12:00p
    MODE     COM      3139   10-20-83   12:00p
    FDISK    COM      6369   10-20-83   12:00p
    BACKUP   COM      3687   10-20-83   12:00p
    RESTORE  COM      4003   10-20-83   12:00p
    PRINT    COM      4608   10-20-83   12:00p
    RECOVER  COM      2304   10-20-83   12:00p
    ASSIGN   COM       896   10-20-83   12:00p
    TREE     COM      1513   10-20-83   12:00p
    GRAPHICS COM       789   10-20-83   12:00p
    SORT     EXE      1408   10-20-83   12:00p
    FIND     EXE      5888   10-20-83   12:00p
    MORE     COM       384   10-20-83   12:00p
    BASIC    COM     16256   10-20-83   12:00p
    BASICA   COM     26112   10-20-83   12:00p
      23 File(s)     28672 bytes free
```

Remember that the CTRL-NUMLOCK key combination temporarily pauses the operation of the computer. This key combination may be used to prevent the top of the directory listing from scrolling off the top of the screen before it has been examined.

The first column of the directory listing contains the names of the files on the diskette. Note that there is an 8 character limit on a filename. Letters, numbers and certain special characters (e.g. the dollar sign, ampersand, and percent sign) may be used in the filename. In general, however, it is wise to get in the habit of using only letters and numbers in the filename because some software packages have tighter restrictions on the use of special characters in naming files and variables. If you develop the habit of using only eight letters and numbers, it is easier to move from one piece of software to another.

The second column of the directory listing is the optional filename extension. It is often used to classify files into types. The extension is limited to the same set of letters, numbers and special characters as described above. Because the extension is limited to three characters, abbreviations are necessary. Some of the common abbreviations and their meanings follow:

BAK	Backup
BAS	BASIC program
BAT	Batch
CAL	SuperCalc3 spreadsheet
COM	Command file (DOS)
DAT	Data
DBF	Data base file (dBase)
EXE	Execute
PRG	Program (dBase)
SYS	System
WKS	Worksheet (Lotus 1-2-3)

The use of an extension allows DOS to have more than one file with the same name and yet be able to distinguish between them. For instance, two payroll files may exist at the same time: PAYROLL.BAS and PAYROLL.DAT. By refering to the above list you can identify the first payroll file as a BASIC program and the second payroll file as a data file. Note the use of the period between the filename and its extension. The period and extension should be given when refering to a file that has an extension; otherwise, DOS may not be able to locate the file.

When working with a file on the default disk drive, the file is refered to by its filename, a period, and its extension as discussed above. This is known as the file specification. When working with a file that is not on the default drive, the file specification must also include an indication of the drive in which the disk containing the file is located. This is done by placing the drive's letter first, followed by a colon and then the rest of the file specification (e.g. B:PAYROLL.BAS). Note that there are no spaces within the file specification.

The third column of the directory listing is an indication of the size of the file in bytes or characters. The fourth and fifth columns are the date and time the file was saved on the diskette. These columns are accurate only if the machine had the correct date and time when the file was saved. See the discussion above on entering date and time.

FORMATTING A DISK

When you first buy a diskette or hard disk it naturally does not contain any information. It is not even able to accept files in its initial condition. In order to accept files the disk must first be initialized or formatted. This formatting process puts the disk into a format usable by DOS and sets up the directory. Because different operating systems have different formats, this process cannot be completed before the diskette is purchased. Even different versions of DOS format the disk differently. Do not be concerned if your execution of the FORMAT command differs from the following example since different versions of DOS allow different amounts of data to be stored on a diskette.

FORMAT B:

Insert new diskette for drive B:
and strike any key when ready

Formatting...Format complete

362496 bytes total disk space
362496 bytes available on disk

Format another (Y/N)?N

When using the FORMAT command, a drive letter followed by a colon should be specified. If none is specified, the default drive is assumed. This can be dangerous because the formatting process erases all existing data on the disk.

The formatting process also analyzes the entire disk looking for defective tracks (i.e. storage locations). Any bad tracks that are found are marked as unusable so that they will not later be used to store data. At the end of the formatting process a status report is issued that indicates the total disk space less the space marked as defective less the space allocated to system files giving the total space available for your files. System files contain the information that is booted into RAM when the machine is turned on. To specify that the system files are to be placed on the diskette as part of the formatting process, place a /S after the FORMAT command.

FORMAT B:/S

The FORMAT command is an external command. This means that in order to execute the FORMAT command it must first be read from disk. Only the external command that is actually being executed needs to be in RAM. This is done to save room in RAM. If DOS cannot find a file called FORMAT.COM then it cannot execute the FORMAT command and an error message is displayed. Note that an external command may be prefixed with a drive letter and colon if the command file is on a drive other than the default drive (e.g. B:FORMAT A: will use the FORMAT.COM file found on the B drive to format the diskette found in the A drive).

An internal command executes immediately. When an internal command is issued, it does not need to be loaded from disk because internal commands are part of the DOS system that was booted when the machine was turned on. For example, because the DIR command is an internal command you will not find a file called DIR.COM on your DOS diskette.

The DOS system, therefore, comes in three main parts. The first part is in ROM all of the time. The second part is booted into RAM when the machine is turned on. The third part of DOS consists of individual external command files which are only brought into RAM when they are to be executed.

The COPY command makes duplicate copies of files. It has the following form: COPY filespec1 filespec2, where filespec is short for file specification, and consists of the optional drive designation (e.g. A:), filename and optional extension. The COPY command does not allow the two file specifications to be the same. This would lead to confusion since two files with the same name and extension would exist on the same device.

There are several ways to abbreviate the two file specifications when entering this command. If the copy of the file is to have the same name and extension as the original file, then only the drive designator needs to be entered in the second file specification. For example

COPY A:PAYROLL.BAS B:

copies the file PAYROLL.BAS from the disk in the A drive to the disk in the B drive and keeps the same name. If all files of a certain description are to be copied then the asterisk (i.e. "*") may be used as a "global filename character" or "wild card". For example, if all payroll files are to be copied from the A to the B drive, regardless of their file extensions, the following command could be used:

COPY A:PAYROLL.* B:

If all command files are to be copied from A to B then the following could be used:

COPY A:*.COM B:

The asterisk takes the place of any zero or more characters in the file specification. The question mark (i.e. "?") is also a "wild card" but it takes the place of any one character.

Recall the form of the COPY command: COPY filespec1 filespec2. Filespecs need not refer only to files on a disk. There are reserved device names for the console keyboard/screen (i.e. CON), parallel printer (i.e. PRN), and asynchronous communications adapter port (i.e. AUX). By substituting the device name for a filespec, you can make the COPY command a very versatile tool. For instance

COPY B:PAYROLL.DAT PRN

prints the payroll data. The following COPY CON command places information from the keyboard into a text file called SAMPLE:

COPY CON B:SAMPLE.TXT

Whatever you enter on the keyboard is placed into the file B:SAMPLE.TXT. This command is used to create a new file and enter data into it. Pressing the F6 key followed by a return brings the COPY CON command to an end. The command

COPY B:SAMPLE.TXT CON

displays the sample text file on the screen. The command

TYPE B:SAMPLE.TXT

is essentially equivalent to the previous COPY command and perhaps a little easier to remember.

Some files cannot be displayed on the screen or printed in any meaningful way using the COPY or TYPE commands. From Chapter 1 remember that any byte or character on the IBM PC can be one of 256 different combinations of on and off bits. Less than half of these 256 combinations have a meaningful printable or displayable equivalent. To illustrate this concept, try using the TYPE command to display various files on your system diskette. Many of the files cause strange things to appear on the screen. If your machine locks up in this experiment, use the ALT-CTRL-DEL key combination to reboot the system.

BACKUP FILES

It is very desirable to have extra or backup copies of important files. These copies should be made after every 15 minutes to half an hour of continuous operation. You continue to work with the original but if anything happens to it, such as accidental erasure, the backup copy can be used. Many application programs have facilities built into them for making backup copies. The DOS COPY command can also be used for this purpose. If after copying the file PAYROLL.DAT from A to B you want to assure yourself that the copy was successful, use the compare files command:

COMP A:PAYROLL.DAT B:

Any differences in the files will be noted on the screen.

At the end of each working day it is desirable to make a special backup of all files changed during that day. This backup copy should be taken home if the data is not sensitive or to a bank safety deposit box if it is sensitive. This off site storage of backup files allows continued business operation even if a disaster destroys the original records.

If for backup file reasons (or any other reason), you wish to copy an entire diskette, the DISKCOPY command is very useful:

DISKCOPY A: B:

The above command formats the diskette in drive B and copies the entire diskette in drive A to drive B. If you want to assure yourself that the copy was successful, enter the disk compare command:

DISKCOMP A: B:

MISCELLANEOUS DOS COMMANDS

DOS has a number of other file manipulation commands. Files may be removed from the directory with the ERASE command. The freed space can be used by other files. For example

ERASE A:PAYROLL.DAT

erases the PAYROLL data file. Care should be exercised in the use of this command especially when using "wild card" characters in the file specification. There is no convenient way within DOS to unerase a file. Even though the data is physically still on the diskette (until another file overwrites it) without a complete entry in the directory the data cannot be accessed. Special utility programs exist that can restore the directory but these programs must be purchased separately.

The DOS RENAME command allows a file name and/or extension to be changed.

RENAME PAYROLL.DAT PAYROLL.BAK

The above command renames the data file as a backup file.

The check disk command is useful in determining the total amount of room on a disk and in memory. It also states the amount of room not currently in use (free) and therefore available for use both on the specified disk and in memory.

CHKDSK B:

```
362496 bytes total disk space
 22528 bytes in 2 hidden files
  4096 bytes in 3 user files
335872 bytes available on disk

262144 bytes total memory
210784 bytes free
```

It is possible to mark a file as a hidden file. When a file is marked as hidden, a normal directory search will not find it. The check disk command is one of the few ways within DOS for a user to detect a hidden file. Two common hidden files within DOS are the system files IBMBIO.COM and IBMDOS.COM. These are the files that are booted into memory when the machine is turned on.

BAT FILES

There are situations where you repeatedly want to execute a series of DOS commands. This can be done easily by placing the commands in a BAT file and executing that file repeatedly. As an example, consider the situation where in the course of the day you may work with five different files. At the end of most work days you wish to copy those five files from the A drive to the B drive in order to back up the originals. If the filenames and extensions do not allow the convenient use of "wild card" characters, then without copying the entire disk it would be necessary to enter five separate COPY commands.

Using the COPY CON command described above in the "Copying Files" section or a word processor such as Wordstar, it is possible to put the five COPY statements (or any DOS commands) into a file with an extension of BAT. By executing that file all of the commands it contains are executed. To execute a BAT file, enter the drive designation (if it is not on the default drive) and the name of the file at the A> prompt.

There is a special type of BAT file known as the AUTOEXEC.BAT file. This file is executed (if it exists on the default drive) automatically after each booting of the system. This AUTOEXEC feature makes it possible to have a favorite piece of software "self loading" any time the system is booted with that software's diskette. For instance, consider an AUTOEXEC file that contains the following three commands:

```
DATE
TIME
DBASE
```

Assuming that the system files and the dBase software are on the same diskette, each time the system is booted with this diskette, the user will be asked for the date and time and then taken into dBase automatically.

PROGRAMMING LANGUAGES

WHAT IS A PROGRAM?

A program is a series of statements that tells the computer hardware what to do. Just as there are several languages (i.e. English, Spanish, German, etc) that people use when talking with each other, there are also several languages available which give the computer commands.

In the previous section, BAT files were discussed. A BAT file is a series of statements that tells the computer hardware what to do; therefore, a BAT file is a program. Although DOS is normally thought of as an operating system, it can also be used as a programming language. It is often difficult to classify a piece of software into just one category.

DOS, when used as a programming language, is a high level language. The term "high level" indicates that each line of the program results in many detailed commands being executed by the processor. When working with a high level language you are able to work at a macro level (i.e. consider the big picture). You do not have to worry about the detailed actions required to complete the task. You are therefore better able to consider what needs to be done rather than how to do it.

Back in the 1940's when electronic computers were first developed, machine language was the only programming language available. Machine language is a very low level language. Each machine language statement is a single command to the processor. Working at such a detailed level was very time consuming. Each computer had a different machine language, so it was necessary to learn a new language for each computer. To make matters worse, the programs often had to be entered in binary code (strings of zeroes and ones). Essentially people were forced to deal with the computer in a manner that was very convenient to the computer but extremely inconvenient for a human.

The development of an assembler made the computer easier to use. An assembler is a piece of software that converts assembly code into machine language. Although assembly code is a low level language, it is easier to work with than machine language. Instead of requiring the programmer to work with instructions in binary code, the programmer can use mnemonics that are easy to learn abbreviations of English commands. Also, instead of forcing the programmer to remember where values are stored in the computer's memory, as is necessary in machine language, assembly code permits the use of variable names.

Assembly code is easier for a person to use but the computer cannot directly execute an assembly language program. The computer can only execute machine code. An assembler program translates the assembly code into the computer's machine language. The assembler performs a function very similar to the role of a human translator who assists travelers in a foreign country who do not speak the native language. (See Figure 2-1)

FIGURE 2-1 PROGRAMMING LANGUAGES

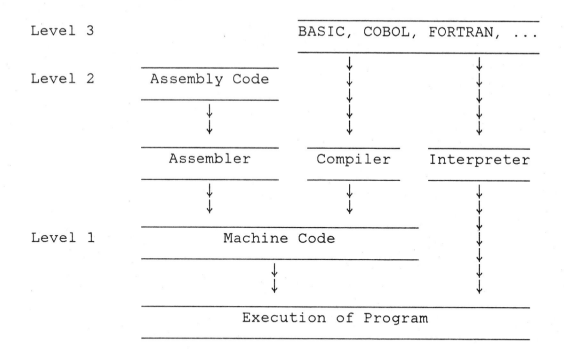

The next advance in the development of programming languages came with the invention of higher level languages and their compilers. A compiler is similar to an assembler in that it converts a programming language into machine language. An assembler translates assembly code whereas a compiler translates one of several higher level languages.

The widespread use of computers has been made possible by higher level languages such as FORTRAN, COBOL, and BASIC. Because each high level program statement has the power of several machine language statements, programs are easier to write. This leverage gets the job done quicker. Also, because there is not a one-to-one conversion of program statements into machine language, the programmer does not have to know the machine language instruction set of each particular computer. COBOL, for instance, on Brand X computer is very similar to COBOL on Brand Y computer. This transportability feature is very important, for instance, when increased processing load or improved technology makes it desirable to convert to a new computer. Often the programs only need to be recompiled with no change to the higher level programs.

COMPILERS VERSUS INTERPRETERS

Using a compiler results in a machine language version of the original program. Assuming that the compiler is well designed, the resulting machine language version will execute in a highly efficient manner. Although the use of compilers results in fast execution of application programs, they are slow in the sense that after writing a program it must be compiled before the program's execution can be observed. This delay can be particularly frustrating in the case of a program undergoing frequent changes.

An interpreter overcomes this problem by directly executing the high level language program. Essentially the interpreter scans a line of the program, interprets or decides what that line means and then the interpreter performs that function. This does not violate the earlier rule that the computer can only execute machine language programs. The interpreter, itself, is in machine language. It is the interpreter that in a sense executes the high level program.

Although the interpreter allows programs to be changed and then executed immediately, the execution speed is low. Each time a line is to be executed, it must be rescanned and reinterpreted before it can be executed. The compiler by translating each line only once saves time when the program is executed. In general an interpreter is most appropriate in situations where frequent changes are being made to a program. Such a situation occurs when a program is first written and problems are being worked out. This process is known as debugging.

A compiler is very useful when a program has been debugged and the program is ready for repeated use. This often occurs in a business environment where, for example, an accounts receivable or payroll program may be run hundreds of times between changes.

EXAMPLES OF HIGHER LEVEL LANGUAGES

The best known language for microcomputers is BASIC. More people have used this computer programming language than any other because it is relatively easy to learn and use. It was developed in 1964 as a streamlined version of FORTRAN. FORTRAN, developed in 1956, was the first higher level computer language. Both BASIC and FORTRAN allow the use of the GO TO command which, by allowing control to be passed to any point in the program, can lead to very confusing program code. Both BASIC and FORTRAN are general purpose programming languages, that are particularly useful for mathematical manipulations.

In 1960, many people saw a need to develop a language that would manipulate files easily. Business programming typically requires the moving and reformatting of large bodies of data with little mathematical manipulation. FORTRAN, the only high level language in existance at that time, was not well suited to that purpose. To fill that void, COBOL was developed. Besides making file manipulation easy, it is also useful in a business environment because its English-like syntax and variable names make it easy to read and understand. This is desirable both for the nonprogramming manager, who may need to know what a program does, and for the programmer who may need to modify the program. More time is spent maintaining the typical business program than is spent developing it, so easy maintenance is important. Because of the above strengths in a business environment, there are more professional programmers of COBOL than of any other language. So many programs have been written in COBOL that it is unlikely to become obsolete in the foreseeable future.

BASIC, FORTRAN, and COBOL are perhaps the best known computer programming languages. There are many others. PL/I is a broad language that attempts to encompass the good points of both FORTRAN and COBOL. LISP is a language that is well suited to manipulating character strings, making it the choice of many artificial intelligence researchers. APL is a very powerful high level language that is particularly adept at matrix manipulations. PASCAL is a language that encourages the use of structured techniques. Structured programs consist of modules, each of which has a single entry and a single exit point, making it easier to read. Many other languages exist and more are being created each year.

INTRODUCTION

Application programs are programs written to solve a particular problem or class of problems. Examples of business application programs that solve a particular problem include general ledger, accounts receivable, accounts payable, payroll, and inventory control packages. Typically these programs are written in a high level language and then are compiled to give a machine language version that executes quickly. Application programs may be programmed by the end user, by a separate in house programming staff or by an independent vendor. A purchased program should be flexible enough to adapt to many different businesses. It is doubtful, however, that any purchased software can fit each company exactly. Typically, a business must adjust its system to the new software.

Other application programs are written to solve a class of problems. Examples of this type of application program include spreadsheets, database packages and word processing programs.

ELECTRONIC SPREADSHEETS

An electronic spreadsheet is an automated form of the manual spreadsheet. It allows for quick and accurate calculation of results. This is particularly useful when several similar spreadsheets must be prepared. After each change to the spreadsheet, all the numbers are recalculated and displayed. Electronic spreadsheets are easy to learn and to use. They increase the productivity of the accountant.

Several spreadsheet packages (including Lotus 1-2-3 and SuperCalc3, which are discussed in this text) allow multiple commands to be stored as a part of the spreadsheet. This programming feature means that such a spreadsheet could be classified not only as an application package but also as a programming language.

DATABASE PACKAGES

Database packages allow the easy manipulation of large bodies of data. A data base package such as dBase, which is discussed in this book, can be used in an interactive mode.

In the interactive mode each command is entered by itself and the results are displayed soon after. The file may be searched for individual records. Reports may be printed on the basis of the entire file.

Another mode available in dBase is the programming mode. Multiple commands are placed into a file and then executed sequentially by giving a single command. As a result, dBase may be classified as a programming language as well as an application program.

WORD PROCESSING

Word processing application software is part of the recent thrust to automate the office. A good word processing program can speed up one time typing tasks. The real strength of word processing, however, lies in its ability to allow easy modifications to documents after they have been keyed in. The word processing package Wordstar is covered in Chapter 14.

REVIEW QUESTIONS AND PROBLEMS

1. What is software? Why is software important to the computer?

2. Distinguish between systems software and application software.

3. What is an operating system?

4. Explain the direct and indirect use of the operating system.

5. Explain why the entire operating system is not already in the machine when it is turned on.

6. Explain booting the system. Why is this process necessary?

7. Suppose that a diskette contains too many files to be displayed on the screen at one time. How can you see the entire directory?

8. Make an appropriate file specification for the following files:
   (a) BASIC program to compute payroll
   (b) Data base file of inventory in dBase.
   (c) Inventory data file
   (d) Backup of inventory data file

9. Distinguish between an external command and an internal command.

10. Describe the functions of the CHKDSK command.

11. What is a BAT file? Describe the advantages of using BAT files.

12. What is a program?

13. What is meant by the term "high level programming language"?

14. What are the disadvantages of machine language?

15. Distinguish between an assembler and assembly code.

16. Distinguish between an assembler and a compiler.

17. Discuss the relative advantages and disadvantages of compilers and interpreters.

18. What are the advantages of higher level languages?

19. List examples of higher level languages and describe the important characteristics of each language.

20. Describe what an application program is and give examples of business application programs.

The following problems require access to a computer:

21. Boot the system. Observe how long it takes for the system to be booted. Do the same thing on another computer. Explain the difference in time, if any, that you observe.

22. After booting the system intentionally enter a bad date and time. What errors, if any, does the computer catch and flag as an error. Using the DATE and TIME commands, try other errors.

23. Change the default drive from A: to B: and then change it back.

24. Display the directory of your DOS diskette using the following three commands. Compare and contrast the results.
    (a) DIR
    (b) DIR /P
    (c) DIR /W

25. Format a blank diskette.

26. Make a backup copy of the DOS diskette using the COPY command.

27. Make a backup copy of the DOS diskette using the DISKCOPY command. Compare the backup copy with the original diskette and with the backup copy created in problem 26.

28. Make a file called EXERCISE.TXT by entering the following statement: "This is an exercise of creating a file by typing on the keyboard." Display it on the screen.

29. Rename the file EXERCISE.TXT created in problem 28 as PROB28.TXT.

30. Erase the file renamed in problem 29.

31. What is the function of the EDLIN program which is part of the DOS system? Use it to create EXERCISE.TXT as in problem 28.

PART II: ELECTRONIC SPREADSHEETS

OVERVIEW OF ELECTRONIC SPREADSHEETS

CHAPTER 3

In 1978, Dan Bricklin, a Harvard Business School student, and Robert Frankston, a programmer of considerable talent, developed what became the first major electronic spreadsheet software, VisiCalc from VisiCorp. The success of the electronic spreadsheet has been so great that some have attributed the tremendous success of the microcomputer industry to this one type of software. Electronic spreadsheets have consistently lead the charts as the best selling software for the microcomputer. In the short six years that electronic spreadsheets have been on the market, they have become required knowledge for all accountants as well as for most business professionals regardless of their discipline.

Why have electronic spreadsheets gained such overwhelming popularity within the business community? This success may be attributable to two characteristics of electronic spreadsheets:

* The matrix organization of the spreadsheets
* The cell referencing capability

Accountants have used the matrix form of analysis with its rows and columns, since the days of Luca Pacioli. From the simple listing of inventory to the final year-end working trial balance, the worksheet has proven to be a very valuable aid to the accountant in the performance of accounting work. In a very real sense, the electronic spreadsheet is simply a computerization of the traditional, well known, manually prepared worksheet.

The capability of referencing by cell address throughout the spreadsheet gives the electronic spreadsheet the what-if power that allows the accountant and other business professional to analyze the complex transactions that makes up today's business world. Thus, by changing one cell in the worksheet, a completely different analysis of the problem is available. Accountants are able to view the bottom-line effect of a complex transaction before its completion. The results of this increased analytical power are seen in the more complicated transactions common in today's business world. To remain competitive, today's accountant is required to become a user of electronic spreadsheets.

OVERVIEW OF SPREADSHEET SOFTWARE

From its beginning as a tool to solve a student's homework, VisiCalc quickly became the standard spreadsheet software. Today, VisiCalc is still widely used; however, it does have certain limitations when entering labels. Most spreadsheets are anywhere from one-third to two-thirds labels. When entering labels or text material, VisiCalc limits the user to the column width, i.e. the number of characters allowed per cell. For example, if the default cell size of nine characters is assumed, a user would be required to enter "Accounts" in the first cell, "receivabl" in the second cell; and "e" in the third cell. At the very least, this procedure makes use of VisiCalc very inconvenient.

The widespread use of VisiCalc encouraged competing electronic spreadsheets. The most successful of the pure spreadsheet packages has been MultiPlan and SuperCalc. MultiPlan is very similar to VisiCalc, however, it has eliminated many of the VisiCalc's inconveniences. SuperCalc, by Sorcim (micros spelled backwards) has most of the same features of MultiPlan plus a color screen (assuming a color monitor.) However, all electronic spreadsheets owe their beginnings to VisiCalc.

The second generation of electronic spreadsheets, the integrated software packages, incorporate some data base management and graphics with an electronic spreadsheet. The undisputed leader of the second generation is Lotus 1-2-3. The electronic spreadsheet in Lotus 1-2-3 is superior to all others in its number of features, speed, and user friendliness. Its data base management capabilities are usable, though limited in the amount of data that may be manipulated; its graphics capabilities are very usable. Of course, the ability to integrate these functions in one package was an innovation worthy of note. Also, Lotus 1-2-3 is unique among the second generation spreadsheets in that it is the only one that was developed and written by a team of programmers all of whom had previous experience writing software for microcomputers. In addition, Lotus 1-2-3 was written for the IBM PC, thus it utilizes all the keyboard features of the IBM PC. Lotus 1-2-3 was the best selling business software throughout the year 1984. Coming into the mid-1980's, Lotus 1-2-3 is the standard for electronic spreadsheets.

Not to be outdone by Lotus on the east coast, in 1983 Sorcim Corporation (of California) produced SuperCalc3. Also an integrated software package, SuperCalc3 has most of the same features of Lotus 1-2-3, though there are notable exceptions. On the whole, SuperCalc3 is a very competitive electronic spreadsheet. It has limited sorting and query procedures but more graphing capability than Lotus 1-2-3.

The obvious question is "Which spreadsheet software should be used?" Both software companies have established aggressive marketing strategies. Without question, Lotus 1-2-3 is the leading electronic spreadsheet. However, SuperCalc3 is a competing product that is available to many college students. The other electronic spreadsheets are not as readily available. Thus the final decision for this book is easy. Lotus 1-2-3 is the market leader, some say the best, and SuperCalc3 is a price competitive, acceptable alternative. It should be noted that all spreadsheets utilize the same matrix form of analysis, with rows and columns, and have the what-if capability gained with the ability to reference by cell address. Once any one spreadsheet is mastered, the knowledge will be readily transferable to other spreadsheet software.

The specific electronic spreadsheet software discussed in the following chapters will be Lotus 1-2-3 and SuperCalc3. However, before discussing the specific software, some general concepts of electronic spreadsheets, applicable to both, will be discussed.

BASIC CONCEPTS OF ELECTRONIC SPREADSHEETS

The basic element of the electronic spreadsheet is the cell. The spreadsheet is divided into rows and columns of cells. One cell is one column wide and one row high. By default, columns are nine characters wide and rows are one character high, thus, a cell normally contains nine characters. The rows are commonly identified by numbers and the columns by letters. Accordingly, each cell on the spreadsheet may be referred to by its "cell address", with the column first and the row second. Thus "A1" refers to the upper left-hand corner of the spreadsheet, Column A, Row 1. It is the ability to reference to the individual cells that gives the spreadsheet its "What-if" power.

Spreadsheet models are built by entering labels (text material) or values (numeric data or formulas) into the cell. Spreadsheets are made up of numbers, labels, and formulas. If the same number, label or formula needs to be referred to at a later time, the reference to the number or formula may be made by its cell address. While labels may not be referenced, they may be copied from cell to cell. One of the guiding principles of spreadsheet design is

"Enter a number only once--Use cell referencing thereafter."

Electronic spreadsheets also utilize "functions." Functions are pre-programmed formulas. While the same results may be obtained by entering the formula, the use of functions is faster and easier, more user-friendly. For example, to add the numbers in cells A1 to A10, the following formula may be entered:

+A1+A2+A3+A4+A5+A6+A7+A8+A9+A10

Alternatively, the SUM function may be used as follows:

In Lotus 1-2-3, @SUM(A1..A10)
In SuperCalc3, SUM(A1:A10)

The results are the same either way, but the use of the function is more convenient.

Note that the function referred to the ten cells by referencing the beginning point, A1, and the ending point, A10. (The beginning and ending cells are separated by two periods in Lotus 1-2-3 and by a colon in SuperCalc3.) Referring to a group of cells in this manner is called a "range." In Figure 3-1 several ranges are diagrammed. Note that only rectangular shapes are allowed as ranges. L-shape references are not allowable as ranges. Ranges are not always required to be in the same row or column. Note the range C5..D7 includes cells both in different rows and different columns. Some spreadsheet software allow more flexibility in the use of ranges than others.

FIGURE 3-1 RANGES

```
F15:                                                                    READY

           A        B        C        D        E        F        G        H
 1    _____
 2   :  A    R :             _____
 3   :  C    A :            :    NOT  ACCEPTABLE     :
 4   :  C    N :            :    RANGE               :
 5   :  E    G :            :               _____:
 6   :  P    E :            :              :
 7   :  T      :            :              :
 8   :  A      :            :              :
 9   :  B      :            :_____:
10   :  L      :
11   :  E      :
12   :_____:             _____
13                          :_____:  <------ACCEPTABLE RANGE
14
```

Another basic concept in electronic spreadsheets is the use of "Commands." Spreadsheet commands are used to aid in the design of spreadsheet models or templates, to interface with peripheral equipment such as printers and disk storage, and to perform the data based management and graphics functions in the integrated spreadsheets. The commands begin with the slash key, the / key on the right side of the space bar on the IBM PC and similar keyboards. The names of the commands vary with the software package being used, but their purpose and result are the same. The commands may normally be entered by typing the first letter of the command, however, Lotus 1-2-3 provides a full-word command menu from which to select commands. Figure 3-2 has been designed to indicate the similarity of the commands between Lotus 1-2-3 and SuperCalc3.

FIGURE 3-2 COMPARISON OF COMMANDS

DESCRIPTION OF COMMAND	Lotus 1-2-3	SUPERCALC
Blank or erase a cell or range of cells	/R E	/B
Clear or erase the entire spreadsheet	/W E Y	/Z Y
Delete an entire row or column	/W D R of C	/D R or C
Edit the definition of any cell	Function key 2	/E
Format the cell	/R F	/F
Adjust column width	/W C S #	/F C #
Insert additional rows or columns	/W I R or C	/I R or C
Move cell or range of cells	/M	/M
Print part of spreadsheet with printer	/P P	/O P
Replicate or copy a cell to another cell	/C	/R
To interface with disk storage to save a file	/F S	/S

WHAT-IF ANALYSIS

What-if analysis, a form of sensitivity analysis, is a method of analysis that measures changes of expected values in decision models based on changes in key variables. The what-if analysis available with electronic spreadsheet allows the accountant to review the effect of changes not just on key variables, but on the entire financial statement, budget, or other financial analysis. With the printing capabilities available, the accountant may easily produce finished reports for presentation or publication.

It is worth repeating, the what-if capability results from the ability to reference cells and construct interrelated formulas and functions in spreadsheet models or templates. Once constructed, the template output is readily available for use in decision-making. What-if analysis is based upon interaction between the user and the spreadsheet. When the first template is constructed, the what-if capabilities will be obvious and impressive.

STEPS TO FOLLOW IN USING ELECTRONIC SPREADSHEETS

The first step in using electronic spreadsheets is to load the spreadsheet software into the primary memory. To accomplish this procedure the accountant must use the operating system to "boot the system" and then call the execute file to "load" the spreadsheet program. Commonly the "exec" file is some abbreviation of the software name. For example, to load SuperCalc3 from DOS, simply type "SC3"; to load Lotus 1-2-3, "123". It must be emphasized that once the program is loaded into the primary memory, the software system disk is only used for "Help" files. The entire program is in primary memory. In fact if the help capabilities are not needed, the system disk may be removed without interfering with the use of the spreadsheet.

Once the spreadsheet is loaded into primary memory, the accountant is ready to use the spreadsheet. The first skill to learn is how to move around the spreadsheet. The primary devices for moving around the spreadsheet are the four arrows keys on the right side of the keyboard. These keys will move the cursor (the small hyphen sign or minus sign that indicates the current cell, i.e. indicates the location within the spreadsheet where the current entry will be entered) in the direction of the arrow, one cell. Thus, to move from cell A34 to A35, the down arrow is typed one time. To move from B5 to C5, the arrow to the right will be typed one time. To move at a much faster rate over greater distances, the "GO TO" key may be used. This key will move the cursor to the cell entered by the accountant. There may be many times you wish to tell the spreadsheet where to go; the GO TO will do just that. Within each spreadsheet software, additional moving around keys may be used. These are discussed further within the specific software.

TEMPLATES

Once the spreadsheet is designed and all the formulas entered into the appropriate cells, and the spreadsheet has been proofed for accuracy, the spreadsheet is referred to as a "template." Thus a template is simply a spreadsheet that may be reused for analysis of similar transactions. Many accountants market their templates through a variety of microcomputer magazines. Other accountants simply pass their templates along to others in the spirit of professionalism. Still others consider their templates proprietary and keep strict control over their use. In either case, the template is nothing more or less than a spreadsheet in which all the formulas and cell references have previously been entered. Using the template requires no more than loading the spreadsheet file into the primary memory and using it. For example, if you have a template to compute depreciation with the filename "DEPR.WKS" (the file type ".WKS" indicates it is a Lotus 1-2-3 worksheet file), simply load the file (the command is /FR DEPR <enter>.)

With the template in place, the next step for the accountant is to enter data into the spreadsheet. Data entry is simply typing the numbers or labels requested by the template. No formulas should be required. After the data is entered, the accountant moves to the output area of the spreadsheet and views the results. To utilize what-if analysis, the accountant moves around the spreadsheet to the input area, changes the inputs, recalculates if necessary, and views the changed results. When the final results are determined, the accountant "Saves the spreadsheet" by writing it to the disk storage. The spreadsheet may then be recalled for further analysis at a later time. When it is written to the disk storage, the spreadsheet is actually still in primary memory, and it will stay there until the machine is turned off, another file is loaded in its place, it is erased (or Zapped in SuperCalc3), or the spreadsheet software is replaced with a different program. If the spreadsheet file is saved as a text file or print file, it may be transferred to another software package for further analysis or printing. For example, a spreadsheet may be printed with a word processing program or a graph printed with a plotter. To save a spreadsheet in SuperCalc3, the command is /S filename <enter>.

The spreadsheet may be printed with the print command of the spreadsheet software. The print commands provide for many options. For example, the printer may be "setup" or instructed to print in a compressed mode (approximately 17 characters per inch) or in expanded mode (approximately 5 characters per inch.) Simply stated, the full capability of the printer is available with the spreadsheet setup options in the print command.

DESIGN OF SPREADSHEETS

With all the power of the electronic spreadsheet, the 63 or more columns, and the 254 or more rows, there is a tendency to assume that the spreadsheet may be haphazardedly put together with little or no planning. The problem with this approach (in addition to being sloppy) is that the limit on the use of electronic spreadsheets lies in the amount of primary memory available. With the IBM PC, that memory is limited to 640 K. Thus, it is important to plan your spreadsheet. Of course, the available commands provide the opportunity to easily change the spreadsheet. The minimum planning required is the same that would be required if a manual spreadsheet is prepared. In designing the spreadsheet, a basic rule should be "KEEP IT SIMPLE." Recall that the computer does not get bored crunching numbers or performing repetitive tasks. Thus, the more simple the design of the spreadsheet, the better. After all some mere human may have to understand the spreadsheet a month after it is done.

The spreadsheet will be more readily understood and used if it is designed with a definite MENU RANGE, INPUT RANGE, and OUTPUT RANGE. The menu range should tell the user how to use the spreadsheet, where the input range is located (the cell address), the purpose of the spreadsheet, the location of key results of the spreadsheet, the location of the output range, and any other information that is needed to properly use the spreadsheet template. The input range is the location within the spreadsheet where the variable

information or data is entered. Once it is entered, the
input is utilized throughout the spreadsheet by using cell
references to the input range.   The input range in some
cases may be quite large or may be included as part of the
output range.   For example, if a balance sheet is being
entered, the input and output range will be the same.
However, if a five year, month by month cash flow projection
is being done, the rate of increase in the monthly expenses,
cash collections, and beginning balance will be entered once
in an input range. The output will be computed by reference
to the input range.

In a recent issue of INFOWORLD,* Jack Grushcow,
president of Consumers Software, listed ten steps to better
spreadsheet design.   The steps he lists are similiar to
those discussed above and are listed here for your
information.

1. Start with a plan
2. After the spreadsheet is completed, use cell
   protect to prevent unintended changes to the
   spreadsheet
3. Make your spreadsheet resemble existing forms
4. Use the input area as a data capture form
5. Enter data in either rows or columns, not both
6. Use manual recalculation when entering data into
   large spreadsheets
7. Place instructions and indentification in the
   spreadsheet
8. Back up your files
9. Always test your spreadsheet
10. Don't mingle entry areas with calculations

Accountants are more users than programmers.
Accountants are not programmers and probably there are basic
reasons why, i.e accountants do not like programming. While
there are obviously exceptions, users, like accountants, do
not like to spend time documenting the purpose of a
spreadsheet. Complete documentation of a spreadsheet would
parallel that required by any computer program. However,
minimum documentation requires a menu range in every
spreadsheet. While the menu range could be anywhere in the
spreadsheet, the most logical and convenient place is the

----

*Doran Howitt, "Avoiding Bottom-line Disaster", INFOWORLD,
 February 11, 1985, pp 26-30.

HOME screen, cells A1 to H20. Thus, by convention, this space should be reserved for documentation through the use of the menu range.

THE FUTURE OF ELECTRONIC SPREADSHEETS

Lotus 1-2-3 and SuperCalc3 are second generation electronic spreadsheets. They have changed the way accountants go about doing their work. In the future accountants are certain to use more graphic analysis, due mainly to the availability of the graphing capabilities of the electronic spreadsheet software. By the end of the 1980's, the auditor's working papers are expected to become a box of diskettes, most of which will be filled with electronic spreadsheets. Projections of cash flows, returns on investments, and capital budgeting decisions are currently done with either electronic spreadsheets or large mainframe programs. Unquestionably, electronic spreadsheets are here for the long haul.

What is the future of electronic spreadsheets? More uses will be found. More users will be trained. More software packages will be forthcoming. Already the third generation of software is available. SYMPHONY is an upgrade of Lotus 1-2-3 from the Lotus Development Corporation. FRAMEWORK is considered a new programming concept in integrated software packages from Ashton-Tate Corporation. Both of these packages have spreadsheets, word processing, data based management, graphics, and communications in one integrated package. Early reviews indicate that Framework is the better software package, but that the Lotus 1-2-3 electronic spreadsheet is a better spreadsheet than either SYMPHONY or FRAMEWORK. The fourth generation is on the drawing boards. What it will bring is not known. The major problem with spreadsheets today is their high primary memory requirements. Perhaps the fourth generation will solve the RAM limitation.

While the future requires predictions, the present requires only an observation. Electronic spreadsheets are a major tool for use by the accountant. Knowledge of spreadsheets is required of all accountants. In the following chapters, Lotus 1-2-3 and SuperCalc3 are discussed. It is assumed that the student will have one or the other available for use. Within each chapter, short exercises will be available to give you practice in using the software. In Chapter 10, longer problems are given to put your knowledge to use in solving problems that directly relate to accounting. The time to begin is now.

USING LOTUS 1-2-3

CHAPTER 4

Lotus 1-2-3 is an integrated business software package that has an excellent electronic spreadsheet, a good graphics package with five types of graphs, and basic database management capabilities. As this is written, Lotus 1-2-3 is the undisputed best selling electronic spreadsheet for business use. The three types of operations are fully integrated, thus each is available though a command. Files generated by Lotus 1-2-3 are automatically given a filetype of .wks or worksheet. Accordingly, electronic spreadsheets prepared with Lotus 1-2-3 are normally referred to as "worksheets". That convention will be followed here. The accountant will find Lotus 1-2-3 an exciting way to use a microcomputer. Let's get started.

GETTING STARTED

When you first break the seal on Lotus 1-2-3, there will be five diskettes--a system disk, a back-up system disk, a graph program disk, a utilities disk, and a tutorial disk. None of the disks will have any operating system files on them, thus the first step will be to "install" the disk by copying those files necessary to provide an operating environment from an IBM DOS diskette, or other operating system that you may be using. The Lotus 1-2-3 manual provides step by step instructions on installing the Lotus 1-2-3 disks. Once installed, you will be able to use the system disks to create worksheet files. In computerease, the installation will be "transparent" to the user. The system disk and the back-up system disk may be used interchangeably; however, the purpose of the back-up system disk is to assure that Lotus 1-2-3 is available in case the system disk is damaged. Thus, using both disks is risky. The system disks are copy-protected, both legally and physically. The disks may not be copied with the DOS copy programs. There is copy software available to copy the disk, but to do so is a violation of the licensing agreement. (One corporation ignored the restrictions of the licensing agreement; Lotus Development Corporation sued and won a two million dollar judgement.) The ethnical standards of the accounting profession also prohibit the unauthorized copying of programs.

With DOS installed on the diskette, you insert the system disk in the default disk drive, normally the A drive on the left, and turn the computer on. The DOS Autoexec program will check out the system and prepare the computer for your use. The date and time will be requested, unless your machine has an internal clock/calendar that will automatically enter the current date and time. Next the autoexec file loads part of Lotus 1-2-3 into the primary memory. At this point the screen will show the "Lotus 1-2-3 Access System" as shown in Figure 4-1.

The Lotus Access System allows you to access the Lotus 1-2-3 spreadsheet, the utilities programs, the print-graph program, and to exit to the operating system. The utilities programs use DOS files to copy, erase, rename, reorder, and format or prepare disks. The File Manager operates on files; the Disk Manager, on disks. The Translate option uses programs on the Utility disk to translate or convert files from VisiCalc, dBASE II, or other DIF files to a Lotus 1-2-3 Worksheet file. The Translate programs are menu driven with substantial on screen instructions. The translation works well and is very useful in the difficult task of interchanging files between software packages. The main focus of this discussion of Lotus 1-2-3 is the selection of commands that make up the electronic spreadsheet.

FIGURE 4-1 LOTUS 1-2-3 ACCESS SYSTEM

```
Lotus Access System  V.1A  (C)1983 Lotus Development Corp.           MENU
-------------------------------------------------------------------------
1-2-3  File-Manager  Disk-Manager  PrintGraph  Translate  Exit
Enter 1-2-3 -- Lotus Spreadsheet/Graphics/Database program
=========================================================================




                          Tue  01-Jan-80
                          0:54:51am
```

```
           Use the arrow keys to highlight command choice and press [Enter]
       Press [Esc] to cancel a choice; Press [F1] for information on command choices
```

LOTUS 1-2-3 WORKSHEETS

From the Lotus Access System, the Lotus worksheet may be entered by using the left or right arrow keys to move the reversed video rectangular menu cursor to "1-2-3" and typing the enter key. The screen will then show the Lotus 1-2-3 copyright notice, as shown in Figure 4-2. Alternatively, from the DOS A> prompt, you may type "123", which will bypass the Lotus Access System and go directly to the 1-2-3 copyright notice. On the copyright notice screen, you are instructed to "Press Any Key To Continue." While literally any of the white keys on the keyboard will do, the space bar is the largest key on the keyboard and the easiest to find. Thus, press the space bar.

The screen will show the "home" screen of the Lotus 1-2-3 spreadsheet, shown in Figure 4-3. Refer to Figure 4-3. Note in the upper right-hand corner of the screen, the

FIGURE 4-2   LOTUS 1-2-3 COPYRIGHT NOTICE

1 - 2 - 3

Copyright (C) 1982,1983
Lotus Development Corporation
All Rights Reserved
Release 1A
*

(Press Any Key To Continue)

mode indicator. At this time 1-2-3 is in the "READY" mode, i.e. it is ready for user action. From the READY mode, all the features of 1-2-3 are accessable. Note the ROW NUMBERS down the left side of the screen and the COLUMN LETTERS across the top of the screen. The upper left-hand corner indicates the cell address where the worksheet cursor or cell pointer (in the words of Lotus) is located.

The modes of Lotus 1-2-3 are important because of the limitations placed on user action by the modes. Also, the meaning of certain keys varies with the current mode. The Lotus 1-2-3 modes are READY, MENU, EDIT, HELP, VALUE, LABEL, POINT, ERROR, WAIT, and FIND. In the READY mode there are no limitations on user action. The user may move to any other mode, enter data, formulas, or labels, call up the command menu, or any other feature of Lotus 1-2-3. The other modes are not so generous. In the MENU mode, the user may only select from the menu--no data, labels, values, formulas, or any other step may be taken until either the user exits the menu mode or selects from the menu. Similarly, in the EDIT mode, the user may only edit the current cell, or exit the edit mode. No other action is allowed. While in HELP mode, the user has access to the entire help menu, but again the help menu must be exited before any action may be taken. The VALUE and LABEL modes indicate the type of entry being made. The POINT mode

FIGURE 4-3   LOTUS 1-2-3 HOME SCREEN

```
A1:                                                                    READ

           A       B       C       D       E       F       G       H
   1
   2
   3
   4
   5
   6
   7
   8
   9
  10
  11
  12
  13
  14
  15
  16
  17
  18
  19
  20
```

indicates that the arrow keys and other movement keys may be used to enter formulas. The use of the POINT mode will greatly speed the entry of formulas and will be discussed in detail below. The ERROR and WAIT modes are self-explanatory. The FIND mode indicates that the Find command in the database management command is being used. Again, when in modes other than READY, user action is limited. Thus, if the operation you are attempting does not work, check the mode indicator. It may be that the action you are trying to take is not allowed in the current mode.

THE CONTROL PANEL

The top three lines of the worksheet is the control panel. Refer to Figure 4-4 as each of these lines is discussed. You will find it very useful to keep an eye on that control panel. Any action you take will first appear on the control panel before it is entered into the worksheet. Many errors may be avoided before they are entered by keeping a watchful eye on the control panel during data entry.

FIGURE 4-4   THE CONTROL PANEL AND THE COMMAND MENU

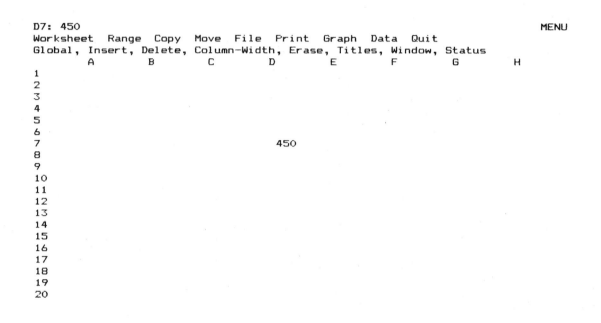

```
D7: 450                                                              MENU
Worksheet  Range  Copy  Move  File  Print  Graph  Data  Quit
Global, Insert, Delete, Column-Width, Erase, Titles, Window, Status
          A         B         C         D        E       F        G        H
 1
 2
 3
 4
 5
 6
 7                                      450
 8
 9
10
11
12
13
14
15
16
17
18
19
20
```

The top row of the control panel displays the cell address and the contents of the current cell, i.e. the cell where the rectangular worksheet cursor or cell pointer is located. Note the top row of Figure 4-4 indicates that the current cell is D7, the contents of cell D7 is the number 450, and we are in the MENU mode. The second row is the "action line." Any action taken by the user will first appear on this line. Also, when the command menu is displayed (see Figure 4-4) the command that is selected will appear on the second row, the action line. The third row of the control panel is the "information row." In the MENU mode, additional information about the commands will be displayed on the third row. The information ranges from short descriptions of the command, to a listing of the subcommands.

THE COMMAND MENU

The commands in Lotus 1-2-3 are selected from the command menu. The menu displays full word commands. The command menu is brought to the screen by pressing the "slash key" (/) on the right side of the keyboard. The full word command menu will be displayed as shown in Figure 4-4. The commands that may be selected are listed on the second row of the control panel. To select from the menu, move the menu cursor (the reversed video rectangle) to the desired command, and type the enter key. For example to select the FILE command, you press the slash key (/), move the cursor to the FILE command by typing the right arrow key four times, and type the enter key. Alternatively, the command may be selected by typing the first letter of the command. Thus to select the FILE command, the user may type / F. Once the commands are somewhat familiar to you, it will be more efficient to simply type the first letter of the command. However, the beginning user should move the cursor to the command and press the enter key. Doing so will allow the beginner a chance to read the brief descriptions of the commands that appear on the information row of the control panel.

SOURCES OF HELP WITH LOTUS 1-2-3

Help with Lotus 1-2-3 is available from five sources. First, Lotus 1-2-3 comes with a 356 page reference manual. The manual is very useful to refer to when a problem arises. However, it is not a very good place to start. Secondly, with your Lotus 1-2-3 software package, you will receive the Lotus 1-2-3 Tutorial disk. The electronic tutorial has six lessons that will lead you through many of the features of Lotus 1-2-3. However, to benefit from the tutorial, you must diligently read each line that appears on the screen. You must be on guard against lapses of attention.

The third source of help is a book like this that is designed to lead you through the features of Lotus 1-2-3 and give you guidance in using the software. A fourth source is to talk to other users. The importance of trying, failing, asking someone what happened, and trying again can not be overstated. The last source of help is the Lotus 1-2-3 on-

line help facility. Refer to Figure 4-5 for the topics
discussed. The HELP menu is brought to the screen by typing
Function Key 1 (F1) located on the left side of the
keyboard. In order to use the help facility, the system
disk must remain in the A disk drive. The help screens are
not loaded into primary memory like other features of Lotus
1-2-3. Only the help screens requested from the menu are
put in RAM. If you are in the process of entering a
command, value, formula, label, or function, Lotus 1-2-3
anticipates your problem, selects a possible help screen
when you type F1, goes to the program disk in the A drive,
and loads and displays the help Also an abbreviated menu
will be given, where one of the options is the full HELP
menu. The menu selections are made by using the arrow keys
to move to the desired help menu item, and pressing the
enter key. To return to the screen, press ESC.

FIGURE 4-5   LOTUS 1-2-3 ON-LINE HELP FACILITY MENU

A1:   HELP

###
Help Index   Select one of these topics for additional Help

How to use The Help Facility   How to Start Over
"Beep!" -- Errors and Messages   How to End a 1-2-3 Session

Special Keys   Moving the Cell Pointer
The Control Panel   Cell Entries
Modes and Indicators   Erasing Cell Entries

Formulas   Operators
"@" Functions

Cell Formats -- Number vs. Label   Column Widths

1-2-3 Commands   Keyboard Macros
Command Menus   Function Keys

Ranges   Menus for File, Range, and Graph Names
Pointing to Ranges   Filenames
Range-Editing Keys

MOVING AROUND THE WORKSHEET

As mundane as it sounds, one of the best features of Lotus 1-2-3 is its ability to move around the worksheet. Recall that an electronic spreadsheet is made up of rows and columns. Many have 63 columns and 256 rows. Lotus 1-2-3 has 256 columns and 2048 rows! It has been reported that if the Lotus 1-2-3 worksheet was printed in its entirely, it would be approximately 21 feet by 42 feet in size. Thus, moving around the worksheet is no small task.

Lotus 1-2-3 was originally designed for the IBM PC. Thus, it is one of the few electronic spreadsheets utilizing the entire IBM PC keyboard. While the keyboard was discussed in Chapter 1, it will be useful to review the uses of the keys in Lotus 1-2-3. The primary movement keys are the four arrows keys on the right side of the keyboard. These keys perform two functions in the READY mode. (Recall the use of the keys varies according to the current mode.) The arrow keys move the cursor one cell in the direction of the arrow--up, down, left, or right. In addition the arrow keys act as an enter key in the READY mode. Thus, to enter data into the worksheet and move the cursor one cell to the right, all that is necessary is to type the right arrow key. The user should consciously try to use the arrow keys for data entry from the beginning.

It is also possible to move around the worksheet by pages. One page of the worksheet is 20 rows by 72 characters (eight nine-character columns-- the default column-width.) To move up and down the worksheet by pages, the "Pg Up" and "Pg Dn" keys are used. They are located on the right side of the keyboard on the number 9 and number 3 keys. To move across the columns, the tab key is used. The tab key is on the left side of the keyboard, to the immediate left of the letter Q. The tab key has two arrows on it, one pointing to the right, and one, to the left. Thus, the tab key will allow the user to move across the columns, one page, i.e. eight nine-character columns at a time.

To move even further distances throughout the worksheet, the HOME and END keys may be used. The HOME key generally returns the cursor to the HOME screen, i.e. to cell A1, the upper left-hand corner of the worksheet. The END key will move the cursor to the end of the occupied area, or to the end of the unoccupied area of the worksheet, as the case may be. For example, refer to Figure 4-6.

Assume that the cursor is located at cell B15. To move to cell A1, press the HOME key. To move from cell A1 to the end of the column of numbers A1 to A10, press the key combination END and down arrow key (on the number 2). The result is to move the cursor to the end of the occupied area, cell A10. To move across the unoccupied area (A11 to A13) to cell A14, again type the end key followed by the down arrow key. Note that when the end key is typed, the word "END" appears in the lower right-hand corner of the screen. You will find the use of the end key in combination with any of the four arrow keys to be a very efficient way of entering formulas and moving around the worksheet. The END HOME key combination moves the cursor to the lower right hand corner of the worksheet. Knowing the cell address of the lower right hand corner is useful in identifying print ranges and in locating vacant worksheet space.

FIGURE 4-6   USE OF END KEY

```
         A    |    B    |    C    |    D    |    E    |    F    |
      |-----------------------------------------------------------------
 1  |       45                         NOTES
 2  |       12
 3  |       36              The END key in combination with
 4  |       23        2     the arrow keys will move the
 5  |       44        5     cursor across empty space to
 6  |       25        8     occupied cell and across occupied
 7  |       69        4     cells to empty cells.
 8  |       78        9
 9  |       91        1     For example, if the cursor is at
10  |       43        7     the HOME cell, A1, the END --> key
11  |                 3     will move cursor to D1, where NOTES
12  |                 8     is entered.
13  |
14  |If the cursor is located in cell B4, the END down
15  |arrow key, will move the cursor to cell B12.
```

There are times when you will want to tell Lotus 1-2-3 where to go. That is the purpose of the Function Key 5, the GO TO key. Typing the F5 key enters a prompt on the action line of the control panel asking the user to "Enter the address to go to:". The user may type the address of any cell in the worksheet and the enter key. The result is that the worksheet cursor (or cell pointer) goes directly to that address. The GO TO key is very useful in setting up indexes within a worksheet. The key portion of the worksheet may be listed on the HOME screen along with their cell address. To view any part, the user will simply type F5 and the correct cell address, then the desired part of the worksheet will appear on the screen.

Throughout our discussion of Lotus 1-2-3, exercises are provided to give you hands on experience with the software. These first exercises are designed to give you practice in the basics of turning the computer on, loading Lotus 1-2-3, using the command menu, and moving around the worksheet. These basic skills are necessary before worksheets are actually designed.

In order to work the following exercises, you will be required to RETRIEVE a FILE from the COURSE DISKETTE provided with the book or from your instructor. In order to do this, the FILE RETRIEVE command will have to be used. The FILE command is fully discussed in Chapter 5. At this point only FILE RETRIEVE is discussed. First, type the right hand slash key, /. The command menu will appear on the action line of the control panel. Select the FILE command by moving the cursor to the right four commands--use the right arrow on the number 6 key. (Note--If the results is four 6's on the action line, check to see if the Num Lock key is toggled on. If it is, the symbol "NUM" will appear on the lower right-hand corner of the screen. Pressing the Num Lock key once will toggle it off.) With the command menu cursor on the command FILE, press the enter key. The sub-commands will now appear on the action line in the control panel. The first of these commands is RETRIEVE. The cursor will be on this command, thus, all you have to do is to type the enter key. At this point the files from the B disk drive will be listed on the action line in rows of eight filenames. Using the arrow keys, move the reversed video cursor to the desired file and type the enter key. The FILE RETRIEVE command will erase the current worksheet, go to the B drive, retrieve the desired file and display it on the screen. The worksheet cursor will appear in the worksheet at the location it was when the file was saved. As a rule of thumb, worksheets should always be saved with the cursor at the HOME cell.

EXERCISE 4-1 -- MOVING AROUND THE WORKSHEET

Retrieve the filename "MOVING" from your course diskette.
Below are several cell addresses from that worksheet. Using
the moving keys that have been discussed above, move the
cursor to these cells and in the blank beside the cell
address (or another sheet of paper), write the contents of
the cell. In moving around use the page keys, the GOTO key
as well as the arrow keys.

Cell address	Contents of cells
A1	_____
C2	_____
C22	_____
A2	_____
I2	_____
R49	_____
AB50	_____

CORRECTING ERRORS

During data input, some accountants may occasionally make an error. With Lotus 1-2-3 there several ways to correct errors. If the entry is still on the action line, i.e. it has not yet been entered, the ESC key will blank the action line allowing you to enter the correct information. Also, before the ENTER key is typed, the backspace key may be used to move one character to the left, erasing that character. If the erroneous entry has previously been entered and consists of only a few characters, the easiest thing to do is to type over the error. By typing over the error, the correcting entry will replace the error. If the error is in a long entry, it is more efficient to use the EDIT mode, entered by typing Function Key 2 (F2). While in the EDIT mode, corrections are inserted to the left of the cursor. The "Del" key, the delete key, will delete the character directly above the cursor. The backspace key will move the cursor to the left one character and erase that character.

In the EDIT mode, the movement keys operate differently. The lateral movement keys, the left and right arrow keys and the tab key, move the cursor along the edit line. The left and right arrows keys move to the left or right one character at a time. The tab key moves the cursor left or right five characters at a time. While in the EDIT mode, the HOME and END keys will move the cursor to the beginning or end of the line being edited. Thus if the error is in the first half of the line, use the HOME key to move to the beginning of the line, the tab key to move to the right five characters at a time, and the right arrow key to move to the specific character to edit. If the error is in the last half of the line, use the SHIFT and tab key to move to the left five characters at a time and the left arrow key to move to the erroneous character. The vertical movement keys, the Pg Up, Pg Dn, Up arrow key, and Down arrow key will leave the EDIT mode and return to the READY mode. Also, typing the ENTER key will return you to the READY mode.

ERASING THE WORKSHEET

There will be times when you simply start off wrong. At times like these, it is more efficient to start over rather than trying to correct all the errors. In this case, the entire worksheet may be erased by using the WORKSHEET

ERASE command. To use the command, type the right slash key (/) to call up the menu, the cursor will be on WORKSHEET, so type the ENTER key to select the WORKSHEET command. ERASE is the fifth sub-command listed. Move the cursor to ERASE and press the ENTER key. At this point, Lotus 1-2-3 will ask if you are sure that you want to erase the worksheet? If you enter "No", the command sequence will be cancelled and you will return to the READY mode. If you enter "Yes", the entire worksheet is erased. Once erased, the information may not be retrieved; it is gone. Frequently, it is not the entire worksheet that you want to erase, rather only part of it. In this case do not use the WORKSHEET ERASE command. The RANGE ERASE command will erase only a part of the worksheet; the part that you specify by giving the appropriate range address. To erase the current cell, i.e. the cell where the cursor is currently located, point to the following commands:

/ RANGE ERASE   Enter key

Thus to erase part of the worksheet, use RANGE ERASE; to erase the entire worksheet, use WORKSHEET ERASE.

EXERCISE 4-2 -- EDIT EXERCISE

Load the file named "EDIT" from your course diskette. Follow the instructions that are given on the screen. The purpose is to give you practice using the various methods of correcting errors. That is, type over short errors, EDIT longer ones. Use the tab key, arrow keys, backspace keys, and delete key. We suggest that you use the techniques in the order they are discussed. Recall that the Lotus 1-2-3 worksheet is on the disk storage, thus, it will not be erased by the WORKSHEET ERASE command. To use the file after using WORKSHEET ERASE, you will have to reload the file from disk storage. Also recall that a range may be as small as only one cell, thus, the RANGE ERASE command may be used to erase the current cell.

Worksheet templates or models are made by entering labels, formulas and numbers or values into cells. Lotus 1-2-3 makes several assumptions as to the nature of the information that is being entered. These rules or conventions must be followed or Lotus 1-2-3 will "beep at you" to indicate an error has been made.

Labels make up anywhere from one-third to two-thirds of a worksheet. The ability to type will be a very useful tool in the use of Lotus 1-2-3 or any other spreadsheet. When entering labels, Lotus 1-2-3 will assume that any character may be a label. Thus, A1 is a label, not a cell address or a value. Any entry that begins with one of the 26 letters of the alphabet, a space, or any other non-value character will be assumed to be a label. In the upper right corner of the screen, the mode indicater will display "LABEL" after the first character is typed. In this way the user will know if a label is being entered. Again, any character may be a label.

Lotus 1-2-3 follows the English convention of right justifying all labels. At times you will want labels to be left justified or centered in the cell. If you begin a label with a double quote ("), the label will be right-justified in the cell. If a caret ( ) precedes the label, the entry will be centered in the CELL, but not the page. As a general rule, labels of columns should be right-justified. This way if the column-widths are expanded, say to 20 characters, the column label will remain right justified, as all values must be. One of the sub-commands of the RANGE command is designed to aid you in obtaining the proper alignment for labels. RANGE LABEL-PREFIX allows you to left justify, right justify, or center the labels within the range specified. To use the command, enter the right slash key (/), move the cursor to RANGE, type the ENTER key, move the cursor to LABEL-PREFIX, type ENTER, enter the range of the worksheet containing the labels, type enter, select LEFT, RIGHT or CENTER, and type enter. Thus, all existing future labels (but only the existing ones) in that range will be so justified.

If the first character typed is a number, +,-,.,(,@,#, or $, Lotus 1-2-3 will assume that a value is being entered. After the first character is typed, the mode indicator will display "VALUE". Lotus 1-2-3 allows cell referencing only

71

for values, thus if a reference to A1 is intended, the first character typed must be a value. Otherwise a label will be assumed. Lotus 1-2-3 suggests that + or - be used. Therefore, if the cell reference to cell A1 is intended, +A1 should be entered. If the reference is to be entered as a negative number, -A1 may be used. Values are always right justified and they may only be right justified. It should be noted, entering the cell address in upper case or lower case does not matter. In this discussion, they will be typed in upper case, but either is fine with Lotus 1-2-3. Of course this applies in typing formulas also.

Values are entered as numbers with decimals. No symbols such as a $ sign or a % sign are entered. To display symbols, the cell must be formatted with a FORMAT command. Decimal points must be entered, but the number of decimal places displayed results from a FORMAT command. The FORMAT command determines the form of the display that appears on the screen, and that is printed by a printer. You enter only the numbers and the decimal point. The rest is left to Lotus 1-2-3.

If a number is to be used as a label, the value assumption must be overridden by the user. Lotus 1-2-3 uses the single quote to indicate a label. Thus, if a single quote precedes a number, it will be entered as a label, not a value. For example, ZIP Codes are never used as numbers; they are always labels and should be preceded with a single quote (') when entered.

POINT MODE

Many spreadsheet operations are intended to be performed on a range of data. Thus, the ability to enter ranges quickly is very useful. Lotus 1-2-3 provides this capability through the use of the "POINT" mode. The POINT mode allows you to use the arrow keys to "point" to a cell rather than having to enter the cell address. When a range is "pointed to" using the POINT mode, the range identified will be displayed in reversed video, i.e. green, light blue, or other, depending upon the monitor being used. The POINT mode may be used anytime that a range or cell address is required to be specified. For example, the MOVE command is designed to move data entered in one cell to a different cell. To use the MOVE command, press the right slash /, move the cursor to the MOVE command, and type the enter key. At this point the user is prompted to "Enter the address to move from:". At the same time, the mode indicator reports that you are in the POINT mode. Thus, the arrow keys may be used to point to the cells to be moved. As the arrow keys are typed, the cell address of the then current cell is entered on the action line as the response to the MOVE command. When the desired location is reached, typing the enter key will enter the current location of the cursor or cell pointer, as part of the MOVE command.

The POINT mode will save many key strokes and therefore, many hours. In addition, frequently it will be easier to move the cursor to the desired cell rather than trying to read the borders to determine the correct cell address. The POINT mode may be used to the great advantage of the user.

Lotus 1-2-3 attempts to help the user by anticipating the desired begining point of the range. Recall that a range is any rectangular grouping of cells in the worksheet. A range has a beginning point and an ending point. In Lotus 1-2-3, the beginning and ending points of a range is separated by two dots (..). Thus A3..C6 indicates the nine cell range beginning with A3 and ending with C6. In the POINT mode, typing the ESC key will unlock the beginning point and allow the user to "point" to a different cell as a beginning point. Typing one period (.) will lock in the new beginning point. Even though the user types only one period, Lotus 1-2-3 will put two periods (..) in its place, the normal manner ranges are identified by Lotus 1-2-3.

Mathematical symbols are somewhat uniform on all microcomputer software. The symbols and the mathematical operation that they perform for the most common functions are listed below.

Mathematical Function	Symbol
Addition	+, the plus sign.
Subtraction	-, the minus sign.
Division	/, the slash key on the right side of the keyboard.
Multiplication	*, the asterisk.
Raise to exponential power	$\wedge$, the caret.

One special key that deserves note is the backward slash key (\) on the left side of the keyboard. This key is a repeating key; it will cause a cell to be filled with any character that follows it. Thus, \- will fill a cell with minus signs, which will resemble an underline; \=, may be used to create a double underline.

LOTUS 1-2-3 FUNCTIONS

Lotus 1-2-3 has several functions built into the program. Functions are no more or less than pre-programmed formulas that are frequently used. Figure 4-7 list the various functions provided by Lotus 1-2-3. The functions all have a similar format and have the following common characteristics. First, Lotus 1-2-3 functions are always values; they may never be labels. Thus, they may be added, subtracted, or manipulated in any desired mathematical equation. A reference to the cell containing a function is a reference to a value. As values, Lotus 1-2-3 functions may be incorporated with other functions or formulas. Accordingly, "nested" functions are possible, for example @SUM(@SUM(A1..B5), A20..B23). In sum, any way a value may be used, a function may be used in the same manner.

Secondly, the Lotus 1-2-3 functions all have the same format. They begin with the at sign, @, located on the number 2 of the typewriter number keys. The @ sign is followed by a function name, and in most cases, a parenthetical expression. The parenthetical expression varies with the specific function. Many times it is a range which identifies the part of the worksheet on which the function is to be performed. For example, the function @SUM(a2..a6) sums or adds the values in the five cells A2 to A6. Note, the function names may be entered in all caps, lower case, or mixed. Lotus 1-2-3 will respond with all caps.

In the following paragraphs, the more commonly used functions are discussed. Discussion of the database statistical functions is deferred until after the DATA command is discussed.

ROUND FUNCTION--@ROUND(x,n)

The @round(x,n) function will round the value "x" which may be a cell address, formula, or any other value, to the nearest nth place. For example to round the number 2.456 to the nearest whole number, the function will be entered as follows: @Round(2.456,0). To round the number to the

FIGURE 4-7   LIST OF LOTUS 1-2-3 FUNCTIONS

Below are listed the Lotus 1-2-3 functions. They all have
the following characteristics:

All 1-2-3 functions are values, never labels. Two special
functions (@NA and @ERR) appear as labels but Lotus 1-2-3
considers them values. All 1-2-3 functions begin with the
at sign, @. Most have an "argument" that is enclosed in
parentheses.

The functions listed below are grouped according to type.

MATHEMATICAL FUNCTIONS

Most useful to accountants:

@ROUND(x,n) Round number x to n decimals places
@RAND   Random number between 0 and 1
@SQRT(x)   Square root of x

OTHERS:
    @ABS(x)   @EXP(x)   @SINx)
    @ACOS(x)   @INT(x)   @TAN(x)
    @ASIN(x)   @LN(x)
    @ATAN(x)   @LOG(x)
    @ATAN2(x,y)   @MOD(x,y)
    @COS(x)   @PI

LOGICAL FUNCTIONS

@FALSE   0, which stands for false
@TRUE   1, any non-zero value is true
@ISNA(x)   1, True, if x = NA
@ISERR(x)   1, True, if x = ERR
@IF(cond,x,y)   x if cond is true; y if cond is false

SPECIAL FUNCTIONS

@NA   The value NA   @ERR   The value ERR

@CHOOSE(x,v0,v1,..vn) Short table lookups, if x is 1,
        results is v1; if x is 0, result is v0;
        x is n, results is vn.
@HLOOKUP and @VLOOKUP(x,range,offset) See text.

FIGURE 4-7 Continued

FINANCIAL FUNCTIONS

@IRR(guess, range)	Internal rate of return
@NPV(x, range)	Net present value of range cash flows at x%
@FV(prin,int,term)	Future value
@PV(prin,int,term)	Present value
@PMT(prin,int,term)	Payment to amortize a liability

DATE FUNCTIONS

@DATE(yr,mo,day)	Numeric value of day, may be formatted
@DAY(yr,mo,day)	Day of month of specified day
@MONTH(yr,mo,day)	Month of specified day
@YEAR(yr,mo,day)	Year of specified day, last two digits
@TODAY	System date's number, may be formatted

STATISTICAL FUNCTIONS and DATABASE STATISTICAL FUNCTIONS

@COUNT(list) and @DCOUNT(imput range,col offset,crit range)
            Number of values in list or range.
@SUM(list) and @DSUM(input range, col offset, crit range)
            Sum of values

@AVG(list) and @DAVG(	same as before)	Average of values
@MIN(list) and @DMIN(	same as before)	Minimum value
@MAX(list) and @DMAX(	same as before)	Maximum value
@STD(list) and @DSTD(	same as before)	Standard deviation
@VAR(list) and @DVAR(	same as before)	Variance

nearest tenth (one decimal place), the function will be entered as @Round(2.456,1); to the nearest ten, @Round(2.456,-1). Lotus 1-2-3 computes each calculation correct to the fifteenth place. At all times each computation is based upon the fifteen decimal number. The number may be displayed with any number of decimals by using a FORMAT command; two is the most common. However, even though the number appears on the screen as if it has been rounded off to two decimals, it has not. Thus, some mathematical operations may appear incorrect, when in fact they are not. For example, if the numbers 22.4533 and 11.4422 are added and displayed with only two decimals, the results would appear as follows: 22.45 + 11.44 = 33.90.   In some situations, this result is not acceptable.   The @Round function is useful in these types of cases.   If the formula is changed to read @Round(22.4533,2) + @round(11.4422,2), the result will be 33.89.   Instead of only appearing to have been rounded to the nearest two decimals, in fact the values will have been rounded.   Thus, the @round function is very useful when preparing schedules for presentation to others parties or other times when accuracy to the nth place is required.

THE IF FUNCTION--@IF(condition, vtrue, vfalse)

The IF function is very useful to classify values and compare values.   The IF function is similar to the logical IF statement in most programming languages.   The form is demonstrated by the following formula: @IF(al=1,2,3).   In plain english, this function says that if the value in cell al is equal to 1, enter the value 2 in the current cell.   If the value in cell A1 is not equal to 1, enter the value 3 in the current cell.   The condition may be made very complex by adding other functions as part of the condition.   For example, the function @if(al=@if(bl=4,5,6),1,2), will equal to 1 if A1 equals 5 and B1 equals 4.   If both conditions are not satisfied, the result will be the false values.   The disadvantage of @IF functions is that they require a large amount of memory, however, they are very flexible and powerful.

FINANCIAL FUNCTIONS

Lotus 1-2-3 has programmed formulas computing the present value of an annuity in arrears (an ordinary annuity).   These formulas are a tremendous help in financial analysis.   Five functions, based upon the present value concepts are available:

Internal rate of return	@IRR(guess, range)
Net present value	@NPV(x,range)
Future value	@FV(principal, interest rate, term)
Present value	@PV(payment, interest rate, term)
Annuity payment	@PMT(principal, interest rate, term)

The internal rate of return requires a guess, or an estimated rate, though in normal cases, the guess only needs to be between 0 and 1.   Lotus 1-2-3 performs 20 iterations before it will give up.   The required range is the range within the worksheet where the cash flows are listed. The range must include at least one change in direction, i.e. go from negative to positive. If all the cash flows are positive, Lotus 1-2-3 will attempt to compute the return on a zero investment--the results are undefined. In the normal case, the first cell in the range will be negative, representing the investment. The following cells in the range contain the returns. Thus, the rate computed is the rate of return for the investment and returns that are entered in the specified range.

The net present value requires only a discount rate expressed in decimal form and a range within the worksheet that contains the cash flows. The list of uses of this financial function is long. Computation of the fair market value of a bond or other series of payments, analysis of a capital budgeting decision, comparing various loan terms and many more may be named. However, the computation is of an ordinary annuity, not an of an annuity in advance.

The @FV, @PV and @PMT all use basically the same information, i.e. the principal of the mortgage amount, the interest rate, the term, and in the case of the @PV only, the payment amount. It is important to remember that the interest rate and the term must be expressed in the same time period. Thus, if the interest rate is expressed as a yearly rate, the term must be a number of years. It should be recalled that the monthly rate is the annual rate divided by 12; the daily rate is the annual rate divided by 360 (or 365 depending upon the convention.)

STATISTICAL FUNCTIONS

The Lotus 1-2-3 statistical functions are the workhorses of the functions. They all have the same form, i.e. @name(list or range). The functions perform the simple task that their name implies. The function and its purpose are listed below. In each case, blank cells are ignored and labels are treated as 0's. Recall that all @functions result in values and may only contain values.

> @COUNT(list)--Responds with the number of non-blank cells in the list or range of the worksheet.
> @SUM(list)--Adds the values in the list or range of worksheet.
> @AVG(list)--Computes the simple average of the values in the list.

@MIN(list)--Compares   the   values   in   the   list   and
          displays the minimum value in the list.
@MAX(list)--Compares   the   values   in   the   list   and
          displays the maximum value in the list.
@STD(list)--Computes   the   standard   deviation   of   the
          values in the list.
@VAR(list)--Computes the variance of the values in the
          list.

Other Lotus 1-2-3 functions will be discussed later.
The functions serve the accountant well.   They are very
useful and may be easily combined into formulas.   The
formulas may be, in the words of the Lotus manual, " . . .
as complex as your courage allows".   However, recall that
some mortal soul will have to read what you have done at
some point.   Remember, the primary objective is to keep it
simple!

EXERCISE 4-3 -- SIMPLE DATA ENTRY

Retrieve the file named "SIMDAENT" from your course diskette. The purpose of this exercise is to give you practice in entering values, labels, and formulas. The task is simple and fully explained in the the file with instructions appearing on the screen. Follow them.

EXERCISE 4-4 -- STUDENT'S GRADE POINT AVERAGE

The purpose of this file is to compute a student's grade point average. The required inputs are name, address, university, college, major, term, courses, credit hours for each course, grade received, entered in numeric form.

The output is the grade point average for the current term followed by a editorial comment regarding the performance.

The input begins in cell A25.

The GRADE POINT AVERAGE is computed in cell G52.

NAME: I. M. Accountant   UNIVERSITY: Masse College

ADDRESS: 342 South Street   COLLEGE: Business
         South Boston, MA
                                 MAJOR: Accounting

GRADES: A = 4.0
        B = 3.0
        C = 2.0
        D = 1.0
        F = 0.0

TERM: Fall

COURSES	CREDIT HR	GRADE	QUALITY PTS.	COMMENTS
ACCOUNTING 3111	3	3	9	NA
ACCOUNTING 3211	3	2	6	NA
ECONOMICS 3111	3	1	3	ERR
FINANCE 3111	3	3	9	NA
MARKETING 3111	3	4	12	NA
CHILD DEVELOPMENT 1	3	1	3	ERR
	--		--	
TOTALS	18		42	2.333

EXERCISE 4-5 -- LOTUS 1-2-3 FUNCTIONS

Retrieve the file named "FUN". The purpose of this exercise is to gain familiarity with the Lotus 1-2-3 functions that discussed above. Full instructions are contained in the file and will be displayed on the screen.

LOTUS 1-2-3 COMMANDS

CHAPTER 5

The Lotus 1-2-3 commands are used to design the worksheet by copying, moving, or deleting data; to format the worksheet; to interface with the printer and disk drive; to use the graphing capabilities; and to use the database management capabilities of the spreadsheet. The commands are organized in a hierarchy of command. From the nine main commands, the command menu is divided into several sub-commands or steps. To select a command, the user first selects from the main menu--the options are WORKSHEET, RANGE, COPY, MOVE,FILE, PRINT, GRAPH, DATA, OR QUIT. Then to complete the command, the user selects from a variety of subcommands. With each selection from the menu, another step is taken to complete the function to be performed. The Lotus 1-2-3 menu, unlike most other spreadsheets, presents the user with a full word menu, rather than a single letter. In addition, the information line of the control panel displays the sub-commands or a single line description of the command. With a familiarity of spreadsheet commands in general, an accountant will be able to read the menus and determine the steps necessary to complete the desired command function.

In this discussion, the menu command to be selected will be typed in all capitals. Recall that to enter the command menu, the slash key (/) on the right side of the keyboard is pressed. To select a specific command, the user may either type the first letter of the command, or move the cursor to the command and type the enter key. The beginner is advised to move the cursor to the command and type the enter key. In this way, the short descriptions of the command will be displayed on the information line in the control panel. In Chapter 4, Figure 4-4 displayed the main menu as it appears on the screen. Figure 5-1 lists the main menu commands and the first level of sub-commands. Refer to Figure 5-1. By reading the various sub-commands, you can get a feel for the types of command functions available with each main command. Before we begin our discussion of the commands, the use of the ESC key and CTRL BREAK key needs to be discussed.

FIGURE 5-1 LOTUS 1-2-3 COMMANDS

Main Command	Sub-Command
WORKSHEET	Global, Insert, Delete, Column-width, Erase, Titles, Window, Status
RANGE	Format, Label-prefix, Erase, Name, Justify, Protect, Unprotect, Input
COPY	From, To
MOVE	From, To
FILE	Retrieve, Save, Combine, Xtract, Erase, List, Import, Disk
PRINT	Printer v File, Range, Line, Page, Options, Clear, Align, Go, Quit
GRAPH	Type, X,A - F Range, Reset, View, Save, Options, Name
DATA	Fill, Table, Sort, Query, Distribution
QUIT	When you said QUIT, you've said it all.

The ESC key, the escape key, is the key that will undo your mistakes in selecting from the command menu. In selecting from the menus, it is not uncommon to start down the hierarchy of commands from the wrong main command. To travel back up that hierarchy, the ESC key may be used. Each time ESC is pressed, the previous menu level will appear on the action line of the control panel. From the main menu, the ESC key will return you to the READY mode. At times it will be useful to quickly move from the MENU mode to the READY mode. The key combination CTRL BREAK will do just that. From any point in the menu, CTRL BREAK will return to the READY mode. This is important because in the MENU mode, you will recall, the only action that may be taken is to select from the menu. The remainder of this chapter discusses the major commands and gives examples of how and when to use them. The commands are discussed in the order they are listed on the command menu. Advanced features of several commands are deferred to Chapter 6. It is suggested that you read through these commands until you reach Exercise 5-1. Then in working this exercise you will most likely need to refer back to the command. Thus, this chapter will be used as a mini manual for the Lotus 1-2-3 commands. Recall that you also have the on-line help facility available. Do not be reluctant to use it. For a quick look at the commands refer to Figure 5-1.

WORKSHEET COMMANDS

WORKSHEET commands are used to modify the worksheet to the satisfaction of the user. The WORKSHEET commands will affect the entire worksheet, row or column, not just a range or part of the worksheet. The WORKSHEET commands may also be used to configure the hardware that will be used with Lotus 1-2-3. The overall format of the worksheet may be set with the WORKSHEET command, and the order of calculation may be set. Lastly, columns or rows may be added or deleted and if the worst happens, the entire thing may be erased in order to start over with a new worksheet.

WORKSHEET GLOBAL COMMAND

The WORKSHEET GLOBAL command sets worksheet settings that will affect every cell in the worksheet. The settings are specified through additional sub-commands. Be aware that it will be slow going at first because of the number of keystrokes that will be required to use the command strings. However, once familiar with the commands, they may be entered by simply typing the first letter of the command. Using this technique will greatly speed the use of the WORKSHEET GLOBAL commands.

WORKSHEET GLOBAL FORMAT (/WGF)

The WORKSHEET GLOBAL FORMAT command sets the FORMAT for every cell in the worksheet. The setting will remain in effect until it is reset with either a subsequent /WGF command or a RANGE FORMAT command. If a cell has been formatted with the RANGE FORMAT command, the WGF command will not affect that specific cell, i.e. the RANGE FORMAT command will overrule the WGF command. Figure 5-2 lists the formatting options and gives examples of each. The GENERAL format is the default format. Decimal places are determined by the size of the column-width and the number needed to reflect the result with a upper limit of fifteen places. In other format options, the number of decimal places may be varied from 0 to 15, at the option of the user.

The FORMAT commands listed in Figure 5-2 are the same for both WORKSHEET GLOBAL FORMAT and the RANGE FORMAT command. As a matter of practice, most accountants find it more convenient to use the RANGE FORMAT command more so than WORKSHEET GLOBAL FORMAT. It is a rare worksheet where every cell in the worksheet is formatted the same way. When RANGE FORMAT is discussed, you will be referred back to Figure 5-2.

FIGURE 5-2 FORMAT OPTIONS

Format	Description	Examples
General	Trailing zeros are suppressed; significant numbers are entered to the extent cell column-width will allow. Large numbers are displayed in scientific format.	23.12345 -4.25 1.3E+12
Fixed	Fixed number of decimal places, 0 to 15. User must specify the desired number.	1.12345 34.000
Scientific	Exponent scientific notation. User specifies the number of desired places. Rarely used by accountants.	-4.3E+00 1.2E+01
Currency	Typical dollars and cents format. A dollar sign precedes each number to its immediate left. The user must specify the number of decimals. Negative amounts displayed in parentheses.	$12.34 $1,234.56 ($12.345) $35
,(Comma)	Identical to the currency format except no dollar sign is displayed. Useful in listing of dollar amounts where dollar sign only appears at top of list.	12.34 1,234.56 (12.345)
Percent	Percentage format, the % sign is added following the number. Note percent is the value enter times 100, thus 12 is 1200%; .12 is 12%; and -.02, -2%.	45% 3.55%
Text	Entry in cell is displayed as entered. Thus, formulas are displayed as entered limited by the cell column-width. Helpful in debugging templates.	+A1 +a3/d4 34.8
Date	Dates in Lotus 1-2-3 are stored as the number of days since January 1, 1900 (which equals 1). Once entered using the @DATE function, they may be displayed as the examples indicate.	15-Jan-85 15-Jan Jan-85 31062

WORKSHEET GLOBAL LABEL-PREFIX *(Left, Right, or Centered)*

The WORKSHEET GLOBAL LABEL-PREFIX (/WGL) command allows the user to set the alignment of all labels in the worksheet. The default setting is left alignment. As a general rule, it is better to use the RANGE LABEL-PREFIX command since side headings should be left aligned. The decision will depend on the number of side headings versus the number of column headings. If side headings dominate, RANGE LABEL-PREFIX will prove more useful. Otherwise, the WORKSHEET GLOBAL LABEL-PREFIX will be preferable.

WORKSHEET GLOBAL RECALCULATION (/WGR)

The RECALCULATION command allows the user to set when to recalculate the worksheet and the order in which it is to be recalculated. Accountants will find the ability to set when recalculation takes place to be more useful. By default, Lotus 1-2-3 will recalculate every formula in the worksheet each time a value is entered or added to the worksheet. When a worksheet is complexed, i.e. contains many formulas, the time for recalculation will seem very long. While, the time for calculation is measured in terms of seconds, the wait will seem like hours. Accordingly, the /WGR MANUAL command turns off the automatic recalculation. When automatic recalculation is off, recalculation occurs only when you calculate the worksheet by pressing the Function Key 9 (F9), the Calc key. For many simple worksheets, the time saved will be insignificant. However, when the time between each value entry seems long, the automatic recalculation may be turned off with the /WGRM command.

The order of recalculation may also be changed from the default, natural order. However, in most cases the natural order will be preferred. The options, COLUMNWISE OR ROWWISE, should be used only in those cases when the worksheet specifically has been designed to calculate in that order. The number of times the recalculation is performed, i.e. the number of iterations, may be set by the /WGR ITERATION command. The default setting is one; one is normally all that is required.

WORKSHEET GLOBAL PROTECTION (/WGP)

The concept of protection of the cells is important. Once a worksheet template is completed, tested, and declared usable by others, then no addition changes should be made by a user of the template. Changes may occur by accident. One way to add a safeguard to the worksheet is to PROTECT the worksheet. With PROTECTION turned on or ENABLED, no changes may be made to the cells. However, the worksheet may still be erased. PROTECTION may be DISABLED for the entire worksheet by the user, or only a part of the worksheet may be UNPROTECTED with the RANGE UNPROTECT command. To PROTECT the worksheet the command is

/WORKSHEET GLOBAL PROTECTION ENABLE.

To UNPROTECT the worksheet, the command is

/WORKSHEET GLOBAL PROTECTION UNENABLE.

WORKSHEET GLOBAL DEFAULT (/WGD)

The DEFAULT option will display the configuration of the software. In addition to changing the configuration of the printer, the default disk drive for storing files may be changed. Normally, with a two floppy disk drive system, the default drive will be the B disk drive. Thus, the default setting is the B disk drive. Hence, the drive prefix, B:, will not be required when saving or retrieving files. If a hard disk drive is used, the default disk drive must be changed to C.

WORKSHEET INSERT (/WI) OR DELETE (/WD)

The WORKSHEET INSERT OR DELETE commands allow the user to add or delete rows or columns in the worksheet. INSERT will add new rows or columns throughout the worksheet in all columns or rows. For example, if column B is inserted, it will be inserted in rows 1 to 2048. Similarly, if row 33 is added, it will be added in all columns, from column A to column IV. The addition will be throughout the entire worksheet, not just in the area that may be seen on the screen. In the same way, if a row or column is deleted, it is deleted throughout the worksheet not just from the area that may be seen on the screen. Thus, as a rule of thumb, insertions may be made with little fear or concern of error. But, deletions should be made only with extreme caution. Once the column or row is deleted, it is GONE, and may not be retrieved. When working with worksheet templates or worksheets that have several formulas already entered, it is advisable to use the MOVE command over which you have more control rather than the WORKSHEET DELETE command.

Insertions are made to the left of the current column if inserting a column, and above the current cell, for rows. When insertions are made, all cell references or formulas are automatically adjusted. For example, if a new column is to be inserted to the left of column E, the new column will be E and the old column E will become new column F. Similarly, each column to the right of the current cell is renamed. If a column or row is deleted, again all the columns or rows will automatically adjust for the change in location of the cell being referenced. If a value referenced in a formula is located in a deleted column or row, the formula will indicate a problem by displaying "ERR" in the cell. Deletion or insertion within a range, i.e. not the endpoint, will simply adjust the length of the range--insertions will lengthen; deletions will shorten the range.

WORKSHEET COLUMN-WIDTH SET (/WCS)

The default width of each column in the worksheet is 9 characters. In you desire to set column-width of the current column alone, the WORKSHEET COLUMN-WIDTH SET command will allow you to set the width of the current column, i.e. where the cursor is located, to any width from 1 to 72 characters. To reset the column width to the global column-width, initially 9 characters, the RESET option is used. Thus, Lotus 1-2-3 provides two commands to set the column-widths. The WORKSHEET GLOBAL COLUMN-WIDTH, will set the widths of all columns in the worksheet; the WORKSHEET COLUMN-WIDTH SET will set only the current column-width. In either case, to specify the desired width, you may either type the number of characters desired, or use the left or right arrow key to point to the new width. Using the POINT mode will allow you to see the width on the screen before you set the width. After pointing to the desired width, type the ENTER key to set the width. The need to set the column-width will be evident by a row of asterisks (*****) that will fill the current cell. Thus, if asterisks appear after entering a value in a cell, the column-width needs to be adjusted.

WORKSHEET ERASE (/WEY)

As discussed above, the WORKSHEET ERASE command allows you to start over with a new screen. All labels, values, and formulas will be erased from the worksheet. So be careful; once erased, they do not reappear. To activate the command, simply answer YES to the menu question--Do you want to erase the worksheet?

WORKSHEET TITLES (/WT)

While entering data to a worksheet, frequently you will want certain rows and/or columns to stay on the screen. The WORKSHEET TITLES command allows you to lock the titles of the rows (VERTICAL title lock), columns (HORIZONTAL title lock), or BOTH. To unlock the title lock, use the CLEAR command. To use the command, move the cursor to the top of the worksheet, one row below the columnar headings, then select HORIZONTAL lock (/WTH) from the command menu. To lock the row labels, move the cursor to the first column to the right of the label and select VERTICAL title lock (/WTV). To set both row labels and column labels at the same time, move the cursor to the upper left hand corner of the worksheet, just below and to the right of the row and column labels, then select WORKSHEET TITLES BOTH (/WTB).

The WORKSHEET TITLE command will prevent rows or columns locked on the screen from scrolling off the screen. The remaining rows and columns will move as before, only those locked on the screen will be affected. The HOME key will not move into the title locked area. In effect, the home cell is redefined to be the upper lefthand corner of the unlocked range. With title lock in place, you will must use the Function key 5, F5, the GO TO key, to move the cursor into the title area. Once in the title area, you may make any changes desired.

WORKSHEET WINDOW (/WW)

The WORKSHEET WINDOW command allows you to split or divide the screen into two parts. With the window in place, you will be able to view two parts of the worksheet at the same time. Furthermore, you may set the scrolling to allow independent movement within the two windows of the worksheet by selecting UNSYNCHRONIZED. To allow the windows to scroll together, i.e. the same rows appear in a vertical window and the same columns in a horizontal window, select SYNCHRONIZED. The two windows will be two separate worksheets in that they may have separate GLOBAL settings.

The WINDOW command is very useful to allow the accountant to view two parts of the worksheet at the same time. For example, to view the effect of a change in Sales on Net income, the HORIZONTAL window may be selected. The cursor in the top window may be moved to Sales; the cursor in the bottom window, moved to Net income. Function key

90

6,F6 the window key, is used to move the cursor between the two windows.

WORKSHEET STATUS (/WS)

The WORKSHEET STATUS command will display the amount of primary memory remaining that may be used for further expansion of the worksheet. In addition, the current worksheet global settings for recalculation, format, label-prefix, column-width, and protection will be displayed. Recall that electronic spreadsheets store everything in primary memory--the program, the data, the formulas, values, everything. Thus, to keep track of the memory available for use, the WORKSHEET STATUS command is very useful.

RANGE COMMANDS

The RANGE commands are very similar to WORKSHEET commands. The distinction lies in the fact that a RANGE command will affect only the specified range of the worksheet, not the entire worksheet. Accordingly, the RANGE commands allow more flexibility than the WORKSHEET commands. Because of the greater flexibility, RANGE commands have proven more useful than their counter part in the WORKSHEET command. However, the relative usefulness of RANGE and WORKSHEET commands is debated among various users. Of course, we are right.

RANGE FORMAT (/RF)

The RANGE FORMAT command allows you to use the same format options discussed under the heading WORKSHEET GLOBAL FORMAT and listed in Figure 5-2. The only difference is that you have to specify the range within the worksheet to be formatted. Recall that a range is any rectangular area of the worksheet. To define a range you must give the beginning point and the ending point separated by periods, e.g. A33..F44. The order of use of the command is to select RANGE FORMAT, specify the type of format (CURRENCY for example), specify the number of decimals if requested, and specify the range using its cell address or name, discussed below.

RANGE LABEL-PREFIX (/RL)

The RANGE LABEL-PREFIX command operates similarly to the WORKSHEET LABEL-PREFIX command. The options LEFT,

RIGHT, and CENTERED are the same and are selected the same way. The difference is that the RANGE command operates only on the range specified by the user.

RANGE ERASE (/RE)

The RANGE ERASE command allows you to erase any range in the worksheet. The suggested range is the current cell. The range may be specified by typing in the beginning and ending cell address or by pointing to the range with the arrow keys. Like the WORKSHEET ERASE command, RANGE ERASE will erase all entries in the cell. However, the erased cells will not free up memory for alternative uses. In order to get Lotus 1-2-3 to release the memory, the file must be saved with the FILE SAVE command, and then retrieved with FILE RETRIEVE command. The retrieved file will utilize memory equal to the occupied rectangular area of the worksheet. The erased cells will no longer require memory. However, if the cell is formatted, memory will be required to support the format of the cell even if the cell is empty.

RANGE NAME (/RN)

The RANGE NAME command is unique to Lotus 1-2-3. Lotus 1-2-3 requires the user to specify many ranges, e.g. the range to format, copy, move, print, and write to disk. RANGE NAME allows you to identify a specific name, any fifteen characters, with a specific range of the worksheet. For example, to add the range A5..A20, the function @SUM(A5..A20) may be used. But if the range A5..A20 is assigned the name "TURKEYS", the same results may be obtained with the function @SUM(TURKEYS). Similarly, to go to A5, the GO TO key (F5) may be pressed, followed by the range name "TURKEYS". The range named may be any size, from only one cell to many cells. Use of range names allows you to more easily remember the location of important parts of the worksheet. Also use of range names in formulas makes it easier to understand the purpose of the formula, and therefore, easier to understand the purpose of the worksheet. Lastly, use of range names makes it possible to set up an index using the GO TO key, F5, and to easily use those commands where ranges must be specified.

Range names are created with the RANGE NAME CREATE command. In answer to the prompt on the action line of the control, you will enter the name to be used. As noted above, any fifteen characters may be used. While the manual states that spaces are allowed, it suggests that they be avoided. The underline key (_) is frequently used to give the appearances of spaces. It is also suggested that mathematical symbols not be used, nor any name that appears like a cell address. Lotus 1-2-3 might get confused as to just where you want it to go.

The other options allow the user to DELETE an individual range name, to RESET all range names, or to automatically associate a range of labels with the cell to their left, right, above, or below the label, the LABELS option. Lastly, when in the POINT mode, the Function key 3, F3, the NAME key, will give you a listing of all range names that have been created in the worksheet. With the name menu, displayed on the action line of the control panel, you may use the arrow keys to point to a name and the enter key to select that name, thereby eliminating the need to type the name. Recall, the slowest part of the microcomputer is the person typing in the data, i.e. you.

RANGE JUSTIFY (/RJ)

The RANGE JUSTIFY command allows you to reblock a string of labels in the same manner that a word processor blocks sentences. Accordingly, a group of labels, perhaps even sentences, may be spread over a range so that they will fit in the range that is specified with a "ragged right" justification. With this command, Lotus 1-2-3 is quite usable as a word processor for short memos. In fact, some accountants use it as the only word processor.

RANGE PROTECT (/RP), RANGE UNPROTECT (/RU)

The RANGE PROTECT and UNPROTECT commands are operative only if the WORKSHEET GLOBAL PROTECT ENABLE command is used first. Then the RANGE UNPROTECT may be used to unprotect the range specified; the RANGE PROTECT may be used to again protect the range. RANGE PROTECT and UNPROTECT only operate on the range specified. Thus, they may to used to make simple modifications in worksheet templates that have been protected. Also, RANGE UNPROTECT may be used to set up a form input to be used with the RANGE INPUT command.

RANGE INPUT (/RI)

The RANGE INPUT is used in connection with the protect commands discussed above. The INPUT option allows you to "fill in the blanks". The cursor will move only to those cells that have been unprotected with the RANGE UNPROTECT command. The arrow keys will move the cursor in the direction of the arrow, but only to the next unprotected cell in that direction.

COPY (/C)

The COPY command creates new cell entries that are copies of existing entries. The COPY command allows you to quickly create large worksheets with complex computations that generate large quantities of numbers. From the standpoint of designing and preparing worksheets, the COPY command is the most important command. The COPY command interacts with the user to copy a part of the worksheet from one range in the worksheet to a second range. At the completion of the COPY command, there will be two copies of the range in the worksheet. The key to the use of the COPY command is to specify TWO ranges: the range to copy FROM, and the range to copy TO.

After the COPY command is selected, the user is requested on the action line of the control panel to "Enter the address to copy FROM:". At this point you will specify the range to be copied. Lotus 1-2-3 will suggest the current cell as the range to be copied. Thus, it is suggested that all copy operations be started with the cursor in the upper left-hand corner of range to be copied. However, any range may be specified. Note that upon entering the COPY command, you are put in the POINT mode. Thus you may use the arrow keys to point to the range you wish to copy. If the cursor is not at the upper left-hand corner of the range, you may type the ESC key to unlock the beginning point, move the cursor to the desired beginning point, press one or two periods (it doesn't matter) to lock in the beginning point, point to the desired ending point, and type the enter key to complete the first step, i.e. specifying the range to copy FROM.

The second step is to answer the prompt on the action line of the control panel, "Enter the range to copy TO:". At this point you are asked to enter the range where you want the worksheet entries to be copied. Recall in the first step, you entered the range to copy FROM. Now, you are asked to enter the second range, the range to copy TO. Again, you are automatically in the POINT mode; thus, you may use the arrow keys to point to the receiving range. In specifying the receiving range, only the upper left hand corner needs to be specified if you are copying a multi-cell range. If you are copying a single cell, but you want multiple copies of that single cell, you will need to specify a multicell range. Refer to Figure 5-3 and the related discussion for a step by step example of the COPY command. If the range copied to has some cells in which information has previously been entered, the COPY command will overwrite those cells and the information therein will be lost. Care should be taken to insure that the range copied TO is vacant.

FIGURE 5-3 THE COPY COMMAND

	A	B	C	D	E	F
1			THE COPY COMMAND			
2						
3			PRINCIPAL AMOUNT	$10,000		
4			INTEREST RATE	15%		
5			TERM IN YEARS	10		
6			PAYMENT	$1,993		
7						
8		PAY #	BEG PRIN	INTEREST	REDUCTION IN PRIN	
9						
10		1	+D3	+C10*$D$4	+$D$6-D10	
11		2	+C10-E10	+C11*$D$4	+$D$6-D11	
12		3	+C11-E11	+C12*$D$4	+$D$6-D12	
13		4	$8,290	$1,243	$749	
14		5	$7,541	$1,131	$861	
15		6	$6,679	$1,002	$991	
16		7	$5,689	$853	$1,139	
17		8	$4,549	$682	$1,310	
18		9	$3,239	$486	$1,507	
19		10	$1,733	$260	$1,733	
20						

NOTE: The copy from C11 to C12 is a RELATIVE copy.

The copy from D10 to D11 to D12 is a RELATIVE copy of the first term and an ABSOLUTE copy of the second term.

Using the COPY command to copy formulas is particularly powerful. Formulas may be copied in the absolute sense or in the relative sense. If copied in the relative sense, all formulas are adjusted relative to the beginning cell. Thus if the formula in cell B15 is B10*B3 and this formula is copied over two columns and down one row in a relative sense the result will be D11*D4, i.e. each column will be increased by two, and each row will be increased by one. The formula is the same form, but the cell references have been adjusted relative to the amount of movement of the formula. If an exact copy is desired, the COPY command will operate in the absolute sense. In Lotus 1-2-3, for a formula to be copied in the absolute sense, dollar signs must be inserted before the part of the cell address that is not to be allowed to change. Thus if the formula B10*B3 is to be copied FROM cell B15, TO D16, with no changes (copied in an absolute sense), the formula must be entered $B$10*$B$3. The dollar sign before the column reference prevents any adjustments from being made to the column reference. The dollar sign before the row address prevents any adjustments to the row reference. The result is an exact copy.

If part of the formula is to be adjusted while the remainder stays the same, you simply have to be selective where you place the dollar signs. Those cell references which are not preceded by dollar signs will be copied in a relative sense, while those with dollar signs will be copied in the absolute sense. For example, assume the formula +D4*C10 is entered in cell D10. Assume that cell D4 is the interest rate on a loan. The beginning balance for each period is in Column C, beginning at C10 with period one. Then the formula in cell D10 computes the interest for period one. The interest for period two, will be of the same form, i.e. interest rate times beginning balance. But the beginning balance for period two will be found in cell C11. Thus the desired formula in cell D11 is +C11*D4. If the formula in D10, +C10*D4 is copied to cell D11, the result will be +C11*D5, i.e. it will be copied in a relative sense. But if the formula in entered in cell D10 as +C10*$D$4, the last part of the formula will be copied in an absolute sense, and the first, in a relative sense. The result of the COPY command will be, +C11*$D$4, which is exactly what we want. Note that the dollar signs do not affect the computation in any way, only the way the formula is copied. With $ results in an absolute copy; without $, results in a relative copy.

Lotus 1-2-3 provides a useful aid to entering the $'s. If you are using the point mode to point to a range, pressing function key 4 (F4) once will enter $'s before both

the column and row. Subsequent pressing of F4 will move $
to just before row, column or none.

The COPY command will prove very useful in designing
worksheets. It should be practiced a great deal. The
exercises that follow require its use to efficiently prepare
the worksheets.

MOVE (/M)

The MOVE is very similar to the COPY with one very
important distinction. With the COPY command, the contents
of the cells copied will appear in two places in the
worksheet. With the MOVE command, the contents of the cell
will appear in only one place in the worksheet. The danger
of the MOVE command is that you will move information on the
top of previous entries in the cell. With the MOVE command,
the cells being moved will displace the contents of the
receiving cells, whether you want them to or not. Thus,
care should be taken to insure that the receiving cells are
either empty or contain information no longer useful to the
worksheet.

As with the COPY command, the MOVE command requires
two steps and two ranges to be specified. First the cell
address of the range to be moved FROM must be specified.
The second step is to specify the cell address of the range
to be move TO. With this two step command, the range
specified will be moved to the receiving range. Any items
in the receiving range will be lost forever. The methods of
specifying the ranges is the same for the MOVE command as
for the COPY command.

FILE (/F)

The FILE command is used to interface with the disk
storage. The most used options are FILE SAVE and FILE
RETRIEVE. FILE SAVE allows the user to write worksheets in
the primary memory to disk storage. All values, formulas,
and labels are written to a file which is named by the user.
The cursor will be saved at its current location. As a
general rule, it is best if the HOME screen is displayed on
the screen when the file is retrieved. Furthermore, if the
HOME screen is to be displayed when retrieved, the cursor
must be at the HOME screen when the file is saved. The
filename must be no more than eight characters selected from
A to Z, 0 to 9, and the underline key _. The worksheet will
be given a filetype of .wks which indicates a worksheet

file. Blank cells below and to the right of the last worksheet entry are not included in the file on disk storage, thus saving a file and retrieving it later is one way to free memory when a part of the file has been erased. If the file has previously been saved, the same filename will be suggested. If a different filename is desired, it may be typed by the user.

The question of when or how often to save a file is important to consider. Recall that the primary memory with Lotus 1-2-3 is volatile memory, i.e. if the power supply is interrupted, anything in primary memory is lost. Accordingly, it is a good practice to save the worksheet after working on it for a period of thirty minutes. Basically what this says is that if thirty minutes of work is lost, the loss will not be of great importance. If the user's time is of greater value, the time between saving the file may be reduced to fifteen minutes or less. Most users ignore this advice at first, until they have the misfortune to accidentally kick the power supply cord from the plug at two AM, and thereby lose the last four hours of work. From that point on, every thirty minutes the worksheet is saved.

The worksheet may be saved as frequently as desired. Each time it is saved, the action line will ask if you want to REPLACE, i.e. overwrite the existing file, or CANCEL the save command. Each time you elect to REPLACE, you will erase the existing file. Normally when this happens you will be developing the worksheet, updating it as you go. Thus, you want to overwrite. Lotus 1-2-3 will always ask you, so be mindful of the old proverb, "Haste makes waste." Carefully consider if, in fact, you want to overwrite before doing so. There is no backup file automatically created. To create a back-up file on another disk, simply resave the file using the same name. With a different disk, back-ups should be kept for every important file. Certainly, any worksheet it takes two days or longer to develop is important enough to justify the cost of an extra disk. BACK IT UP!

FILE RETRIEVE

The FILE RETRIEVE command is simply going to the disk and loading a file into the current worksheet. The current worksheet will be erased and replaced by the worksheet on the disk. The entire worksheet will be loaded with the FILE RETRIEVE command. If only a portion of the worksheet is desired, the FILE COMBINE (discussed later) command must be be used. On the action line of the control panel, all worksheet files will be listed in rows of eight files at a time. To select one of the files, simply use the arrow keys to point to the desired filename, and type the enter key. The FILE command will search the default disk for the files. Normally, this will be the B disk drive. The default drive may be changed with WORKSHEET GLOBAL DEFAULT, or alternatively, with the FILE DISK command, the default disk for the current Lotus 1-2-3 session may be changed.

FILE ERASE

The FILE ERASE command allows the user to erase a specific file. Once erased it is gone, never to return without reentering all the data again. Thus, use it carefully. The FILE LIST command will display on the screen all the worksheet (.wks) files, the print (.prn) files, or the graph (.pic) files that are on the disk. The FILE IMPORT, COMBINED, and EXTRACT commands are discussed below, immediately following Exercise 5-1.

PRINT   (/P)

The PRINT command allows the user to interface with the printer. Even in the computer age, the printed copy is desired. The user has the option of printing the file to the PRINTER, obtaining a hard copy, or to print to the disk, for insertions in a word processing program or other type of software, the FILE option. The PRINT command may be very frustrating to use at first, but with practice, it to will become simple.

In order to get a hard copy of a worksheet file, the only REQUIRED steps are to first specify the range of the worksheet to be printed--the RANGE option. Secondly, tell Lotus 1-2-3 that the printer is at the top of the page or else apparently random blank spaces will show up in your printed copy--ALIGN. Lastly, GO. The default settings for the margins, the number of lines on a page, and other options are acceptable for most printing. Additional PRINT options are discussed in Chapter 6. The purpose of this limited discussion is to give you sufficient information to print out the following exercises.

EXERCISE 5-1 -- STUDENT'S BUDGET

The purpose of this exercise is to put to use the various commands that have been discussed to this point. Below is information that may be used to prepare a budget for Paula Baynett, for a thirteen week term at school. Following that, is a compressed printout of the completed budget. Your assignment is to prepare the worksheet to complete the budget.

The first step is to enter the labels of the various rows and columns. Then, enter the input information. Most of the labels for the output section of the budget may be copied from the input section. Once the formulas are in place for the first week, the formulas for the remaining weeks may be copied from the first. Remember to use cell referencing whenever possible. The rule is to enter a number only once. Each time thereafter, use cell referencing.

EXERCISE 5-1   PAGE 1

NAME: Paula Baynett

ADDRESS: 3007 Campus Row
                   Blacskburg, VA

SCHOOL: Virginia Tech   BEGINNING BALANCE $1,300

TERM: Fall   FIRST DAY AT SCHOOL   ----->   08-Sep

                   CASH RECEIPTS:
SOURCE   AMOUNTS   PERIODICITY *
----------------   ----------   --------------
PARENTS $600   FIRST OF MONTH
PART-TIME JOB $40   WEEKLY
SCHOLARSHIPS $500   FIRST OF TERM
LOANS   AS NEEDED
INVESTMENTS $200   MONTHLY, AT FIRST OF MONTH
OTHER $300   END OF TERM

                   CASH DISBURSEMENTS

EXPENDITURES   AMOUNT   PERIODICITY *
----------------   ----------   -----------
RENT $300   MONTHLY, FIRST OF MONTH
FOOD $75   WEEK
TUITION $1,000   FIRST OF TERM
BOOKS $300   FIRST OF TERM
OPERATION OF CAR
    AT SCHOOL $25   WEEK
CAR TRIPS HOME $40   END OF MONTH
ENTERTAINMENT $30   WEEK
CLOTHING $100   TERM, AVERAGE PER WEEK
OTHER $500   TERM, AVERAGE PER WEEK

   * Note a term is assumed to be thirteen weeks.

BUDGET ITEMS

WEEK BEGINNING

RECEIPTS:

	08-Sep	15-Sep	22-Sep	29-Sep	06-Oct	13-Oct	20-Oct	27-Oct	03-Nov	10-Nov	17-Nov	24-Nov	01-Dec
PARENTS	600				600				600				600
PART-TIME JOB	40	40	40	40	40	40	40	40	40	40	40	40	40
SCHOLARSHIPS	500												
LOANS													
INVESTMENTS	200				200				200				200
OTHER													
BEGINNING BALANCE	1300	870	740	610	440	810	680	550	380	1050	920	790	620
CASH AVAILABLE	2640	910	780	650	1280	850	720	590	1220	1090	960	830	1460

EXPENDITURES

	08-Sep	15-Sep	22-Sep	29-Sep	06-Oct	13-Oct	20-Oct	27-Oct	03-Nov	10-Nov	17-Nov	24-Nov	01-Dec
RENT	300				300								
FOOD	75	75	75	75	75	75	75	75	75	75	75	75	75
TUITION	1,000												
BOOKS	300												
OPERATION OF CAR AT SCHOOL	25	25	25	25	25	25	25	25	25	25	25	25	25
CAR TRIPS HOME				40				40				40	
ENTERTAINMENT	30	30	30	30	30	30	30	30	30	30	30	30	30
CLOTHING	7	7	7	7	7	7	7	7	7	7	7	7	7
OTHER	33	33	33	33	33	33	33	33	33	33	33	33	33
CASH AVAILABLE END OF MONTH	$870	$740	$610	$440	$810	$680	$550	$380	$1,050	$920	$790	$620	$1,290

COMBINING FILES

In analyzing a complex problem, it is frequently useful to break the problem into smaller parts and then combine the results of each part into the final analysis. For example, in analyzing maintenance costs relating to equipment, it will be useful to accumulate the costs by week, summarize the weekly costs by month, and the monthly costs for the year. The yearly costs may then be compared to the cost of the equipment, the vendor and the location of use, in order to determine if there is any correlation among these factors. The FILE COMBINE and FILE XTRACT commands allow you to interchange information between primary memory and disk storage. Either entire files or only parts of files may be transferred between primary memory and disk storage, and these parts may be added, subtracted, or copied to the current worksheet.

The FILE COMBINE command involves the following steps.

Step 1   Move the cursor to the location in the current worksheet where the information from the saved worksheet is to be inserted

Step 2   Select FILE COMBINE from the command menu

Step 3   Select COPY to copy the labels, formulas, and functions into the current worksheet. Select ADD to add the values from the saved file to the the cells in the current worksheet. Select SUBTRACT to subtract the values in the saved worksheet from the cells in the current worksheet. Note if ADD or SUBTRACT is used, no labels will be combined into the current worksheet.

Step 4   Select ENTIRE FILE if the entire file is to be combined into the current worksheet. Select NAMED RANGE if only a part of the saved file is to to be combined. Note: the RANGE NAME command must be used first to name the range to be combined. The range must be named while the saved worksheet is the current worksheet before the worksheet on the disk is saved. If the range has not been named, stop here, go to RANGE NAME CREATE, and name that range.

Step 5   Type the name of the range that you wish to
          combine, if combining a named range. If
          combining the entire file, this step is
          skipped.

Step 6   Select the filename from the list provided on
          the action line in the control panel.

Step 7   Type the enter key. The result is that the
          worksheet from the disk is combined into the
          current worksheet with the upper left hand
          corner of the combining worksheet at the
          current cell, i.e. where the cursor was
          positioned in the current worksheet by the
          user.

     The FILE XTRACT is just the reverse of the FILE
COMBINE, i.e. rather than moving information from the disk
storage into the current worksheet, the information is moved
from the current worksheet into a file on disk storage. In
this way parts of the current worksheet may be saved in a
file for further analysis or reporting. An additional
advantage of FILE XTRACT is the ability to save only values
as displayed and not the formulas that computed the values.
Thus the information saved is not a function of other cells
in the current worksheet. It may serve as input to another
worksheet for further analysis.

     The steps to use FILE XTRACT are listed below.

Step 1   Select FILE XTRACT

Step 2   Select FORMULAS if you want to save the
          formulas Select VALUES if you want to save
          only the values.

Step 3   Select the filename to which the extracted
          information will be written. If the file is
          an existing file you will be asked if you want
          to REPLACE the file or CANCEL the command. If
          you elect to REPLACE the file on the disk with
          the extracted information the contents of the
          file on the disk will be lost. BEWARE.

Step 4   Specify the range of the worksheet you want to
          extract to the disk. The range may be
          specified as a range name or by giving the
          cell address of the beginning and ending
          points of the range.

Step 5   The result will be that the range of the
current worksheet you selected will be written
on the disk.   The file will be named as you
have selected.

The FILE XTRACT command is useful to change values
resulting from formulas to values alone. Then the values
may be combined into other worksheets for further analysis
or printing.   The advantage of not combining formulas is
that when combined the value in the combined cell would be
the result of the formulas that as applied to the current
worksheet.   The formulas were designed for the worksheet in
disk storage, thus the formulas applied to the current
worksheet may (and normally will) provide erroneous results.
By using FILE XTRACT the values will simply be values, and
not dependent upon formulas. Thus, the extracted values may
easily be combined into other worksheets.

EXERCISE 5-2 UPDATE STUDENT'S GPA

The purpose of this exercise is to practice using the FILE COMBINE and FILE XTRACT commands. You will be using the following files from your course diskette: GPA, which you completed in Exercise 4-4 and UPDAGPA, from your Course diskette. In addition, you are given four semester grades report for I. M. Accountant--one of which is from Exercise 4-4. Below the summary report for the four term period is reproduced. The purpose of this exercise is for you to prepare this summary report by using the FILE COMBINE and FILE XTRACT commands. The following steps are required.

Step 1   Retrieve the file GPA from Exercise 4-4. If you used a different name, adjust accordingly.

Step 2   Name the output range FALL3 using the RANGE NAME CREATE command. The output range is the range of the worksheet in which the courses, grades and GPA are summarized. Save the revised GPA file under the name FALL3.

Step 3   Retrieve the file UPDAGPA. With the cursor at cell A41, use FILE COMBINE to combine the FALL3 into UPDAGPA.

Step 4   Using the old GPA revised to FALL3, change the courses and grades to reflect the SPRING4 report below, use the RANGE NAME CREATE to create a range named SPRING4, and combine into UPDAGPA using FILE COMBINE, beginning one page (20 rows) below FALL3 grades.

Step 5   Repeat Step 4 for the FALL4 and SPRING5 reports. Note, it will be more efficient to prepare the two GPA files before using FILE COMBINE.

Step 6   Use FILE XTRACT to extract the single row for each report that contains the summary information. Use temporary filenames like F3, S4, etc. to receive the extracted information.

Step 7   Use FILE COMBINE to combine the summary information for each term in the file UPDAGPA at the appropriate location. Note, in this case you will combine the entire file, e.g. the temporary file F3, etc.

Step 8   Print   the   summary   report   using   the   PRINT
          command.

          NAME: I. M. Accountant   UNIVERSITY: Masse College

       ADDRESS: 342 South Street   COLLEGE: Business
                South Boston, MA
                                             MAJOR: Accounting
        GRADES: A = 4.0   D = 1.0
                B = 3.0   F = 0.0
                C = 2.0

                              SUMMARY

CUMULATIVE GPA   2.42

TERM   CREDIT HRS QUALITY POINTS TERM GPA

FALL, YR 3   18   42   2.33
SPRING, YR 4   18   48   2.67
FALL, YR 4   18   39   2.17
SPRING, YR 5   18   45   2.50

GRADE REPORTS FOR EXERCISE 5-2

TERM: Fall, YR 3

COURSES	CREDIT HR	GRADE	QUALITY PTS.	COMMENT
ACCOUNTING 3111	3	3	9	NA
ACCOUNTING 3211	3	2	6	NA
ECONOMICS 3111	3	1	3	ERR
FINANCE 3111	3	3	9	NA
MARKETING 3111	3	4	12	NA
CHILD DEVELOPMENT 1	3	1	3	ERR
	--		---	
TOTALS	18		42	2.333

TERM: SPRING, YR 4

COURSES	CREDIT HR	GRADE	QUALITY PTS.	COMMENT
ACCOUNTING 3112	3	3	9	NA
ACCOUNTING 3212	3	4	12	NA
ECONOMICS 3112	3	2	6	NA
MANAGEMENT 3001	3	4	12	NA
ACCOUNTING 4000	3	2	6	NA
CLASSICAL MUSIC 1	3	1	3	ERR
	--		--	
TOTALS	18		48	2.667

TERM: Fall, YR 4

COURSES	CREDIT HR	GRADE	QUALITY PTS.	COMMENT
ACCOUNTING 4220	3	3	9	NA
ACCOUNTING 4500	3	4	12	NA
BUSINESS LAW 4000	3	1	3	ERR
BUSINESS POLICY 4000	3	2	6	NA
LIFE AFTER 40	3	2	6	NA
FIRST AID 2	3	1	3	ERR
	--		--	
TOTALS	18		39	2.167

TERM: SPRING, YR 5

COURSES	CREDIT HR	GRADE	QUALITY PTS.	COMMENT
ACCOUNTING 4111	3	2	6	NA
ACCOUNTING 4200	3	3	9	NA
FINANCE 4011	3	3	9	NA
FINANCE 4200	3	2	6	NA
ACCOUNTING 4700	3	4	12	NA
	--		--	
TOTALS	18		42	2.333

PREPARATION OF FORM INPUTS

Frequently substantial data will be required to be entered into worksheets. This information will normally be time consuming to be entered, and may more efficiently be entered by someone who is a trained typist. However, the trained typist may not be knowledgeable of the use of Lotus 1-2-3. The Lotus 1-2-3 compromise is the RANGE INPUT command. The RANGE INPUT command allows a way to provide form orientated data entry into the worksheet for use by people not familiar with Lotus 1-2-3 to enter data. The command restricts movement with the arrow keys, the END key, and the HOME key to those cells in the worksheet that have been unprotected with RANGE UNPROTECT command. When the RANGE INPUT command is used, the movement keys will move the cursor to the next unprotected cell in the direction of the key.

When used in connection with KEYBOARD MACROS, to be discussed in Chapter 6, the RANGE INPUT command may resemble the preformatted screen that is common with database management software. When used alone, the RANGE INPUT command reduces the number of keystrokes and time devoted to repetitive data entry. To use the command, the entire worksheet is first protected with the WORKSHEET GLOBAL PROTECT ENABLE command. Secondly, those cells where data entry is to take place are unprotected with the RANGE UNPROTECT command. Lastly, the RANGE INPUT command is selected and the input range specified. Normally the input range will be the entire worksheet, thus the range may be specified by use of the END HOME key combination if the beginning point is the home cell. At this point all you can do is to enter data, use the F1 HELP key, the F2 EDIT key, and the F9 CALC key. No commands may be selected. To end the input session, type the enter key twice. You will be returned to READY mode from which the world of Lotus 1-2-3 is at your finger tips. In summary, the use of RANGE INPUT is for a form orientated screen usable by a less trained Lotus 1-2-3 user.

EXERCISE 5-3   TRAVEL REIMBURSEMENT FORM

The purpose of this exercise is to create a simple form that will then be used with the RANGE INPUT command. A common form is a travel reimbursement request form. Retrieve the file EX53 from you course diskette. This file contains the labels and formulas to prepare the TRAVEL REIMBURSEMENT FORM reproduced below. To see how the RANGE INPUT command works, first protect the worksheet with WORKSHEET GLOBAL PROTECT ENABLE command. Next unprotect those cells that will require input from the user with the RANGE UNPROTECT command. Lastly, use the RANGE INPUT to input the information given in the following example.

TRAVEL REIMBURSEMENT FORM

The purpose of this worksheet is to demonstrate the use of the RANGE INPUT command. The worksheet prepares a TRAVEL REIMBURSEMENT REQUEST form. The Form begins one page down, at cell A21. To input the required information, select the RANGE INPUT command, specify the entire worksheet as the INPUT RANGE by typing the END HOME key. (NOTE: The END HOME key combination will move the cursor to the lower right hand corner of the worksheet.)

Enter the information by using the right arrow key (-->). The cursor will move only to those cells requiring user input.

REQUEST FOR REIMBURSEMENT OF TRAVEL COSTS

NAME   Indiana Jones   DEPARTMENT A&S.
ADDRESS   Dept of Archeology   DATE   9-4-84
            Univ. of Louisville
            Louisville, KY

PURPOSE OF TRAVEL Retrieve art of covenant

TRANSPORTATION-coach rate, unless unavailable   500

LOCAL TRANSPORTATION (Bus, Rail,Cab)   50

AUTO-Miles @$0.20   100
     -Parking   20
     -Tolls   10   50

OTHER-Explain   Purchase of Whip   50

LODGING   800

MEALS   200
                                                  ─────
TOTAL   1,650

DISALLOWED AS EXCESSIVE   1,100
                                                  ─────
AMOUNT TO BE PAID   550

SIGNATURE OF TRAVELLER   _____

AUTHORIZED BY   _____

ADVANCED LOTUS 1-2-3

CHAPTER 6

In Chapters 4 and 5, the basics of using Lotus 1-2-3 were discussed. Many accountants who are considered "Lotus users" do not go beyond the commands covered in those two chapters. In this chapter the advanced capabilities of Lotus 1-2-3 are discussed. Included is the graphing command that allows you to prepare five types of graphs. In the future, much of the "action" in using Lotus 1-2-3 will center upon these topics.

USING THE PRINT COMMAND'S OPTIONS

The PRINT commands provides a full range of options to get the most from your printer. The limits on the use of the Lotus 1-2-3 PRINT command are a function of the type of printer available and the amount of creativity you possess. The options with the PRINT command are of three types: Margins, page labels, and Setup codes. The default margins are left, 4; right, 76; top, 2; and bottom, 2. Thus, the default margin allows you to print is 72 characters per line. The default page-length is 66 lines, the normal length for 8 1/2 by 11 paper. For most printing, the default margins are acceptable. However, the margins may be changed to accommodate wider or longer paper. Most wide paper used with microcomputers is 14 inches wide. The margin setting for regular size type is a right margin of 135, for a printing range of 131 characters. In summary, the margins are normally acceptable with no changes. If other than 8 1/2 by 11 paper is used, the page-length and right margin will need to be changed. Also, if compressed type is used, the right margin will need to be changed to 135 for 8 1/2 inch paper or 235 for 14 inch paper. Note in setting the right margin, specify the number of spaces from the left edge of the paper. Thus, you are required to include the spaces reserved for the left margin as well.

The PAGE-LENGTH will have to be reset if you are not using the standard 11 inch paper. The default setting is 66 lines per page, including the top and bottom margins, which is designed for the standard paper. If have shorter paper available, count the lines on the paper, reset the PAGE-LENGTH, print a page, and perhaps reset the length. Trial and error is one of the best ways to learn the print options.

HEADERS AND FOOTERS

The page labels may be at the top of the page, a HEADER, or at the bottom of the page, a FOOTER. Furthermore, repetitive row labels or columnar labels may be entered with the BORDER options. HEADERS or FOOTERS may be written on the left side of the page, the center of the page, or the right side of the page. See Exercise 6-1 for examples. To position the HEADER or FOOTER on the page, the vertical line key (|) is used. For example, if "||Header" is entered in response to the prompt to enter the header, the word "Header" will be entered on every page with the letter "r" even with the right margin. Similarly, "|Header" will center the word "Header" at the top of each page; and "Header" will put the word "Header" at the top of each page with the letter "H" even with the left margin. In the same manner, Footers may be positioned at the bottom of each page. Lotus 1-2-3 provides two special characters for use with HEADERS and FOOTERS. The # sign when used in a HEADER or FOOTER will generate page numbers, i.e. numbers, beginning with one that will increment by one each page. The numbers should be identified as page numbers by including "PAGE #" in the HEADER or FOOTER. Recall that the header or footer may be located at the right, left, or center of the page. The second special symbol is the @ sign. When placed in a header or footer, the @ sign will print the system date, which should always be the current date (i.e. today.) Thus, most companies will have a standard header that gives the company's name, today's date, and page number. For the Peanut Company, the following header would be enter in response to the prompt for the HEADER LINE:

Peanut Company|@|PAGE #.

BORDERS

The BORDER options allow you to identify a range of the worksheet as the borders for the rows or the columns of the worksheet. For example, if a weekly cash budget is being prepared for a year, all 52 weeks will not fit on one page. The budget items will be the same for each week, thus the row labels should appear in the left column for each part of the year. The ROW BORDER may be established to print the row labels on each page automatically. Similarly, if columnar labels for each page are desired, the BORDER COLUMN may be specified.

SETUP CODES

Lotus 1-2-3 allows full use of the printer's type fonts through the use of SETUP codes. Use of SETUP codes require knowledge of the specific printer that you are using. The printer's manual will provide a listing of ASCII Control codes and Character Fonts. Similarly, in the appendix to the Lotus 1-2-3 manual, a listing of Lotus 1-2-3 Setup Strings cross referenced to the Decimal ASCII Codes is provided. Thus, by comparing both tables, you may set your printer to use any of the 128 settings supported by Lotus 1-2-3.

The Lotus 1-2-3 setup strings are entered in response to the prompt from the PRINT OPTION SETUP command. The form of the SETUP string is a backward slash - followed by the three digit Decimal ASCII code. For example, with the Espon Dot Matrix printer, the ASCII Decimal code 15 turns on the compressed mode. The result prints 135 characters on standard 8 1/2 by 11 paper. The 1-2-3 SETUP string is, \015. Compressed Mode will remain on until the printer is turned off, which resets all settings to default, or the Compressed Mode is turned off with -018. One of the very useful printer control codes is \069 which turns the Emphasized Mode on. Again, once set on, it will remain on until either the printer is turned off or the control code \070 is entered. Some of the control code must be preceded by "ESC", for example the Emphasized Mode. In these cases, the 1-2-3 setup string would begin with \027, the Lotus 1-2-3 equivalent for "ESC". Thus, to turn on the emphasized mode, the 1-2-3 setup code is \027\069. You must be willing to experiment with the various codes to achieve the special effect you desire. The SETUP code will remain in the worksheet until cleared or erased. Thus, be careful not to keep adding codes on top of codes. The results may not be as expected.

OTHER OPTIONS

The OTHER option allows you to choose As-Displayed or Cell-Formatted, and Unformatted or Formatted. The As-Displayed option is the default. The result is the printed copy will appear the same as appears on the screen, i.e. the printed copy will be as displayed. The Cell-formatted option is useful for documenting the worksheet. The result is a printout of the formulas, values, or labels for each cell, beginning with cell A1 and continuing to the last cell in the worksheet, exactly as entered, i.e. as displayed on the first row of the control panel. Thus, the printout may become a printed documentation of the worksheet. The Formatted option is the default setting and it results in page breaks, headings, and footings. The Unformatted setting suppresses or turns off, these settings. The Unformatted setting is useful when the worksheet is to be printed to a FILE for insertion in another software application, such as a word processor.

The CLEAR option will clear ALL settings, the RANGE setting, the BORDERS setting, or the FORMAT setting. Thus, it is easy to reset to the default settings any of the PRINT commands options.

EXERCISE 6-1 -- PRINT EXERCISES

Below are portions of a Lotus 1-2-3 worksheet which demonstrate the following print features that are in common use by accountants. Your assignment is to recreate these print examples.

Example one is EMPHASIZED print, Lotus 1-2-3 setup code, \027\069.

Example two is EXPANDED MODE, FOR LENGTH OF LINE, setup code -014.

Example three is COMPRESSED MODE, setup code \015.

Example four is normal type with a header and a footer.

While these exercises have in no way exhausted the features of the Lotus print command, they are representative of what can be done. You must be willing to try it, and try it again. Through experimentation, you will find your desired print format.

EXERCISE 6-1 -- EXAMPLES OF PRINT SETUP CODES

EXAMPLE 1   EMPHASIZED MODE   \027\069

This is the emphasized mode; use setup code \027 as ESC, \069
         to set emphasized mode on.   Note results.

EXAMPLE 2   EXPANDED MODE   \014

THE EXPANDED MODE IS FOR TITLES.
Only the first line printed is expanded.

EXAMPLE 3 COMPRESSED MODE \015

The compressed mode allows 135 characters including margins, on regular size paper. It is very useful to get those long worksheets
on one page. You may have to clear the previous setups before you can get compressed mode.

EXERCISE 6-1   PRINT COMMAND   PAGE 1

EXAMPLE 4   HEADERS AND FOOTERS

These are used to identify the worksheet.   Normally the company's
name and the current date are included.

VIRGINIA PEANUT CO.   04-Feb-85

EXERCISE 6-1   PRINT COMMAND   PAGE 2

The GRAPH command allows the accountant an opportunity to put into practice the old adage, "A picture is worth a thousand words." Lotus 1-2-3 provides five types of graphs that may be prepared quickly and easily with the GRAPH command--a LINE graph, a BAR graph, a STACKED-BAR graph, a PIE graph, and an X-Y graph. The availability of this capability should eliminate the reluctance that accountants have shown to use graphs to represent financial information. In fact, many accountants have already said that they are now putting graphs, prepared by Lotus 1-2-3, into annual reports, monthly reports, and special analysis, where in the past they did not use graphs.

Lotus 1-2-3 requires only three steps to prepare a graph. First, select the TYPE of graph. If a TYPE is not specified, no graph may be prepared. Secondly, identify the range of the worksheet that contains the data to be graphed. Lotus 1-2-3 allows six ranges of data, range A to range F, to be specified by the user. In addition the user may specify the values for the X-axis, but it is not a required step. The final required step is to VIEW the graph. Assuming that you have the correct hardware (your computer must have a graphics card installed) these three commands will produce a graph on your screen. The additional commands are optional commands used to enhance the appearance of your graph and allow you to print out the graph with the Graph Program Disk that comes with Lotus 1-2-3. Once the graph has been defined, you may return to the worksheet, modify the data in the ranges being graphed, and view the graph of the modified data. To view the last graph without reentering the GRAPH command, type the Function key 10, F10 (View). The graph will be displayed on the screen.

The SAVE command saves the graph in a .PIC file which can be printed with the PrintGraph command on the Graph Program Disk. The SAVE command writes the current graph on the default disk from which it is later printed. The NAME command allows you to assign a name to the graph through the GRAPH NAME CREATE command, and later USE that graph, by name, to view it. While these two commands appear similar, they are quite different. The SAVE command writes the current graph to the disk. The NAME command will simply assign a name to the current graph while it is in primary memory. If the worksheet as a whole is saved with FILE SAVE, the name will still be associated with a specific graph in that worksheet and may be used when the worksheet is later loaded with FILE RETRIEVE. Thus a saved graph, using the SAVE command, exists outside of the worksheet. The named graph only exists within the worksheet.

The importance of the distinction is that a change in the data being graphed will have no effect on a saved graph, but it will change a named graph. The named graph reflects the data in the range of the current worksheet being graphed. A change in that data is immediately reflected in the named graph. The saved graph has its underlying data saved along with it, thus, it is not affected by any change in the worksheet. The ability to regraph the same range of the worksheet allows graphical display of data that changes over time. Thus, sensitivity analysis in the graphical form may be done.

DISPLAY OPTIONS

The OPTIONS with the GRAPH command allow you to modify the display of the graph to enhance its appearance. The LEGEND Option displays a legend for the data in the ranges. The FORMAT option allows you to set the method for displaying the data points in a LINE or XY graph. The available methods are to use lines connecting the data points, to use symbols, to use both, or to use neither. The default is to use lines.

TITLES

The TITLES option allows you to enter a two line title for the graph, a one line title for the x-axis, and a one line title for the y-axis. The GRID option allows you to overlay horizontal or vertical lines to help the reader identify the plots. The SCALE command allows you to set the scale for the x and y-axis. The default scale is normally acceptable and is the most used. The default scale takes the difference between the high point and the low point in the data range and spreads the difference evenly over the space available. The COLOR option allows you to view the graph in four colors--black, white, a shade of pink, and a shade of blue. The shades will vary with the quality of color monitor you have available. There is little advantage of color with Lotus 1-2-3. The DATA-LABELS allows you to specify a range in the worksheet where the labels for the data ranges have been previously entered.

The common problem in using the GRAPH command is correctly identifying the ranges in the worksheet where the data is found. Like many other parts of Lotus 1-2-3, practice greatly reduces the likelihood of errors. Figure 6-1 is an example of a graph using many of the options discussed. Exercise 10 is designed to give you a chance to practice designing a graph. With the GRAPH command, you may present pictures to tell your story with very little additional effort.

FIGURE 6-1   EXAMPLE OF LOTUS 1-2-3 GRAPH

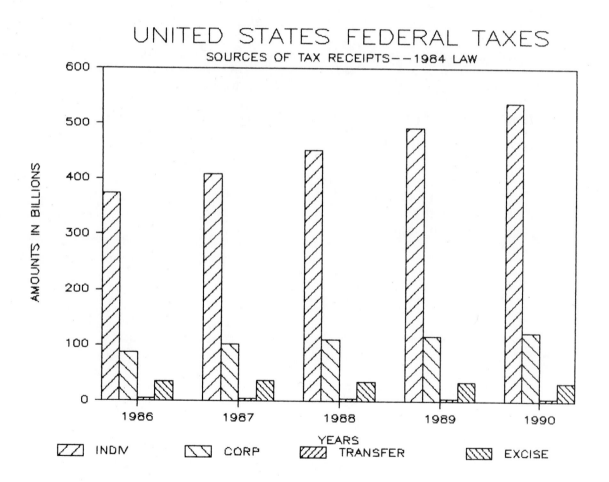

Retrieve the file named "GRAPHS" from your course disk. The data in this worksheet is the federal taxes paid by type of taxpayer under current law. The data served as the basis for the BAR graph in Figure 6-1. For this exercise you are to use the data in the file GRAPHS and prepare a line, pie, bar, stacked bar, and XY graph. For each graph, create a title and legend for the graph, save the graph, and print the graph. To use the GRAPH PROGRAM, the following steps are required.

Step 1   Insert the Print Graph Program disk in disk drive A. If you are in the Lotus Access System, you may select the PrintGraph menu item and you will be prompted to insert the disk in drive A and type the enter key. If you are in DOS, type "GRAPH", press the enter key, and you will get the graph menu.

Step 2   Select the graph (the .pic file) to be printed

Step 3   ALIGN the printer to the top of the page, and select GO. The graph will be printed with the default configuration. If the configuration you are using is different, you will have to reset the configuration. The default configuration is:

Files   Pictures from the B disk drive; Fonts from the A disk drive. Thus, the Print Graph program disk must stay in A disk drive.

Device   Epson MX-80/100, single density (120 x 72) dots

Page   Length 11.0
              Width   8.0

Interface Parallel

The other options are menu driven and explained on the third line of the control panel. We will leave them for you to experiment with. The Lotus 1-2-3 manual provides some information on the use of the various options, but you will still have to try and error your way through.

DATA COMMANDS--DATA BASE MANAGEMENT

The Lotus 1-2-3 DATA commands constitute the database
management capabilities of Lotus 1-2-3, the third segment of
this integrated package. Also the DATA command is the most
limited of the three segments of Lotus 1-2-3. As will be
seen in the discussion of dBASE II or III, the Lotus 1-2-3
DATA command is a limited database management program. The
full discussion of what is a data base, the purpose of a
database management system, and the parts of a data base is
deferred to the discussion of dBASE II and III. However,
Lotus 1-2-3 does perform several operations that are very
useful tools in spreadsheet analysis. The DATA FILL and
DATA TABLE commands are very useful in designing "What-if"
analyses. Accordingly they will be considered first.

DATA FILL

The DATA FILL command fills a range of the worksheet
with numbers. The numbers may start with any number,
positive or negative; step up or down by any number; and
stop either at a specified level or when the limits of the
range is reached. The steps involved are first select the
DATA FILL command. Secondly, specify the range of the
worksheet that is to be filled with numbers. Thirdly,
specify the number to start with, the step between two
numbers, and the number to stop with. The step may be of
any magnitude and either positive or negative. Examples of
uses include generating a list of numbers for checks,
invoices, receivables, inventory of part numbers, etc. Any
number may be generated. Restrictions include that the step
between each number must be constant. Hence 1,2,3 or 2,4,6
are acceptable; 1,4,6,10 is not. The range must be
specified. Ranges may be specified by cell address or by
range name. Furthermore, the range specified may be much
larger than will be needed to reflect the numbers desired;
thus, the end point will be determined by the stop value.
Alternatively, the stop point may be unrealistically large
in which case the end point will be determined by the ending
point of the range. For example, if the range A1..A5 is
specified and the start is 0, step is .05, and the stop is
1, the last value will be .20 in the ending cell A5. The
same results is obtained if the stop value is .20 and the
range is A1..A400. The method used to specify the fill
numbers will depend upon the actual application. As a
general rule, in automated worksheets, i.e. MACRO keystrokes
discussed below, the stop will more likely than not be

determined by the stop value. Any of the values may be specified by cell reference. Thus, the stop value of .2 could have been entered in cell D14 and referenced in the DATA FILL command, i.e. the stop value could have been specified as +D14. Again, the purpose of the DATA FILL command is to fill a range with numbers.

DATA TABLE

DATA TABLE provides the extremely useful capability of preparing a one or two way table to compute the results of an equation which is the function of one or two other values specified by the user. The table may be based upon one or two input variables. Figure 4-12 displays the form of the one input variable and the two input variables DATA TABLE. The steps involved are to first select DATA TABLE; specify the range of the table, which must be set up in the correct form; identify the cell containing the governing formula, the formula that computes the values in the table, and identify the cell or cells containing the input variable or variables. The result is a table of computed values, computed from the formula specified after varying the inputs. In setting up the table, input variable one will be the left-most column, input variable two will be the top row of the table. In a one input table, the formula is located in the cell at the top of the column reporting results of the formula. In a two input table, the formula is specified in the cell that constitutes the upper left hand corner of the table range. See Figure 4-12 for a computed table of mortgage amounts with varying interest rates and monthly payments. Note, in the preparation of a table, the DATA FILL command will be of great use. Lastly, the Function key 8, F8 Table, will recompute the last table that has been specified by the DATA TABLE command. The DATA TABLE command allows a wide range of tabular comparisons to be prepared.

FIGURE 6-2   DATA TABLE COMMAND

```
       A   |   B   |   C   |   D   |   E   |   F   |
   |-----------------------------------------------------
 1 |2*C1
 2 |                              IMPORTANT POINTS
 3 |
 4 |   ONE INPUT TABLE       TABLE RANGE         A7..B12
 5 |-----------------|
 6 |       X        Y |     INPUT CELL 1 is C1 - i.e. CELL C1
 7 |             +B1  |     WILL ASSUME THE VALUES LISTED IN
 8 |       1        2 |     THE LEFT MOST COLUMN.
 9 |       2        4 |
10 |       3        6 |     NOTE THE FORMULA IS REFERENCED AT
11 |       4        8 |     THE TOP OF THE SECOND COLUMN IN
12 |       5       10 |     CELL B7.
13 |-----------------|
14 |                        FURTHER NOTE THE CELL AT THE TOP
15 |                        OF THE FIRST COLUMN, i.e. CELL A7
                            IS BLANK.
```

VALUES IN B8.B12 ARE COMPUTED BY THE DATA TABLE COMMAND.

```
       A    |   B   |   C   |   D   |   E   |   F   |
   |-----------------------------------------------------
 1 |(C1*2 + D1*3) -- > ENTERED IN CELL B1.
 2 |
 3 |INPUT CELL 1          INPUT CELL 2
 4 |
 5 |C1 VALUES   *********  D1 VALUES   **********       C
 6 |   +B1          3        6       9       12         O
 7 |     1         11       20      29       38 --|     M
 8 |     2         13       22      31       40   |     P
 9 |     3         15       24      33       42   -- > U
10 |     4         17       26      35       44   |     T
11 |     5         19       28      37       46 --|     E
12 |                                                    D
13 |
14 |NOTES:   Reference to formula is now in upper left hand
15 |         corner of range, i.e. cell A6.
16 |         Range is A6..E11.
             Input cell 1 is C1, whose values are
                listed in cells A7..A11
             Input cell 2 is D1, values listed in cells
                B6..E6.
             Note BOTH Input Cells MUST appear in FORMULA.
```

Thus, the computed values are a function of the input cell 1 and input cell 2.

EXERCISE 6-3 -- DATA TABLE

Retrieve the file MPG from you course diskette. Using the
information referred to in the menu of that file, compute
the Miles per gallon.

EXERCISE 6-4 -- FINANCIAL LOANS

Retrieve the file MORT from your course diskette. Using the
information referred to on the menu of that file, compute
the amount of mortgage that may be borrowed for each of the
interest rates and monthly payments given. Use DATA TABLE.
Also, report each amount rounded to the nearest $100, using
the @ROUND function.

DATA SORT

The DATA SORT and DATA QUERY commands are the database operations that most closely resembles database management software. DATA SORT command allows the user to sort a range of data, a DATA RANGE, in either ASCENDING or DESCENDING order according to either a PRIMARY KEY and/or a SECONDARY KEY. The SECONDARY KEY will be operative only if there is a tie in the PRIMARY KEY. The key step is correctly specifying the range of the worksheet containing the data to be sorted. Interesting results may occur if the range is not correctly specified. In the DATA command, each row of data is one "record", or one set of information about an entity. If the DATA RANGE is incorrectly specified, perhaps by leaving out one column of information, the result may hopelessly mismatch data such that the remaining data is useless. For example, one accountant (who will not be named) sorted a series of checks but left check numbers out of the DATA RANGE. As a resulted, the checks were sorted by account numbers, but the check numbers displayed did not go with the checks indicated. The resulting information was hopelessly mismatched. That accountant learned to back-up files. As a result of the error, he had to reenter all the information about each record, i.e. each check, one at a time [sic].

The steps required to use the DATA SORT command are discussed in Exercise 6-5. In that exercise each step has been pre-specified to aid you in walking through the DATA SORT command. The command is limited by the amount of primary memory available. Recall that with Lotus 1-2-3 everything is stored in the primary memory. Thus, all fields of each record, or each column of each row of data must be stored in primary memory. Realistically, the limit on the number of records will be lower than the 2,000 stated maximum. The limit will depend upon the amount of memory each record requires. The database management operations in Lotus 1-2-3 are more suited to a small database and analysis of small amounts of data. Thus, analysis of checks written on a certain account, departmental personnel records, continuing education records, telephone lists, client or customers list, and other data bases of individual interest to the accountant are appropriate uses of the DATA command.

EXERCISE 6-5 -- THE DATA SORT COMMAND

Retrieve the file CHECKSOR from your course diskette. CHECKSOR is a file with twenty checks may payable to a variety of payees and accounts. The DATA commands are used to summarize these checks by account numbers and may be used to explore the limits of DATA SORT. All of the required steps have been done, thus you will be able to simply select the various commands and observe the correct entry on the first line of the control panel. For the first look, you are advised to make no changes. That is, the only keys you should type are the arrow keys to move along the command menu, and the enter key to enter the prespecified answers to the DATA SORT prompts.

After you have taken a look at each step involved in using DATA SORT, select the DATA SORT RESET command to eliminate all settings. Try to reenter the commands. If you incur problems, retrieve the CHECKSOR file. All settings will still be intact for your additional review.

The required steps are as follows.

Step 1   Select the DATA SORT command

Step 2   Select DATA RANGE; specify the range of the worksheet. It is important to specify the data range without the columnar headings--the field names. Note the DATA RANGE in the file CHECKSOR.

Step 3   Specify the PRIMARY KEY, i.e. the column or field to be sorted. The PRIMARY KEY is specified by entering the cell address of the first row in the desired column, or in database terms, the cell address of the first record in the field to be used for sorting. As a part of this step, you will be asked to specify whether ASCENDING or DESCENDING order is desired for the sorting. Note, either alphabetic or numeric information may be used for sorting. If desired, a SECONDARY KEY may be stated in the same form as the PRIMARY KEY. The SECONDARY KEY is operative only if a tie is incurred in the PRIMARY KEY.

Step 4   GO. The sort is very fast, RAM speed you might say. For a larger DATA RANGE, the speed will be much slower.

DATA QUERY

The DATA QUERY command allows you to search a data base, and write the records that match the criteria specified into another part of the worksheet, referred to as the OUTPUT RANGE. The criteria can be as simple as all checks written on Account 101, or as complex as the checks written on Account 101 to a person whose last name begins with S and the amount is more than $500, but less than $1,000. The criteria may be specified as an "EITHER OR" criteria or as an "AND" criteria, i.e. the desire item must meet two or more criteria to be a match. The operations that may be performed are FIND, which highlights selected records; EXTRACT, which makes copies of selected records in the OUTPUT RANGE; or DELETE, which erases the selected records.

INPUT RANGE

DATA QUERY requires three types of ranges to be specified before it may be used. The first range is the INPUT range. This range contains the database. Every cell that makes the data must be included in the INPUT range, including the field names (the columnar labels.) The range is specified by giving the range name or the cell address of the beginning and ending point.

CRITERION RANGE

The second range is the CRITERION range. The concept of a CRITERION range seems to be the most difficult to understand. The file CHECKSOR, referred in Exercise 13, contains several criterion ranges. It is suggested that they be studied closely. The CRITERION range is a range within the worksheet. The range must be at least two rows wide, but may be more. The first row of the CRITERION range must be an exact copy of the field names or row labels from the INPUT RANGE. To obtain an exact copy, it is suggested that the COPY command be used. The second and succeeding rows, contain the criteria that must be matched. Note, if the space bar is typed, you are entering a blank space in the cell. Thus, frequently, a blank space will be entered in the criterion range. The result is a search for a blank cell, which may not exist. To find that error is difficult. The best solution is to not make that error. So DO NOT ENTER BLANK SPACES in the CRITERION range.

Criteria are specified in true-false form. Thus, if you are searching for checks written on Account 101, the criterion is expressed as +D4=101. That is the value in cell D4 is equal to 101. If true, the criteria is met; if not true, the criteria is not met. The DATA QUERY command checks each cell in the INPUT range beginning with the first cell in the column or field identified and continuing down that column until it reaches the end of the INPUT range. In the cell containing the criteria, the value 1, if criterion true,or 0, if false, will be displayed. The logical operands, #and#, #or#, and #not#, as well as >,<,>=,<=, or <> will operate as part of a criterion. If a value within a range is desired, the cell address of the first item in that field must be evaluated. In the DATA QUERY command, labels may be evaluated as well as values. Thus, the criteria to identify the last name "Smith", may be entered as +C4=Smith, where cell C4 is the first cell under the column, last name. As with any range, the criterion range may be identified by cell address or with a range name. Many accountants will use range names of the form CRIT_1. Like any range name, the name must first be created with the RANGE NAME CREATE command.

An AND criterion - the item being evaluated must meet all criteria, is specified by entering the criteria all on the same row. An EITHER OR criterion - the item being evaluated must meet either of the criteria, is specified by entering the criterion on succeeding rows. Thus, an either or criterion range would be at least three rows: row 1, the field names or columnar labels; row 2, the first criterion; the row 3, the second criterion; and so on if additional criterion is specified. As a normal case, two criterion will identify the desired record.

OUTPUT RANGE

The third range to be specified is the OUTPUT range. The OUTPUT range is simply a portion of the worksheet reserved for the receipt of records EXTRACTED from the INPUT range. The OUTPUT range must begin with an exact copy of the columnar labels or field names. Again the COPY command may be used. The OUTPUT range should be large enough to receive all possible extracted records. If the range is not large enough, an error message will be displayed. If the ESC key is typed, all the selected records that fit, are extracted to the OUTPUT range.

FIND

The FIND operation evaluates records in the INPUT range according to criteria in the CRITERION range, and reports any match by highlighting in reverse video, the matching record on the screen. To move to the second matching record, type the down arrow key. To move to the third, type the down arrow key again, and so on until the last matching record is reached. When the last matching record is found, Lotus 1-2-3 will give you a friendly beep, and refuse to move down any further. To return to the top of the matching items, press the up arrow key.

EXTRACT

The EXTRACT command will find all items that match the criteria in the CRITERION range and write them to the OUTPUT range. At this point, they are simply additional entries in the worksheet and may be so manipulated. The normal procedure is to print out these matching items. The worksheet is not normally saved with items in the OUTPUT range. If the EXTRACT command is repeated, the new matches will replace the previous results.

To change the criteria in the CRITERION range, you must quit the DATA command, return to the READY mode, move to the criterion range, and change the criteria. To repeat the last QUERY operation (FIND, EXTRACT, UNIQUE, or DELETE), press Function key 7, (F7) the Query key. Lastly, the RESET command will eliminate all range settings.

DATABASE STATISTICAL FUNCTIONS

The database statistical functions are very useful for summarizing information according to some criterion. These functions will perform the same statistical function as the normal statistical functions (e.g. @SUM, @MIN, etc.) but they operate on a database rather than a range. The selection process, i.e. the items to be included in the process, are identified with the same selection process used in DATA QUERY. Thus, the database statistical functions require an INPUT range and a CRITERION range in the same form as the DATA QUERY command. In addition, the column to perform the statistical function on is identified as a column offset, i.e. the number of columns from the left of the INPUT RANGE. Unfortunately, the first column is numbered 0, the second,1, and so on. The standard form for the database statistical functions is:

@Dxxx(input range,column offset,criterion range)

The database statistical functions are @DCOUNT, @DSUM, @DAVG, @DMIN, @DMAX, @DSTD, and @DVAR. Their operation is identical to the normal function, however, they operate only on those items matching the criteria in the CRITERION RANGE. Refer to the file CHECKSOR on your course diskette as discussed in Exercise 6-6 for an example of the @DSUM function.

Retrieve the file CHECKSOR from your course diskette.   This is the same file that was used to work with the DATA SORT command in Exercise 6-5.   The setting for the DATA QUERY commands has previously been set.   Review these settings by walking through the command.   First select DATA command from the command menu.   Next, select QUERY, followed by INPUT. At this point you will be prompted to enter the Input range. The suggested range will be correct, so review it first, and then enter it by typing the enter key.   Next, select CRITERION.   You will be prompted to enter the CRITERION range.   Again, this has been done for you.   Review the range that has been entered, and type the enter key to move back to the menu.   Select OUTPUT range to review the previously entered OUTPUT range.   Type enter to return to the menu. Select FIND.   Note that the items matching criteria in the criterion range are highlighted in reverse video.   Press the enter key to return to the menu.   Proceed through the other options.   Note that the option DELETE will delete all those items meeting the criteria.   That will end your review of previously entered information.   Select RESET to eliminate all settings and try it on your own.

While in the DATA command, repeat the FIND operation to test your settings.   Once you are assured that they are correct, quit the DATA command, return to the READY mode, and change the criteria in the CRITERION range to find those checks written on account 102.   Use Function key 8, the QUERY key, to repeat the last QUERY operation you performed, which should be the FIND command.   If along the way you find that you have erased the data, retrieve CHECKSOR again and start over.   Once mastered the DATA QUERY will be helpful.

Keep the file CHECKSOR in primary memory.   Move the cursor to the right one page (72 characters or 8 default columns.)   Review the summary of checks by account that is displayed there.   Note that only the first two accounts are summarized.   Use the @DSUM command to summarize the checks written on the other accounts.   PRINT the summary for these checks.

Lotus 1-2-3 has the capability to activate a string of keystrokes that are stored in a range within the worksheet. Thus, by typing the combination of the ALT key and one letter (from A to Z) that has previously been associated with the string of keystrokes, you will be able to enter complex and time consuming keystrokes. Lotus 1-2-3 refers to this capability as use of MACROS. The addition of MACROS to the electronic spreadsheet has been hailed the most innovative feature of Lotus 1-2-3. It has proven to be of great use for two basic purposes:

Macros are a time saving device for repetitious commands, primarily PRINT commands.

Macros provide the ability to design worksheets that may easily be used by relatively untrained users for data entry.

Macros are set up by entering as a label, each keystroke to be performed, in a range of the worksheet. The range will contain certain special characters used only in Macros and interpreted by Lotus 1-2-3 the same as if the key they stand for had been typed. See Figure 6-3 for a listing of these special characters. The macro range is then assigned a special range name with the RANGE NAME command. The range must be given a name consisting of the backward slash key (\) and one letter from A to Z. Macros are built by using the alternative method of selecting commands from the menu. Recall that commands may be selected by moving the cursor to the command and typing the enter key, or alternatively, by typing the first letter of the desired command. Thus, commands are selected by entering the first letter of each command. For example, to enter a macro to erase the current cell using RANGE ERASE, the keystrokes "/RE" would be entered into a cell as a label, say cell B5. Next the range B5 is given a name beginning with the backward slash key, say "\E". To activate the keyboard macro, type the key combination ALT E. The result is that the current cell will be erased, that is the keystroke string "/RE enter key" has been performed. The tilde (~) key is a special character that represents the enter key in a macro. The special characters and the keys they represent are listed in Figure 6-3.

FIGURE 6-3

Macro keystrokes require the use of several special characters to replace the use of the keyboard. These special characters and what they mean are listed below.

SPECIAL CHARACTER   PURPOSE OR MEANING OF CHARACTER

~   The TILDE takes the place of typing the
                           enter key.
{Down}   Represents the down arrow key on the
                           number 2 of the number pad.
{up}   Similarly, these character string
{right}   represents the other arrow keys
{LEFT}   on the numpad.

{PgDn}   These additional movement macro keys
{PgUp}   take the place of their normal key-
{Home}   board movement keys.
{End}

{esc}   These macro keys stand for the ESC key,
{del}   the DELETE key, and the Backspace
{BS}   key, respectively

MACRO FUNCTION KEYS

{Edit}   F2, the EDIT key
{Name}   F3, the name key
{abs}   F4, the absolute key
{GoTo}   F5, the GO TO key

{Graph}   Function key 10, the graph key allows you to view
                           a graph
{Window}   F6, the window key
{Query}   F7, the Query key
{Table}   F8, the Table key
{Calc}   F9, the Calc key

MACRO INTERACTIVE KEYS

{?}   Pauses and waits for enter key to be typed

/xlmessage location   Use within a macro keystroke, dis-
                           plays a message in the control panel
                           and waits for the user to enter a
                           label which will be entered at the
                           location specified and type the enter
                           key before proceeding.

/xnmessage location   Use within a macro keystroke, display
                           a message in the control panel and
                           waits for the user to enter a VALUE
                           which will be entered in the cell
                           location indicated before
                           proceeding.

/xmlocation   Specifies the location in the work-
                           sheet where the user defined menus
                           will begin.

/xiformula   "Iformula" uses an If-then statement
/xglocation   to either continue in the current
/xq   macro or go to another one. "G
                           location", allows user to move to
                           the execution of a different macro
                           string. "Q" Allows user to quit the
                           macro.

/xcrange and /xr   These commands are similar to a
                           BASIC program sub routine. The /xc
                           allows you to move in the middle of
                           a macro to a different range and at
                           the conclusion of that macro, the /r
                           returns you to the original point in
                           the first and main macro.

\0   The autoexec macro range . Macros
                           with this name are executed upon
                           using the File retrieve command.

    In deciding where in the worksheet to place the macro
range, the only restrictions are the effect on the amount of
memory being used, and the effect of the macro or other
changes in the worksheet on the macro. Recall that for the
efficient use of memory, worksheets should be designed in
rectangular form, with no L shapes. Typically the macro

range will be most efficiently placed at the bottom of the computation range, out of the working area, but not in a location that would create an L-shaped worksheet. The macro will activate the commands row by row until it comes to a blank row. At this point, Lotus 1-2-3 assumes that the macro is completed, thus, in picking a location for the macro, you want to be certain that the macro range will not be changed by inserting or deleting rows, or by action of the macro itself. For example, some macros may be written to erase a portion of the worksheet. If the macro range is erased, the macro can not be activated--it will no longer exist!

The macro should be documented with a listing of the range name for each macro, the purpose of the macro, and the location of the macro in the worksheet. For example, the minimum documentation for the RANGE ERASE command noted above, would be the following:

\E   Erase the current cell   B5

If the macro is rather lengthy, each step in the macro should be explained with comments to the right of the macro range. Of course for short macros, the statement of the purpose will be sufficient. If there is extensive use of macros in the worksheet, a macro menu screen should be added immediately below the main menu screen at the home screen. In any case, the main menu should refer to the location in the worksheet of the listing of macros.

Interactive macros may be constructed allowing you to input additional data when prompted to do so on the screen. The interactive feature is attained by inserting a question mark enclosed with brackets, i.e. {?}, within a macro string. When the question mark is encountered in the macro, Lotus 1-2-3 will pause and wait until you type the enter key. Thus, when prompted to enter information, you will type the requested information and the enter key. The macro will continue from that point forward. In this case, the enter key is not acting strictly as a enter key, rather it is a signal to continue the macro key.

The special macro range name \0, (that is, back slash zero), allows you to design an autoexec macro. That is, the macro will be activated when the file is retrieved. The macro may be the menu macro. Thus, upon retrieving the file, you will move directly to a user defined menu. The macro will operate the same as if it had been entered as a normal macro range name, but it may be activated only through the FILE RETRIEVE command. Typing ALT O will not activate this special macro. If it is possible that you will want to activate the macro from the keyboard, it should be given two names, \0 and another name that can be activated from the keyboard, like \D. The advantage of the autoexec macro is that a relatively untrained user may use the template and only be required to know how to turn on the machine and load a file. Autoexec files may be written to even do part of that process. Thus, with macros in place, Lotus 1-2-3 may be made very user friendly.

MACRO MENUS

Macros may be designed with user defined menus that operate the same as the Lotus 1-2-3 menus. They will appear in the control panel, will be activated by moving to the command and typing the enter key, or by typing the first letter of the menu selection, and will lead to execution of the macro the same as if entered from the keyboard with "ALT letter." The menu macros use the special macro commands, the /x commands. Lotus 1-2-3 gives a warning that the /x commands are only for those who really want to become programmers. The use of the /x opens the door for all the advantages and disadvantages of programming. With these commands you will have a great deal of flexibility in what you do with the spreadsheet. You will also open the door for all the normal errors that may creep into your program as with any other programming efforts. It is this type of errors that may drive you back to the pencil and paper. But recall, even without programming macros, the electronic spreadsheet will substantially increase your efficiency.

The macro menu is entered in the worksheet on two rows. The first row is the main menu word. The second row is a short explanation of the macro. The menu range is identified by entering the cell address as the location of the menu in the special macro "/xmlocation". The actual macro string to be "run" by the menu will begin on the row directly below the short explanation. Thus, the menu will allow the user to specify which macro string to go to through the use of menus like the Lotus 1-2-3 menus. Refer to Figure 6-4 for an example of menus that may be designed with the /xmlocation macro key.

FIGURE 6-4 EXAMPLE OF A MACRO MENU

FIGURE 6-4   MACRO MENUS

The following examples of MACRO MENUS are for your review.
```
                              !          THESE ARE MACRO MENUS              !
MENU OPTION              -->SAVE--NEW                    SAVE--REPLACE
EXPLANATION OF OPTION ->SAVE THE NEW FILE        SAVE THE CURRENT FILENAME
MACRO KEYSTROKES    -->   /xlEnter file name~b9~ /FS~R~
                    -->   /fs
                    -->
                    -->   ~


MENU MACRO ENTRY        \M Macro for USER DEFINED MENU      /xma5.c5~
```

Additional features of macros are beyond the scope of this book. In summary, macros will always the following characteristics.

1. Macros are always entered as labels, thus the single quote must be used to enter Lotus 1-2-3 commands in a macro string. Otherwise the command itself will be executed.

2. Each keystroke that is required to execute a command must be included in the macro string. If the enter key is required to execute the command, it must be in the macro as a tilde (~).

3. The Lotus 1-2-3 manual rule for entering macros is, "What you see of a label in the worksheet is what 1-2-3 uses to do Alternative Typing." That is, the keystrokes that appear on the screen, must include all keystrokes required to activate the command.

EXERCISE 6-7   USE OF MACROS

Part A

Retrieve the file UPDAGPA from your course disk. GO TO cell A200 and write the following macros.

Macro range name	Purpose of macro	Macro keystrokes
\E	Erase the current cell	/RE~
\M	Enters a menu to select file for updating UPDAGPA	/XMA210.D210~
\C	Combine file into UPDAGPA	/FCCNFALL3FALL3~ /FCCNSPRING4SPRING4~ /FCCNFALL4FALL4~ /FCCNSPRING5SPRING5~
\P	PRINT the output range	/PPROUTPUTAG~

Using the macros, combine the files as before, print the output range, and complete the macro menu. To complete the macro menu, the menu terms should be the school terms, the explanation should explain that the files will be combined or printed, and the macros are as above. Note the macros menu will do the same task that the macros do. The point is to learn how to prepare macro menus. Refer to Figure 6-4 for examples of macro menus. In the print macro above, it is assumed that the output range has been named "output". If this is not the case, you must first use RANGE NAME to name the output range "output".

Part B

Retrieve the file LOAN from your course diskette. The purpose of this worksheet is to prepare a table comparing the principal amount of loan that may be obtained with varying the monthly payment and the interest rates. The table is prepared with the DATA TABLE command. Beginning three pages to the right of HOME, the following macro may be entered to complete the worksheet. Enter this macro, give it a macro name, and execute the macro. Be careful to enter all the keystrokes.

LOTUS 1-2-3 DATE ARITHMETIC

Lotus 1-2-3 provides a series of date function to allow you to let Lotus 1-2-3 handle the computation of time. The date functions are entered as the number of days since January 1, 1900, with 1-1-1900 assigned the number 1. The FORMAT options include a date format that will give you three options to display dates--day-month-year; month-year; and day-month. Since the date is entered as value, you may perform any mathematical operation on that value. Thus, to obtain the date when a 90 day note is due, simply add 90 to today's date. Similarly, to obtain a listing of the dates of every Friday in the first quarter, determine the first Friday and add 7 to it for the desired period. The date functions are very flexible.

The date functions are @DATE, @TODAY, @DAY, @MONTH, and @YEAR. @TODAY will give you the system's date which should be the current day's date. Once it is entered, the worksheet will always display the current day's date. In this way you may keep track of the date the report was prepared. The @DATE is the workhorse of the date arithmetic. It is also a bit unconvenient to enter. The form is @DATE(year,month,day). The entry process may be simplified by using a simple macro, named -D and of the form @DATE({?},{?},{?}). The result will be an interactive macro that will ask for the year, month, and day, but will not require your having to type the rather long function name with all of its upper case characters. If you have several dates to enter, you will be surprised at the time saving involved.

The other date functions give you the day of the month, the month of the year, or the year number (the last two digits of the number.) These are provided for inclusion is formulas where these values are needed. Since the dates are values, they may be used in formulas. For example, if you were preparing a schedule of the age of accounts receivable, those over thirty days old may be determined by an @IF statement. Assume that the date of the receivable is January 6, 1986, and today's date is February 11, 1986, the @IF statement would be @IF(@DAte(6,1,86)-@today)>30,@ERR,0). The result will be ERR if the receivable is more than 30 days old, or 0 (zero) if it is not over thirty days old.

THE LOOKUP FUNCTIONS

The LOOKUP FUNCTIONS are very useful to extract information from a table. One of the most frequent uses is to compute income tax liability. The tax rates must be looked up in a table and then included in a tax computation that results in the tax liability. The function is of the form @VLOOKUP(x,range,offset) where x is the value looked up in the table, say taxable income; range is the range in the worksheet where the table is found; and offset is the number of columns from the left in which the value is to be found where the left most column in the range is 0. The left most column is the comparison column, i.e. the column where the value x is looked up. The @VLOOKUP searches the 0 column (the first column in the range) until it finds a value that is greater. Then, the VLOOKUP will drop back one row and over the offset number of columns for the desired value. Since the @VLOOKUP function searches the first column for a larger value, the last value in the column must be larger than any possible value that will be looked up. Likewise, the first value in the range must be smaller than any possible value that is looked up.

The @HLOOKUP is the same as the @VLOOKUP except the x value is looked up across the columns (i.e. you stay in the same row) rather than down the column. The form is @HLOOKUP(x,range,offset) where x is the value looked up, range is the range of the table where the first row of the table is the range in which the x value is looked up, and the offset is the number of rows from the top that you move down to find the desired value. As before, the value looked up must be larger than the first value in the comparison row and smaller than the last value in the comparison row, the first row. See Figure 6-5 for some examples of both @VLOOKUP and @HLOOKUP.

FIGURE 6-5 EXAMPLES OF LOOKUP

	A	B	C	D	E	F
1	(100,000)	0	100	200		
2	0	0.2	400	1,000		
3	2,000	0.4	300	400		
4	5,000	0.6	200	3,000		
5	8,000	0.8	700	478		
6	100,000	1	300	234		
7						
8	3,200		100			
9	8,700		0			
10						
11	@VLOOKUP(A8,A1.D6,1) = .4				VERTICAL LOOKUP	
12	@VLOOKUP(A9,A1.D6,3) = 478					
13						
14	@HLOOKUP(C8,A1.D6,2) = 300				HORIZONTAL LOOKUP	
15	@HLOOKUP(C9,A1.D6,4) = 0.8					

EXERCISE 6-8 -- DATE ARITHMETIC and LOOKUP FUNCTIONS

PART A

The Hardluck Company reports to you the following Accounts receivable. The company's policy is to age the accounts into three classes: current, 30 days or less; past due, more than 30 but less than 90 days; and hopeless, those more than 90 days old. You are to prepare a schedule of aging of accounts receivable. For consistently, prepare the schedule as of January 1, 1986.

DATE	CUSTOMER'S NAME	AMOUNT
December 2, 1985	George Bailey	$ 200.00
November 8, 1985	Clarence Angle	500.00
August 10, 1985	Mr. Thomas Potter	1,400.00
February 2, 1985	Billy Bailey	500.00

In doing this exercise, use the @DSUM function in which the criterion uses date arithmetic.

PART B

The Chicken Parts-R-Parts Corporation reports taxable income of $89,000 in 1985; $105,000 in 1986; and $48,000 in 1987. Throughout the entire period, the tax rates stayed the same. The rates for all these years are .15 on the first $25,000; .18 on the second $25,000; .30 on the third $25,000; .40 on the fourth $25,000; and .46 on any amount over $100,000.

REQUIRED: Compute the tax liability. Use a LOOKUP table in your computation.

USING SuperCalc3

CHAPTER 7

SuperCalc3 is an integrated software package that has a powerful electronic spreadsheet, the ability to produce simple graphs with a few keystrokes, and some aspects of data base management. SuperCalc3 is a revision of SuperCalc1 and 2. SuperCalc was originally written for the CPM operating system, and then later modified for use with DOS. The resulting electronic spreadsheet is an easy-to-use package with most of the features of a good spreadsheet.

GETTING STARTED

When you open the SuperCalc3 package, you will find a "Product" disk, a "Utilities" disk, a manual, a "10 Minutes to SuperCalc3" tutorial booklet, and a very useful Answer Card 1 and 2. The first step in using SuperCalc3 is to prepare a working copy of SuperCalc3 with part of DOS installed on the disk. SuperCalc3 provides a "STARTUP" program with full on screen instructions to prepare the working copy. SuperCalc3 also suggests that a back-up copy of the configured disk be prepared; STARTUP includes step-by-step instructions to do that. Note that SuperCalc3, unlike other software manufacturers, is not copy protected, i.e. you can copy the needed files from the SuperCalc3 product disk to a formatted disk using the normal DOS copy command. However, you should note that the software is legally protected by the licensing agreement, such that wholesale copying by an organization would violate that agreement. Furthermore, the ethnical standards of the accounting profession does not allow copying of software for other than back-up purposes.

Once the working copy has been prepared, you are ready to load SuperCalc3 into primary memory. As with most spreadsheets, the entire program must be loaded into primary memory. The result is great speed but it does require large amounts of primary memory. From the DOS A> prompt, SuperCalc3 may be loaded by entering SC3. However, the working copy may be installed to automatically load the program. The result is the SuperCalc3 copyright screen shown in Figure 7-1. Per the instructions, type the "return" or enter key, and you will enter the world of SuperCalc3.

FIGURE 7-1

```
                    SuperCalc3(tm)
                    Version  1.00
                     I B M   P C
                 S/N-041878 ,IBM DOS

                    Copyright 1983
                    SORCIM CORP.
                    San Jose, CA.
```

```
Enter "?" for HELP or "return" to start.
F1 = Help; F2 = Erase Line/Return to Spreadsheet; F9 = Plot; F10 = View
```

The other materials you receive with SuperCalc3 are helpful aids in using SuperCalc3. The Utilities disk contains programs designed to help maintain the SuperCalc3 files. It also contains DOS programs that help with file maintenance. The "10 Minutes to SuperCalc3" is a short tutorial booklet designed to familiarize you with SuperCalc3 in a short period of time. The booklet is well written and easy to follow. Answer Card 1 includes a brief listing of the SuperCalc3 commands in a very useful decision tree format, and a listing of the SuperCalc3 functions. Answer Card 2 is a quick reference of the Graphic capabilities of SuperCalc3 including examples of the types of graphs that SuperCalc3 will prepare.

THE WORLD OF SUPERCALC3

SuperCalc3 is organized into rows and columns. The rows are numbered from 1 to 254; the columns are identified by letters from A to BK. The bottom four lines of the screen displays the control panel. Refer to Figure 7-2. The first three lines are the Status line, the Prompt line, and the Entry line. The last line lists the definition of the four Function Keys that SuperCalc3 uses. This last line is always on the screen for your information. Function key 1 (F1) enters the SuperCalc3 Help screens; Function key 2 (F2) erases the entry line and returns to the screen so you can start over; Function Key 9 (F9) plots or prints the current graph; and Function Key 10 (F10) displays the current graph on the screen. None of the remaining Function Keys are used by SuperCalc3.

The Status line indicates the status of the current cell and of the spreadsheet cursor. Also any error message will appear in the far right part of the status line. The first character on the line indicates the direction the cursor will move when the enter key is typed. The greater than sign, >, indicates the cursor will move to the right; the less than sign, <, to the left; the caret,∧, indicates the cursor will move up one cell; while the lower case letter v is used to indicate the cursor will move down one cell. Next, the location of the cursor is indicated by its cell address. If the cell is formatted, the type of format is displayed next. In approximately the middle of that line, the contents of the current cell are displayed and identified as "Text" or "Form", where Text refers to alphabetic entry and Form as a formula or numeric value.

FIGURE 7-2

```
    |  A   ||  B   ||  C   ||  D   ||  E   ||  F   ||  G   ||  H   |
 1|EXAMPLE
 2|
 3|
 4|
 5|
 6|
 7|
 8|
 9|
10|
11|
12|
13|
14|
15|
16|
17|
18|
19|
20|
< A1                Text="EXAMPLE
Width:  9   Memory:253 Last Col/Row:A1      ? for HELP
  1>
F1 = Help; F2 = Erase Line/Return to Spreadsheet; F9 = Plot; F10 = View
```

The Prompt line displays one of two types of information. The first (and normal) type is general information about the spreadsheet. First, the width of the current column is reported in terms of the number of characters. Second, the number of kilobytes of primary memory available is displayed. Next, the cell address, column and row, of the lower left hand corner of the utilized spreadsheet is displayed. Finally, you are reminded that the Help screens may also be accessed by typing the ?.

The second type of information displayed on the prompt line appears when you enter the command-entry mode, i.e. you are about to select from the command menu. At this time the prompt line lists the first letter of the commands for your selection. Pressing Function key 1 or ? will display the command help screen which lists the full word description of the commands. As you make selections from the sub-commands, the available options are listed.

The third line is the Entry or action line. Any action you take appears on this line before you enter it in SuperCalc3. To move back to a previous step in the entry process you may type the backspace key. The sub commands or options that are to be selected appear on the prompt line, but are entered on the entry line. When entering data or textual material, the information may be immediately edited before it is entered. Thus, it is good practice to keep an eye on the entry line. Many errors may be avoided at this point. Before discussing how information is entered, you should understand the sources of Help available with SuperCalc3.

SOURCES OF HELP

SuperCalc3 provides help from several sources. The most obvious source is the answer screen available for each step in using SuperCalc3. At any point you may type either the question mark (?) or Function Key 1 (F1), and the answer screen relating to the command, function, or data entry being entered is displayed. While you do not have a choice of topic on which you receive help, the answer screens do provide useful information that should answer most questions relating to the command or other step that you are entering at the moment. In order to use the answer screens, the product disk has to remain in the default disk drive, normally the A drive. The Help file is not loaded into primary memory and is only available from disk storage.

Other sources of help include the manual, this book, and other books like it. The manual is divided into two parts. The first is an eleven lesson tutorial designed to introduce you to the software. It is an interactive tutorial with detailed instructions on how to use the various commands. The second part of the manual is a reference with each command listed in alphabetic order and explained. Examples of various sub-commands are given. Following the commands, the SuperCalc3 functions are listed and explained. Taken together, the two parts of the manual are very good. Compared to other spreadsheet packages, the SuperCalc series of manuals are superior. They are very readable and provide the necessary information. In addition Sorcim, the creator of SuperCalc3, maintains a technical support group to answer questions.

The basic mindset required to learn the use of microcomputers is the willingness to try, make mistakes, ask for help, and try again. The rewards are great. The use of SuperCalc3 greatly increases productivity and makes your product, i.e. your service, more valuable to your employer. The spreadsheet is before you; it is awaiting your data entry. First, you need to learn how to get around in the spreadsheet.

MOVING AROUND THE SPREADSHEET

The primary movement keys in SuperCalc3 are the four arrow keys on the number pad at the right of the keyboard. These arrows move the cursor one cell in the direction of the arrow. If the keys are held down, they act as repeating keys and cause the cursor to continue to move in the same direction. The keys do not act as enter keys; there is only one enter key with SuperCalc3. In addition to entering data, the enter key moves the cursor one cell in the same direction as the last arrow key that was typed. The first character on the status line indicates the direction the spreadsheet cursor moves when the enter key is pressed. Thus, when you are entering a column of numbers, set the direction you want the cursor to move by typing the arrow keys such that the last arrow key typed is in the desired direction, i.e. down for a column of numbers. Next you may turn the number pad on (by pressing the NUM LOCK key) and use the ten key number pad at the right of the keyboard and the enter key to enter the column of numbers. The spreadsheet cursor automatically moves to the next cell. To skip a cell, just type the enter key, i.e. "enter" a blank cell.

In order to move greater distances in the spreadsheet, you may use the GOTO key. To use the GOTO key type the equal sign, =. The prompt line will ask you for the address to go to. You have three options at this point. If you type a cell address, D4 for example, the cursor moves to cell D4. If you type a number, 4 for example, SuperCalc3 assumes that you intend to move to column A, row 4, thus you arrive at cell A4. If you type a letter, D for example, you move to the first cell in that column, D1. Another movement with the GOTO command is to move the cursor to the cell that you want to be in the upper left hand corner of the screen. Type the equal sign and the enter key, but with no cell address. The result is to move the current cell to the upper left hand corner of the screen.

The last movement key to be discussed is the HOME key. The Home screen has been referred to earlier as the normal location of the spreadsheet's index or menu screen. To move to this screen, SuperCalc3 uses the HOME key (located on the number 7 key of the number pad). Type this key once and you will automatically move to cell A1, the upper left hand corner of the Home screen.

EXERCISES

Throughout the discussion of SuperCalc3, exercises are provided which allow you to gain hands on experience with the software. These first exercises are designed to give you practice in the basics of turning the computer on, loading SuperCalc3, using the command menu, and moving around the spreadsheet. These basic skills are necessary before spreadsheets are actually designed.

In order to work the following exercises, you are required to LOAD a file from the COURSE DISKETTE provided by your instructor. In order to load a file, the LOAD command has to be used. First, type the right hand slash key, /. The command menu appears on the Prompt line of the control panel. To LOAD the file named MOVING from the COURSE DISKETTE in disk drive B into RAM, type the following and then press the enter key.

/ L B:MOVING

The contents of the file are loaded into the existing SuperCalc3 spreadsheet. The spreadsheet cursor is located at cell A1, the HOME Cell. The spreadsheet cursor is always located at the cell where it was when the spreadsheet was saved, i.e. when it was written on the disk.

150

EXERCISE 7-1 -- MOVING AROUND THE SPREADSHEET

Load the file named "Moving".

The purpose of this exercise is to give you practice in moving around the spreadsheet. Use the movement keys discussed above to move to the cell requested. In the blank provided or on separate paper, indicate the entries found in the listed cells.

CELLS   WHAT ENTRY DID YOU FIND?

A1   _____

C2   _____

C22   _____

M1   _____

A100   _____

BK254   _____

CORRECTING ERRORS

It is not unusual for users of microcomputers to make errors when using the software. In a sense, that is good; you learn what not to do the next time. Also one criteria of a "good" software package is the way it handles errors, which all users make. Errors are tolerated quite well by SuperCalc3 and there are several ways provided to correct these errors. The choice depends upon the type of error made and the work involved to correct that error.

If you discover an error before it is entered, you may correct it on the entry line. The lateral movement keys, left and right arrow keys and the backspace key, will allow you to move along the entry line without changing the entry. When you reach the erroneous entry, you may delete it or type over it. If you decide the entire entry is erroneous and have not yet entered it into the spreadsheet, you may use Function key 2, F2, to erase the entry and start over.

If the entry has been entered and is very short, the easiest approach to correcting an error is to simply retype the entry. Retyping will overwrite or replace the old entry with the new. If the entry is long, it will be quicker to EDIT the entry. To edit an entry that has previously been entered into the spreadsheet, the EDIT command is used. To call up the commands type a slash key /. The slash key is on the right side of the keyboard. One of the commands that is listed on the prompt line is E for EDIT. Thus, typing /E and the enter key allows you to edit the current cell, i.e. the cell where the cursor is located.

While in the EDIT command, the arrow keys move the cursor to the left or right on the edit line one character at a time. The TAB key, the key with two arrows, located on the left side of the keyboard, just to the left of the letter Q, moves the edit cursor to the end or beginning of the edit line. Type the Tab key once, it moves to the beginning of the edit line; type it again, it moves to the end. In the default setting of the EDIT command the insert mode is off. Thus, any correction typed overwrites the character previously entered. If you desire to INSERT a character, you may type the INS key, the Insert key, once. The last line in the control panel reports that you are in the INSERT mode. When you type a character, it is inserted to the left of the character above the cursor. Alternatively, you may insert blank spaces in the edit line by typing the up arrow key. Then you may type the characters in the line. To DELETE a character, move the cursor to the character and type the DEL key, the Delete key, located in the lower right hand corner of the keyboard. Alternatively, you may use the down arrow key to delete the character where the cursor is located. To exit the EDIT command type the enter key. Any changes you have made are entered into the spreadsheet at this point. Until the enter key is typed, the edited changes are not entered.

There are times when the entry is beyond hope. In fact you may determine that there should be nothing in the cell. In this case, you would like to erase the current cell completely. The Blank command, listed as a B in the command menu does that and more. The purpose of this command is to erase either the current cell alone, or a range of cells. To erase only the current cell, the command is /B and type the enter key. To erase a block or a range of cells, type /B, give the beginning and ending cell address, and type the enter key. For example to erase the ten cells A1 to B5, the command is

/ B A1:B5

Of course, once the cell is erased, to get it back, you have to reenter it.

If things are really bad, the entire spreadsheet may be erased. The command is straight from the West Coast, ZAP. Only with SuperCalc3 may you ZAP a spreadsheet. But as is often the case with well written software you are given a chance to change you mind, or realize you really do not want to erase the entire spreadsheet. You are given three options: Yes, erase all settings and entries in the spreadsheet; No, cancel the Zap; and Contents, erase all entries and all settings except the user defined formats settings (to be discussed later.) After selecting an option, type the enter key. You have zapped your spreadsheet, and whether you wanted to or not, it is gone. To get it back, you must reenter the data. Use Zap carefully. To use Zap, type /Z, select an option (Y,N, or C) and press the enter key.

EXERCISE 7-2 -- EDIT EXERCISE

Load the file named "EDIT" from your course diskette.
Follow the instructions appearing on the screen. The
purpose is to give you practice using the various methods of
correcting errors. Thus, when making the corrections, type
over short entries; EDIT longer ones. Use the tab key, the
up arrow key and the insert key, the down arrow key and the
delete key, the backspace and the left and right arrow keys.
You will be instructed to use the Blank command to erase
some single cells and some ranges. After you have edited
the file once, use the ZAP command to erase the spreadsheet.
Recall that the file is on disk storage, thus you will be
able load it a second time for further practice.

Spreadsheet templates or models are made by entering labels, formulas and numbers or values into cells. SuperCalc3 makes several assumptions as to the nature of the information that is being entered. These rules or conventions must be followed or SuperCalc3 responds with an error message.

Labels make up anywhere from one-third to two-thirds of a spreadsheet. The ability to type is a very useful tool in the use of SuperCalc3 or any other spreadsheet. When entering data, SuperCalc3 evaluates the entry to determine if it is a legitimate formula. SuperCalc3 considers a formula to be any entry that results in a number such as a number, a cell reference to a number or a formula or function that results in a number. In addition a textual value, to be discussed below, is considered a formula. If the entry is not a formula, it is assumed to be a label or text. Thus, SuperCalc3 assumes all entries that qualify to be a value or formula. Other entries are considered text and are so indicated internally in SuperCalc3 by a double quote at the beginning of all text entries. The following entries are assumed to be formulas or values:

a numeric constant, i.e. the characters 0-9 (+ -)

a cell reference or cell coordinate, for example A4

a mathematical, calendar, or special function

a textual constant

No other entries are assumed to be values or formulas, thus they must be labels or text. The nature of the entry is displayed on the status line in the control panel at the bottom of the screen after it has been entered.

SuperCalc3 follows the English convention of left justifying all text material. At times the user desires the text to be right justified in the cell. You may change the justification with the FORMAT command, discussed below, to either TEXTLEFT or TEXTRIGHT. Note that the text is left or right justified in the CELL, but not the page. As a general rule, labels of columns should be right-justified. This way if the column-widths are expanded (with the FORMAT command,) say to 20 characters, the column label remains right justified, as all formulas or values are. In order to center a title on a page, you are forced to use the same method as an old typewriter, i.e. count the characters in the title, subtract from 72 (the total per page), and divide the difference by 2.

If one of the items assumed to be formulas is typed, SuperCalc3 assumes that a formula or value is intended. After the entry is typed, the center of the status line displays "Form=" with the entry displayed following the equal sign. See Figure 7-2, for an example. SuperCalc3 allows cell referencing only for formulas and textual values. To reference a cell, simply type the cell address, A1 for example. If A1 is intended to be a text entry, it must be preceded by the text indicator, the double quote sign, ("). A textual value is a special value provided by SuperCalc3 that allows you to reference what appears to be textual material. A textual value is any label or alphabetic character set that is delimited or enclosed with both double quotes and parentheses, for example ("SuperCalc"). Textual values are limited to nine characters. Once entered in a cell, they may be treated as formulas for purpose of cell references. Their uses are further illustrated below. Formulas are assumed to be positive. If the reference is to be entered as a negative number, -A1 may be used. Formulas or values are always RIGHT justified by default, but with the FORMAT command they may be LEFT justified.

Formulas or values are entered as numbers with decimals. No symbols such as a $ sign or a % sign are entered. To get the symbols, the cell must be formatted with the FORMAT command. Decimal points must be entered, but the number of decimal places displayed results from an option in the FORMAT command. In sum, the FORMAT command determines the form of the display that appears on the screen and that is printed with a printer. The user enters only the numbers and the decimal point. The rest is left to SuperCalc3.

If a number is to be used as a label, the formula assumption must be overridden by the user. SuperCalc3 uses the double quote to indicate textual data. Thus, if a double quote precedes a number, it is accepted as text, not a formula. For example, ZIP Codes are not used as numbers; they are usually labels and should be preceded with a double quote (") when entered.

Many spreadsheet operations are intended to be performed on a range of data. The ability to enter ranges quickly is very useful. SuperCalc3 provides this capability through the use of the ESC key. Basically, the ESC key allows the user to use the arrow keys to "point" to the cell to be entered rather than having to type the cell address. The ESC mode may be used anytime that a range or cell address is required to be specified. For example, one of the useful yet simple functions is the SUM function. To use the SUM function, you type SUM(range). The result is that the values in that range are added. The range to be typed may be identified by sight and the beginning and ending address of the range entered. However, if you type the ESC key, you will be able to point to the first cell in the range with the arrows keys. As you move the cursor in the spreadsheet, the cell address of the cursor appears on the entry line. When you reach the beginning point of the range, type a colon (:). (Note, SuperCalc3 ranges are separated by a colon.) When the colon is entered, the cursor returns to the beginning point. Using the arrow keys again, point or move the cursor to the end of the range and type the ending parenthesis. The current range is entered, but without typing the range address.

The use of the ESC key saves many key strokes. In addition, frequently it is easier to move the cursor to the cell that you desire to reference, rather than trying to read the borders to determine the correct cell address. The ESC key may be used to great advantage by the user.

Mathematical symbols are somewhat uniform on all microcomputer software. The symbols and the mathematical operation that they perform in SuperCalc3 for the most common operations are listed below.

Mathematical Function	Symbol
Addition	+ the plus sign.
Subtraction	- the minus sign.
Division	/ the slash key on the right side of the keyboard
Multiplication	* the asterisk.
Raise to exponential power	∧ the caret.

One of the keys deserving special attention is the repeating text key, the single quote ('). If a character is entered with a leading single quote, that character is repeated until it fills the entire row from point of entry until an occupied cell is encountered. The cell may be occupied with no more than a row of blanks entered by typing a single quote and the enter key. The primary use of the key is to construct underlines (the minus sign repeated for the entire row, i.e. '-) and for double underlines (the equal sign repeated in the row, i.e. '=).

SUPERCALC3 FUNCTIONS

SuperCalc3 has several functions built into the program. Functions are no more or less than pre-programmed formulas that are frequently used. Figure 7-3 lists the various functions provided by SuperCalc3. A function is a specially defined set of characters that is recognized by SuperCalc3 to refer to a specific formula. The functions are always values; they may never be labels. Thus, they may be added, subtracted, or manipulated in any desired mathematical equation. A reference to the cell that contains a function is a reference to a value. As values SuperCalc3 functions may be incorporated with other functions or formulas. Thus, anyway that value may be used, a function may be used in the same manner.

The SuperCalc3 functions are all of the same format. They have a unique name, followed by an argument allowing you to specify the cells used by the function. The function name may be entered in upper, lower, or mixed case. In this discussion, function names will be typed in upper case. The parenthetical expression varies with the specific function. Many times it is a range which identifies the part of the spreadsheet on which the function is to be performed. For example, the function SUM(a2:a6) sums or adds the values in the five cells A2 to A6.

In the following paragraphs, the more commonly used functions are discussed. Discussion of the Calendar functions and some of the special functions are deferred until Chapter 9.

FIGURE 7-3 SUPERCALC3 FUNCTIONS

ARITHMETIC FUNCTIONS--Frequently used by accountants

AVERAGE or AV(list)	Computes the average of the values in the list
COUNT(list)	Returns the number of non-blank cells in the list
MAX(list)	Returns the maximum value in the list Non-numeric cells are ignored
MIN(list)	Returns the minimum value in the list Non-numeric cells are ignored
ROUND(value,places)	Rounds the value off to the nearest "places"
SQRT(value)	Computes the square root of the value
SUM(list)	Adds the numbers in the list, labels are ignored.

OTHERS--Listed for your information

ABS(value)	Absolute value	ACOS(value)	Radian angle of
COS(value)	Cosine,Sine, or	ASIN(value)	Cosine, Sine, or
SIN(value)	Tangent of	ATAN(value)	Tangent value
TAN(value)	radian angle	EXP(value)	e value
LN(value)	Natural log	INT(value)	Integer of value
LOG(value)	Common log	PI	3.141592653589793
MOD(value1,value2)	Produces the remainder from dividing the values.		

LOGICAL FUNCTIONS

IF(expression1, value2,value3)	If expression 1 is true, enter value 2, otherwise, value 3--no labels
AND(value1,value2)	If both value 1 and value 2 are TRUE, expression will equal 1, TRUE.
OR(value1, value2)	If either value 1 or value 2 is TRUE, function will equal 1, TRUE.
NOT(value)	Returns the opposite truth value, e.g. NOT(A1=1) if A1 is 1, function is 0; if not, function is 1.

SPECIAL FUNCTIONS

ERROR or ERR	Returns the word ERROR
NA	Returns the word N/A, for not available
LOOKUP or LU(value,col/row range)	Looks up value in table Discussed in Chapter 9.

ROUND FUNCTION--ROUND(a,n)

The ROUND(a,n) function rounds the value "a" which may be a cell reference, formula, or any other value, to the nearest nth place. For example to round the number 12.456 to the nearest whole number, 12, the function is entered as follows: ROUND(12.456,0). To round the number to the nearest tenth (one decimal place), the function is entered as ROUND(12.456,1); to the nearest ten, ROUND(2.456,-1). At all times each computation is computed to the fifteenth decimal place. The number may be displayed with any number of decimals by using a FORMAT command; two decimals are the most common. However, even though the formatted number appears on the screen as if it has been rounded off to two decimals, in fact it has not. Thus, some mathematical operations may appear incorrect, when in fact they are not. For example, if the numbers 22.4533 and 11.4422 are added and displayed with only two decimals, the results would appear as follows: 22.45 + 11.44 = 33.90. In some situations, this result is not acceptable. The ROUND function is useful in these types of cases. If the formula is changed to read ROUND(22.4533,2) + ROUND(11.4422,2), the result is 33.89. Instead of only appearing to have been rounded to the nearest two decimals, they are in fact so rounded. Thus, the ROUND function is very useful when preparing schedules for presentation to other parties.

IF FUNCTION--IF(expression a, expression b, expression c)

The IF function is useful to classify values and compare values. The IF function is similar to the logical IF statement in most programming languages. The form is demonstrated by the following formula: IF(a1=1,2,3). In plain English, this function says that if the value in cell A1 is equal to 1, enter the value 2 in the current cell. If the value in cell A1 is not equal to 1, enter the value 3 in the current cell. The condition may be made very complex by adding other functions as part of the condition. For example, the function IF(a1=IF(b1=4,5,6),1,2) is equal to 1 if A1 equals 5 and B1 equals 4. If both conditions are not satisfied, the result is one of the false values 6 or 2.

Textual values may be used in IF statements. Thus, an IF function can evaluate a text entry. For example, The IF statement, IF(a1=("male"),a3,a4) will enter the value of a3 if cell a1 contains the textual value ("male"). Textual values add greatly to the clarity of the IF function. A disadvantage of the IF function is that it utilizes memory rapidly, however, it is very flexible and powerful.

FINANCIAL FUNCTIONS

SuperCalc3 has programmed formulas to compute the present value of an annuity in arrears (an ordinary annuity). These are a tremendous help in financial analysis. Five functions, based upon the present value concepts are available:

Internal rate of return   IRR(guess,col/row range)

Net present value   NPV(discount,col/row range)

Future value   FV(principal,interest rate,term)

Present value   PV(payment,interest rate,term)

Annuity payment   PMT(principal,interest rate,term)

The internal rate of return (IRR) does not require you to specify a guess; the default guess is .10. In normal cases, a guess would be made between 0 and 1. SuperCalc3 performs 20 iterations before it gives up. The col/row range is the range within the spreadsheet where the cash flows are listed. The first cell includes the investment and the others in the range, include the cash flows that are assumed to be in equal intervals.

The net present value requires only a discount rate expressed in decimal form and a range within the spreadsheet that contains the cash flows. The uses of this financial function are many, for example, computation of the fair market value of a bond or other series of payments, analysis of a capital budgeting decision, and comparing various loan terms. Remember the computation is of an ordinary annuity; not of an annuity in advance.

The FV, PV and PMT functions all use basically the same information, i.e. the principal of the mortgage, the interest rate, the term, and in the case of the PV and FV, the payment amount. You must be careful to assure that the interest rate and the term are expressed in the same time frame. Thus, if the term is expressed in years, the interest rate must be a yearly rate. It should be recalled that the monthly rate is the annual rate divided by 12; the daily rate is the annual rate divided by 360 (or 365 depending upon the convention.)

ARITHMETIC FUNCTIONS

The SuperCalc3 Arithmetic functions are the workhorses of the functions. They all have the same form, i.e. name(list or range). The functions perform the simple task that their name implies. The function and its purpose are listed below. In each case, blank cells are ignored and labels are treated as 0's.

COUNT(list)--Responds with the number of non-blank non-text cells in the list or range of the spreadsheet.

SUM(list)--Adds the values in the range of spreadsheet.

AV(list)--Computes the simple average of the values in list.

MIN(list)--Compares the values in the list and displays the minimum value in the list.

MAX(list)--Compares the values in the list and displays the maximum value in the list.

Additional SuperCalc3 functions are discussed later. The functions serve the accountant well. They are very useful and may be easily combined into formulas. The formulas may be very complex. However, recall that some mortal soul will have to read what you have done at some point. Remember the primary objective, KEEP IT SIMPLE!

EXERCISE 7-3 -- SIMPLE DATA ENTRY

Retrieve the file named "SIMDAENT" from your course diskette. The purpose of this exercise is to give you practice in entering values, labels, and formulas. The task is simple and fully explained in the file with on screen instructions. Follow them.

EXERCISE 7-4 -- SUPERCALC3 FUNCTIONS

Retrieve the file named "FUN". The purpose of this exercise is to gain familiarity with the SuperCalc3 functions that discussed above. Full instructions are contained in the file and are displayed on the screen.

EXERCISE 7-5 -- STUDENT'S GRADE POINT AVERAGE

The purpose of exercise file is to compute a student's grade point average. The required inputs are name, address, university, college, major, term, courses, credit hours for each course, and grade received, entered in numeric form.

The output is the grade point average for the current term followed by a editorial comment regarding the performance. Note the comments are entered with the special function NA or ERR.

The input begins in cell A25.

The GRADE POINT AVERAGE is computed in cell G52.

NAME: I. M. Accountant   UNIVERSITY: Masse College

ADDRESS: 342 South Street   COLLEGE: Business
         South Boston, MA
                                MAJOR: Accounting

GRADES: A = 4.0
        B = 3.0
        C = 2.0
        D = 1.0
        F = 0.0

        TERM: Fall

COURSES	CREDIT HR	GRADE	QUALITY PTS.	COMMENTS
ACCOUNTING 3111	3	3	9	N/A
ACCOUNTING 3211	3	2	6	N/A
ECONOMICS 3111	3	1	3	ERROR
FINANCE 3111	3	3	9	N/A
MARKETING 3111	3	4	12	N/A
CHILD DEVELOPMENT 1	3	1	3	ERROR
	--		--	
TOTALS	18		42	2.333

SuperCalc3 COMMANDS

CHAPTER 8

The SuperCalc3 commands allow you to perform many operations in designing the spreadsheet. The SuperCalc3 command menu is displayed on the prompt line in the control panel by typing the slash key (/), located on the right side of the keyboard. The menu consists of the first letter of each command and is listed in alphabetic order. If you need more information about the commands, you may display the help screen for the command menu by typing either Function key 1 (F1) or the question mark (?). The full word command and a short description of the command will be listed on the screen. To return to the command menu, type Function key 2 (F2). To select one of the commands, type the first letter of the command. Thus to LOAD a file from the disk drive, the command is entered by pressing / L.

The names used for commands are descriptive of their purpose. For example EDIT, edits a cell; LOAD, loads a file; SAVE, saves a file; and so on. However, some commands perform functions that are not evident from the name of the command. For example, it is frequently necessary to adjust the widths of the columns. The command to do so is an option under the FORMAT command. The commands grouped according to their functions are listed below.

COPY, REPLICATE, MOVE	Aids in entering data
EDIT, BLANK, ZAP, QUIT, INSERT, DELETE	Used for making corrections
LOAD, SAVE, OUTPUT	Peripherals interface, use of disk drive and printer
FORMAT, TITLE	Display format of data
GLOBAL, WINDOW	Design of spreadsheet
APPEND, DATA	Database management
VIEW	Prepare and view graphs
EXECUTE (/X)	Run SuperCalc3 programs

In the following discussion, the commands are discussed in the border listed above. Your goal in reading this discussion is to become familiar with the tasks performed by the command so you will be able to identify which command to use to design spreadsheets. When you are not sure if the command is appropriate, enter the command and press function key 1, F1, to display the answer screen for that command.

SUPERCALC3 FILE DIRECTORY

The DELETE, LOAD, OUTPUT, SAVE, EXECUTE, and QUIT commands have an option that allows you to view a directory of the disk before you complete the command. The SuperCalc3 File Directory responds with a menu as shown in Figure 8-1. The top four lines of the directory reports the current status. The listed options allow you to C(hange) the default disk drive; D(isplay) all files on the disk; S(ee) the .CAL files only, i.e. the SuperCalc files only; E(nter) a filename which returns you to the action line of the spreadsheet; and G(raphs) which display the current graphs in the spreadsheet. To return to the spreadsheet, type F2.

The Change option is very useful. The normal default disk drive is the A drive. Thus, if you do not change the default, each time you enter a filename, you have to type a disk drive designation, for example B:. By changing the default disk drive, you only have to type the filename. The change in the default drive is effective only as long as you keep SuperCalc3 in RAM. When you Quit or the power is turned off, the default is reset to A when SuperCalc3 is loaded into the primary memory. The See option allows you to see or display the contents of cell A1 in each spreadsheet file and to view a listing of each file name.

FIGURE 8-1   SUPERCALC3 FILE DIRECTORY

```
SuperCalc3 Directory Options
Program disk drive is A:
Current data disk drive is A:
Current spreadsheet file is : B:FIG9-1   .cal

   OPTIONS:
      C(hange) data disk drive
      D(isplay) all files
      S(ee) .CAL spreadsheet files only
      E(nter) filename
      G(raphs) - current spreadsheet

   F2 to abort command.
```

```
Type C(hange), D(isplay), S(ee), E(nter) or G(raphs)
   7>/Load,
F1 = Help; F2 = Erase Line/Return to Spreadsheet; F9 = Plot; F10 = View
```

SUPERCALC3 CELL RANGE

Many of the SuperCalc3 commands require that you specify a cell range. Ranges may be specified in a variety of ways. The most common is a rectangular block of cells that may vary from only one cell, to part of a column, part of a row, or a group of cells identified by giving the upper left hand cell and the lower right hand cell. Figure 8-2 lists the various range designations used by SuperCalc3.

SELECTING SUB-COMMANDS

Most of the SuperCalc3 commands also have sub-commands. SuperCalc3 informs you of the sub-commands by the notation "<,> for options." To display the sub-commands on the prompt line, you need to type a comma ,. As a matter of fact, you may always type the comma to select any command or sub-command. Therefore, as a general rule, it is preferable to type the comma to select from the commands. Doing so insures that you always have the related sub-commands presented to you on the prompt line. Otherwise, you may ignore the option prompt and bypass the sub-commands.

FIGURE 8-2   RANGE DESIGNATORS

RANGE DESIGNATION	EXPLANATION
Cell	A column letter followed by row number
Column	Columns are indicated by letters from A to BK.
Partial column	Two cells in the same column, separated by a colon, e.g. A4:A9
Column range	Two column letters separated by a colon. For example, A:G, the range includes all columns from A to G.
Row	Rows are numbered from 1 to 254.
Partial row	Indicated by two cell addresses in the same row, for example D4:R4.
Row range	Two rows numbers separated by a colon. For example 4:43, the range includes all rows from 4 to 43.
Block	The normal range, indicated by the cell address of the upper left hand corner and the lower right hand corner.
All	The range from A1 to the lower right hand corner of the spreadsheet as indicated in the control panel.

COPY COMMAND

The COPY command duplicates the contents of source cells to the designation cells. The number of cells in the designation range must be the same as that in the source range. You are asked to specify two ranges: the range to copy FROM, the from range, and the cell address of the upper left hand corner of the range to copy TO, the to range. The command is used by typing the slash key to display the menu, and the letter C for Copy. You are asked to enter the from range. Next you are asked to enter the cell address of the upper left hand corner, the copy to range. After you have entered the range, if you type the enter key, the range is copied and all formulas adjusted, i.e. the cell addresses are adjusted for the number of rows and columns from the source range to the designation range. For example, if the formula in cell C4 is A4 + B4, when copied to cell C6 and adjusted, the formula in cell C6 will be A6 + B6. That is, each row address has been increased by the number of rows down the formula was copied. Cell C6 is 2 rows down from cell C4, thus, each row in the formula has been increased by 2. If you press the comma rather than the return, the options or sub-commands are listed on the prompt line. The option NO ADJUST results in the identical formula, with no adjustment. In the example above, C6 would contain the unadjusted formula A4 + B4. The option ASK FOR ADJUST, will ask, cell by cell, if you wish to adjust the cell when it is copied. While SuperCalc3 refers to these options of the COPY command as ADJUSTING, other spreadsheet packages refer to this procedure as a RELATIVE or ABSOLUTE copy.

The VALUES ONLY option of the COPY command allows you to copy the value of the source cell and not the formula. Thus, if the result of the formula referred to above in cell C4, .i.e. A4 + B4, was 10, the VALUES ONLY option of the COPY command will result in only the numeric value 10, in cell C6, not the adjusted or unadjusted formula. When copying the results of analysis to other parts of the spreadsheet for printing purposes, it is frequently useful to copy only the results or values. The mathematical manipulation options, +,-,*, and /, allow you to copy one range to another range and either add, subtract, multiply or divide the source range into the destination cell. The result is a numeric constant, not a formula. Thus, you must be careful when using these options. A mistake is hard to find; because, there is no indication of what you have done or where the values came from. The cells will only contain values.

The REPLICATE command is similar to the COPY command except that the REPLICATE command copies one cell range to a multi-cell range. That is, with REPLICATE, you may start with a one cell range as the source range, and copy the cell into a twenty cell range. The ranges that may be used as sources and destinations are a cell range to a cell, partial row, or partial column range; a partial row range to a left partial column, and a partial column range to a top partial row. (Refer to Figure 8-2 for examples of each type of range). For example, if the range A4:D4 is to be copied down the columns from A5 to A10, B5 to B10, C5 to C10, and D5 to D10, the source range is specified as A4:D4, and the destination range is A5:A10. That is, the destination you specified is a left partial column, i.e. the left most column of the full destination range.

The options are the same as for the REPLICATE command as for the COPY command. To select from the options menu, type a comma and select from the menu. The default is to adjust all formulas and may be selected by pressing the enter key. If you want to copy a block of data, you must use the COPY command, not REPLICATE. The key to remember is that REPLICATE copies one cell to many cells down columns or across columns. For example, if you want to copy all entries in the range A5:D7, i.e. a block of the spreadsheet, to A25:D27, the COPY command should be used. You are copying each cell in the source range only once, to the destination range. On the other hand, if you want to copy the entries in the partial row, A5:D5, to the next 20 rows, i.e. A5 is to be copied to 20 different cells (A6 to A25), the REPLICATE command should be used.

The COPY command is commonly used to copy parts of a spreadsheet to a different area in order to be printed or further analyzed, that is, when an exact copy is required. The REPLICATE command is used to copy formulas from the first row of an analysis down the column to the following rows to complete the spreadsheet. The REPLICATE command is normally used more than the COPY command in the design of spreadsheets, thus, try it first.

MOVE COMMAND

The MOVE command allows you to move a ROW or a COLUMN to another location on the spreadsheet. The MOVE command may be distinguished from the COPY command. Copy creates two copies of the same information, the original and one copy. The MOVE command moves the row or column to another location. Thus, afterwards the information appears in the spreadsheet only once. Blocks of information may not be moved, only rows or columns. Any number of rows or columns may be moved. To use the command, select M from the command menu, specify the ROW range or COLUMN range to move, type a comma to specify the current row or column as the beginning point, and specify the designation row or column followed by the enter key to complete the move. For example,

/ M R 5 , 9

moves the old row 5, all columns thereof, to become the new row 9. The old row 9 is now the new row 8. All formulas in the spreadsheet are adjusted to account for the move. At times it seems like magic, but all the remaining formulas are correctly adjusted to account for the moving of the row or columns. In fact, there is no provision to move rows or columns without adjustment.

EDIT COMMAND

The EDIT command was discussed in Chapter 7. The major point to remember about the EDIT command is that the command edits the contents of any cell, only after information has been entered into the cell. To EDIT a cell, move the cursor to that cell, type /E and the enter key. Only individual cells may be edited, not blocks or ranges.

BLANK and ZAP COMMANDS

The BLANK and ZAP commands erase all or part of the spreadsheet. The BLANK command erases one cell or a range of cells. The ZAP command erases the entire spreadsheet. A major difference between the two erasing commands is that the BLANK command will not affect a protected cell, only unprotected cells. Also BLANK does not affect the Column, Row or Global display formats. Graphs may also be erased by specifying the graph range. To select the BLANK command, type / B and enter a range or type enter key. The ZAP command completely erases the entire spreadsheet, protected cells and all. The only survivor will be the user defined format table (discussed later) and it is saved only if you select the CONTENTS option. To use the command, press / Z enter key.

QUIT COMMAND

The QUIT command allows you to get out of SuperCalc3 back to DOS, and go home. You must remember that if you have not SAVED you spreadsheet before you QUIT, it is completely wiped out when you press the enter key. Thus it is better to always save your file before you QUIT, even if you later decide to erase that file. SuperCalc3 gives you an opportunity to reconsider before you QUIT. At the prompt, you must type a Y to erase the spreadsheet and QUIT. If you type a N for NO, the QUIT command is cancelled and all is well. One very useful feature of the QUIT command is the ability to QUIT TO another program. That program may be any program that runs on your machine. For example, if you complete a SuperCalc3 spreadsheet, output it to a disk where it is given a .PRN filetype, and want to go directly to a wordprocessing software package, WordStar for example, you may QUIT TO WS. The Wordstar program disk must be in the default disk drive. Thus, you do not have to exit to DOS and then load WordStar.

INSERT and DELETE COMMANDS

The INSERT and DELETE commands both operate on either a row range or a column range. INSERT adds a row, a group of rows, a column or a group of columns to the spreadsheet. The rows are inserted above the row range specified; columns are inserted to the left of the column range given. For example, if you specify a row range of 6:8, the three rows 6,7, and 8 will be inserted above the current row 6. The old row six becomes new row 9 and every row below is similarly adjusted. All formulas are adjusted according to the insertion. The rows above old row 6 are not affected by the insertion except for any formulas in those rows referencing row 6 or lower, which are adjusted to reflect the insertion.

The DELETE command can be a dangerous command. The DELETE command deletes row or column ranges. The deletion affects the entire column or row. Thus, if the portion of the row that appears on the screen is incorrect, that does not mean that the remainder of that row, the part you do not see on the screen, is also incorrect. DELETE erases not only the portion of the row that you see, but also the portion of the row that is not seen. Proceed with great caution. The row or column that is deleted is the row or column that you specify. For example, to delete rows 6 to 8, the row range 6:8 is specified. The result is that the entire row 6, 7, and 8, from column A to column BK, is gone; totally, completely, irrecoverably gone. Again, use DELETE with caution.

DELETE provides the option of deleting a FILE that is stored on the disk drive. To erase the file, press / D F and specify the name of the file. If the file is not on the default drive, the drive must also be specified. Furthermore the SuperCalc3 File Directory may be accessed to allow changing the default disk drive and displaying the files on the disk. If the last file loaded is desired, you may type the ESC key to display that filename on the entry line. Files that are deleted, are gone. There is no way to get them back without reentering all the data. Be cautious.

PERIPHERAL INTERFACE -- LOAD, SAVE, OUTPUT

Peripheral equipment are devices that are connected to the central processing unit. SuperCalc3 supports or helps you use three of these units, the monitor, the disk drives, and the printer. Of the leading spreadsheet software packages, SuperCalc3 makes the best use of the color monitor. No user action is required to utilize color. If you have a color graphics card and a color monitor, SuperCalc3 displays a blue border and uses color to highlight errors and other messages. Thus, SuperCalc3 support of your monitor is transparent. To interface with the disk storage, the LOAD and SAVE commands are used to do just what their names implies. We will begin with the LOAD command.

LOAD COMMAND

To use the LOAD command, the first step is to select LOAD by typing / L. The second step is to specify the filename that you wish to load from the disk storage. Pressing the ESC key displays the last file that was loaded during the current session with SuperCalc3. You rarely reload the same file; however, when you start over, modify only part of the file at a time, or want to display the file in steps, you may use the ESC key to display the current filename. You may also display the SuperCalc3 File Directory by typing the enter key. Finally, you may type the disk drive, filename and the enter key.

The third group of options allows you to select the portion of the file that you want to load into the current spreadsheet. The options are to load the entire file, ALL; to LOAD only a PART, which may be a cell, a row range, column range, or a block of cells; to CONSOLIDATE the stored file and the current file; or to load a graph range, i.e. graphs numbered one to nine. The most common choice is to LOAD ALL of the file. The spreadsheet in disk storage is loaded into the spreadsheet that is displayed. The files are matched cell by cell. If a cell in the stored spreadsheet is blank and the corresponding cell in the displayed spreadsheet has data entered in it, the displayed cell remains as a part of the new spreadsheet. Therefore, before a stored spreadsheet is loaded, the current spreadsheet should be ZAPPED. Otherwise, the resulting spreadsheet will be a compilation of erroneous information. However, there are occasions when this feature of the LOAD command is useful.

Another choice is to LOAD only a PART of the spreadsheet from disk storage. In this way, you can combine the contents of a stored spreadsheet to the current spreadsheet. At the prompt, enter the source range, the range from the stored spreadsheet, that is to be combined into the current spreadsheet. Type a comma, and you are prompted to enter the upper left hand corner of the destination range, i.e. the location in the current spreadsheet where the stored spreadsheet is to be added. If you press the enter key, the current location of the cursor is entered as the upper left hand corner of the destination range. The part of the spreadsheet loaded from disk storage overwrites any occupied cell in the destination range. Typing the comma again, allows you to select whether or not to adjust the formulas loaded into the spreadsheet. The default is to adjust, selected by typing the enter key. Alternatives are NO ADJUST, ASK FOR ADJUST, VALUES ONLY, +,-,*,/. These options are the same options available in the COPY command and were discussed above.

Another LOAD option is to CONSOLIDATE the two spreadsheets. CONSOLIDATE will add the values of the current spreadsheet to the values of the corresponding cells in the stored spreadsheet. The resulting spreadsheet is a combination of the two spreadsheets. CONSOLIDATE does not affect the labels, only the values are added. Thus, the disadvantage of the fact that the LOAD command does not erase the spreadsheet before loading a file, becomes an advantage when you want to consolidate two spreadsheets into one. It should be noted that CONSOLIDATE operates to combine entire files only. To achieve the same results with only part of a file, use the PART option followed by the + options.

The last option of the LOAD command is to LOAD GRAPHS. The graph descriptions are loaded by graph number. For simplicity, the graph option is deferred until graphs are discussed in the following chapter.

SAVE COMMAND

The SAVE command is the reverse of LOAD. Its purpose is to transfer the spreadsheet from primary memory to disk storage. By selecting the PART option, you may save only a part of the spreadsheet. To select the SAVE command, type / S. The first step is to specify the filename to be assigned to the spreadsheet. Typing the ESC key enters the current name of the spreadsheet, if it has one. Typing the enter key displays the SuperCalc3 File Directory. If the file has previously been saved, you have to specify whether to CHANGE NAME, BACKUP, or OVERWRITE the file, thus, you have to tell SuperCalc3 how to handle the duplication. Two files may not have the same name on the same disk.

The CHANGE NAME option allows you to change the name of the current spreadsheet before it is saved to disk storage. The BACKUP option allows you to create a backup copy of the spreadsheet. Backups should be made for every important file. If it takes one day to create a spreadsheet that will be used many times in the future, it is certainly worth $1 in cost of disk space to make a back-up copy. The reason for the back-up copy is to insure against loss in case the file is accidently erased or overwritten. Thus, with the SuperCalc3 BACKUP option, the file appears on disk storage two times, once as a .CAL file, the normal SuperCalc3 filetype; and once as a .BAK file, the SuperCalc3 backup filetype. For added security, the file should be copied to another diskette that may be maintained in a separate location. If you no longer desire to keep the file on the disk you may select the OVERWRITE option. The file on the disk is replaced with the file in primary memory. The file that was, is no more. Be careful how you specify your file names.

The OVERWRITE option is used frequently. Recall that any interruption in power erases all information stored in RAM. Power interruptions may be caused by a variety of reasons, most outside your control. Therefore, it is better to frequently save your spreadsheet rather than risk losing it to a power interruption. Thus, you should frequently OVERWRITE a file by saving it often while you are developing it.

OUTPUT COMMAND

The last peripheral that SuperCalc3 supports is the printer. In most cases, the last step in preparation of any spreadsheet is to print the results on paper. Printers are powerful machines. Even the most inexpensive has the power to print very elaborate labels, typestyles, and characters. The key to unlocking that power is SETUP codes. Use of setup codes requires that you have a printer manual and the SuperCalc3 table of ASCII codes, Appendix J in the manual. Setup codes are more fully demonstrated and explained in the next chapter. The task here is to explain how to get printed copy with the default settings.

The command used to interface with a printer is the OUTPUT command. There are many options with the OUTPUT command; only the basic ones are discussed at this point. More follow in the next chapter. The command is selected from the menu by typing / O. The first option is to print the DISPLAY, as you see it on the screen, or to print the CONTENTS, that is the formulas and text that you have entered into the spreadsheet. If DISPLAY is selected, the output as it appears on the screen is printed. If the borders appear on the screen, i.e. the column letters and the row numbers, they are printed as displayed. To remove the borders, a GLOBAL command, GLOBAL BORDERS, /G B, must be used. The / G B command acts as a toggle switch, entered once, it turns the borders on, and entered again, it turns them off. DISPLAY prints what you see on the screen. If CONTENTS is selected, the formulas of the cells are listed one cell at a time, beginning with the upper left hand corner, normally A1, and proceeding across each row, printing the contents of each cell. The usefulness of this output is to document the contents of the spreadsheet. Also, it may help in debugging a spreadsheet that should, but does not work.

After selecting between DISPLAY or CONTENTS, the next step is to specify the range of the spreadsheet that is to be printed. The range is specified by stating the upper left hand corner and the lower right hand corner of the area of the spreadsheet that you desire to print. Alternatively, you may type "ALL"; and the range from A1 to the lower right hand corner of the spreadsheet, displayed on the status line in the control panel is specified for you. If you are using SuperCalc3 to write a short memo, you must be careful to specify a range that includes the entire screen area. While, SuperCalc3 allows you to overwrite textual material into blank trailing columns, the portion that is overwritten is not printed unless the overwritten cells are included in the output range. Thus, be certain to include the entire screen area in the output range you specify if you want to print what you see on the screen.

The next group of options determine the device you used for the output. The options are PRINTER, SETUP, CONSOLE, and DISK. The PRINTER is most frequently used, and of course, the result is printed output. CONSOLE writes the output to the screen for your review before printing. The DISK option allows you to print a worksheet file to disk storage with a .PRN filetype. This allows you to combine the file into a wordprocessor or other software package. Alternatively, the file may be printed with DOS, or otherwise, without having to use SuperCalc3. SETUP allows several changes in the printed copy and its discussion is deferred to the next chapter.

If you selected to write to the PRINTER or to the CONSOLE, you have no additional options to select. The printer will do its thing and you will have the printed page. If you selected DISK, you still have to specify the filename as with LOAD and SAVE above. You have the same options to OVERWRITE, CHANGE NAME, BACK UP, or display the SuperCalc3 File Directory.

To summarize, to print your spreadsheet, the required steps are to select the OUTPUT command, select DISPLAY, specify the range (ALL is frequently appropriate), select PRINTER, and wait for the printer to finish. While at times the use of the printer is frustrating, the rewards are real. The concept of totally error free printed pages is a realistic goal with electronic processing.

FORMAT COMMAND

The FORMAT command allows you to display the values and labels in the spreadsheet in several different format or appearances. As with most electronic spreadsheets, SuperCalc3 requires that you enter the data without any symbols. Thus, to enter $5.00, type the number 5 and then use the FORMAT command to add the symbols that you desire. It is important to remember that you only enter the numbers, and never the symbols. Of course, you must type the decimal in the correct place or otherwise, SuperCalc3 will not know where to put it.

To select the FORMAT command, type / F. The first required step in the FORMAT command is to specify the range of the spreadsheet that you wish to format. The options are GLOBAL, COLUMN, ROW, and ENTRY. The GLOBAL option formats every cell in the spreadsheet. The GLOBAL option may be overridden with any of the other ranges, i.e. ROW, COLUMN, or ENTRY. In fact SuperCalc3 sets up an order of precedence. The first priority is an Entry range. The next is a ROW, followed by COLUMN, with GLOBAL having the lowest priority. Once the range is identified, the next step is to select a format option. The FORMAT options include more than just symbols to identify the type of number referred to. Figure 8-3 lists the typical FORMAT options common to most spreadsheet software.

FIGURE 8-3   COMMON FORMAT OPTIONS

Format	Description	Examples
Integer	Displays numbers as integers, rounding when necessary to reflect whole numbers	1.34 = 1 1.79 = 2
General	Displays integers or decimals as they are entered if column-width is large enough.	1.3 = 1.3 1 = 1
$ Money	Displays numbers with two decimal places, negatives in brackets, but no $'s	3 = 3.00
R L	Right justifies formula values Left justifies formula values	
TR TL	Text Right, right justifies text entries. Text Left, left justifies text entries.	
U(1-8)	User-defined format options including $'s, see Figure 8-4	
Hide	Hide causes the cell to display as blank.	
(0-127)	Enter a number to set the column-width of the current column.	

LEFT AND RIGHT JUSTIFICATION

SuperCalc3 provides additional formating options, including some that are not common in electronic spreadsheets. The left or right justification of textual material is very common. The TR option, TEXT RIGHT, causes all text or labels to be RIGHT justified, which means that the last letter of the labels is lined up at the right edge of the cell. If the label is longer than the column width, TEXT RIGHT will cause the first part of the label to be truncated. If this happens, your choices are to widen the column width or revert to TEXT LEFT. The TL option returns the text justification setting to the default with the first letter of the label or text lined up on the left edge of the cell. SuperCalc3 does not provide a way to center the label in a cell. An uncommon option allows you to left or right justify values or formulas. The L option lines the number up with the left edge of the cell; R, returns it to right justification, the default justification for values. All values including dates and textual values may be either left or right justified.

The * option provides the ability to display asterisks to represent numbers. In this manner, you may prepare simple linear graphs of numbers in the spreadsheet. The number of asterisks printed is scaled based upon the maximum value in the range. With the greater graphical power of SuperCalc3, it is unlikely that you will be using this form of graphical representation.

USER-DEFINED FORMATS

SuperCalc3 supports a table containing eight sets of format combinations that may be set by the user. These are appropriately enough, referred to as "USER-DEFINED FORMATS" To use one of these formats you select the FORMAT option USER-DEFINED FORMAT TABLE (1-8), identified as U 1-8. To complete the table, select the DEFINE option. There are seven items in the table that may be varied. Figure 8-4 lists the items that may be varied and explains what they mean. The most important is the first, FLOATING $. The only way to display numbers with dollar signs in the spreadsheet is to use the USER-DEFINED FORMAT. If the format you define says Y for yes in the row labeled Floating $, then the range formatted with the user-defined format displays leading dollar signs. If you attempt to enter dollar signs into a column of amounts, the dollar signs do not line up unless all the numbers are the same number of digits. The only way to display a straight row of $ is to define a one character column and enter $ in each cell of that column using the REPLICATE command. Typically only the first and total row of a column of dollar amounts have leading dollar signs. The remaining entries have only two decimals. Thus, the fact that dollar signs do not line up is not a problem.

HIDE FORMULAS

The HIDE option of the FORMAT command allows some security in the use of your spreadsheet. The key formula or input may be formatted "HIDE", thus, it does not appear in

FIGURE 8-4

```
                      User-defined formats
                      1  2  3  4  5  6  7  8

Floating $           Y  Y  Y  Y  Y  Y  Y  Y

Embedded Commas      Y  Y  Y  Y  Y  Y  Y  Y

Minus in ( )         N  N  N  N  N  N  N  N

Zero as Blank        N  N  N  N  N  N  N  N

%                    N  N  N  N  N  N  N  N

Decimal Places       2  2  2  2  2  2  2  2

Scaling factor       0  0  0  0  0  0  0  0


F2 to return to worksheet.


  B5               Text=" 1|
Y(es) or N(o) ?
 15>/Format,Define
F1 = Help; F2 = Erase Line/Return to Spreadsheet; F9 = Plot; F10 = View
```

the spreadsheet, nor does it print with the OUTPUT command. It is, however, listed on the status line of the control panel. Thus, spreadsheets containing sensitive data may be printed for distribution to others without the sensitive information being printed.

ADJUSTING COLUMN-WIDTH

The last FORMAT sub-command listed is the column-width option. On the menu it appears as (0-127). With it you may set the column-width of the range you specified to vary from 0 to 127 characters in width. The default is 9 characters which is acceptable much of the time. If the default column-width is not sufficient to display the formatted value, the cell is filled with greater than symbols, e.g. >>>>>. When the cell is expanded, the correctly formatted value is displayed. It is important in SuperCalc3 to be aware of the column-width when printing. Recall that the OUTPUT command only prints the range specified; none of the cell that overwrites the following cells is printed. Note that when you are setting the column width, the entire spreadsheet may be specified as the appropriate range if, in fact, the entire spreadsheet column-widths are to be set. The status line in the control panel reports the column-width of the current column.

The FORMAT command dresses up a spreadsheet, making it suitable for viewing by others. The FORMAT options are sufficient to provide attractive reports; there is really no excuse for sloppiness.

TITLE COMMAND

The purpose of the TITLE command is to lock columns, rows, or both on to the screen so that they do not scroll off. The usefulness comes when you have a large spreadsheet that contains several columns of information relating to each row. The label for the row may scroll off the screen and inhibit you from appropriately entering the data. That is, you are not be able to see the row labels. The TITLE VERTICAL command locks the column containing the row labels on the screen. The current column and all columns to the left of it are locked on the screen. Similarly, the rows that contain the columnar labels may be locked on the screen with the TITLE HORIZONTAL option. The HORIZONTAL option locks the current row and all rows above it on the screen. The BOTH option locks both the HORIZONTAL and VERTICAL titles. The CLEAR option removes the TITLE lock.

TITLE command is saved with the spreadsheet, but it will not operate with the OUTPUT command. Thus, if you are printing a spreadsheet and want the titles to repeat on each page, you must move to the proper location, insert additional rows or columns as needed, and copy the titles to that location. Then you may print the spreadsheet as normal and the titles will be there. When the TITLE locks is operative the arrow keys will not move the cursor into the title area, but the GOTO key, the equal sign (=), and the HOME key will operate as normal. Once you are in the area changes or additions may be made.

THE GLOBAL COMMAND

The GLOBAL command allows you to specify settings for the entire spreadsheet. The most useful options are the BORDER DISPLAY and the MANUAL or AUTO recalculation. The default settings for the other options are acceptable for most operations.

The default setting for the BORDER DISPLAY is on, that is the row numbers and column letters appear on the screen and are printed with the OUTPUT command. For all but the final draft of a report, it is both useful and acceptable to have the borders printed. However, for the final draft, it is preferable to turn the borders off. The GLOBAL BORDER option acts as a toggle switch to turn on and off the borders. Thus, if the borders are displayed, typing / G B turns the borders off; retyping / G B restores the borders to the display.

The MANUAL or AUTO options set the timing of the recalculation of the spreadsheet. The default setting is AUTO, thus, each time you enter data the spreadsheet will recalculate each and every formula in the spreadsheet. While the recalculation is at RAM speed, i.e. the recalculation is electronically performed, as the spreadsheet increases in size, the time for recalculation seems long. The time for recalculation is only a matter of seconds, but if you have to wait 20 seconds between each entry of data, it seems more like an hour. The solution is to select GLOBAL MANUAL, which turns off the automatic recalculation feature. Thus, SuperCalc3 recalculates the formulas in the spreadsheet when you tell it to. The recalc key, which is the exclamation point (!), recalculates the spreadsheet.

The order of recalculation is important and should be thoroughly understood. SuperCalc3 provides two alternative orders of recalculation, ROW and COLUMN. The default is ROW-wise calculation. This means that the formulas in the spreadsheet are calculated one row at a time starting with cell A1 in Row 1. Refer to Figure 8-5. Note that the formula for cell B1 is a function of cell C1 which is in turn a function of cell D1. If the recalculation order is set to COLUMN, Column A will be calculated first, B second, and so on. Thus, in the case of Figure 8-5, a change in the entry in D1 is not reflected in the first calculation of cell B1; B1 is calculated before cell C1. To obtain the correct answer, you have to recalculate with the recalc key,

(!). Alternatively, if you set the recalculation order to ROW, row 1 is recalculated first, followed by row 2, and so on. Formulas that are dependent on amounts in a lower row will be incorrectly computed until the spreadsheet is recalculated. Refer to Figure 8-5. If the spreadsheet is calculated on a row basis, all the formulas are correctly computed. None of the formulas are a function of a lower row.

FIGURE 8-5 ORDER OF RECALCULATION

```
|   A    ||   B    ||   C    ||  D   ||  E   |
1|  3         A1+C1    D1+E1      5        3
2|  5         A2+C2    D2+E2      8        1
3|  A1+A2     B1+B2    C1+C2
```

The importance of the order of calculation is its effect on design of your spreadsheet. With SuperCalc3, it is important to build spreadsheets going down the columns. In such spreadsheets, the formulas are based upon cells in the preceding rows. Thus, the default row-wise recalculation will be acceptable. If you are not certain the spreadsheet has been properly designed to handle the potential problem of the order of calculation, you should recalculate the spreadsheet with the recalc key, (!). The recalculation is very fast. Some accountants suggest that as a matter of course, you recalculate each spreadsheet three times before you consider yourself finished. After all, that is the purpose of the recalc key.

The other GLOBAL command options and their purposes are listed below. Recall, the default settings are acceptable for most accounting applications.

OPTION   PURPOSE

GRAPHICS   GRAPHICS option displays the settings that controls the way your graph looks, some hardware options, and allows changes to each.

184

FORMULA DISPLAY	FORMULA DISPLAY is a toggle switch, on or off. If on, the contents or formula of the cell is displayed. If the switch is off, the values of the cell are displayed. The reason to display the formulas themselves is to document the spreadsheet. The default is FORMULA DISPLAY OFF.
NEXT	The NEXT option turns off/on the spreadsheet cursor auto-advance feature. The default is ON.
TAB	The TAB option allows you to set the cursor lockout option on or off. If the TAB is set ON, the cursor moves only to non-blank, non-protected cells. Thus, by protecting all cells except those that are to receive data, the cursor only moves to the cells that are to receive data. In this way a relatively untrained user may efficiently enter data. When used in connection with the EXECUTE commands (discussed in Chapter 9) a "canned application" may be created.

WINDOW--CREATES A SPLIT SCREEN

The WINDOW command allows you to split the screen into two parts so that you may view two parts of the spreadsheet at once. The screen may be split either horizontally or vertically. The split is above or to the left of the current cell. The result is two separate, independent spreadsheets. By default the two spreadsheets move together; they are synchronized. If you want them to scroll or move independently, you should select UNSYNCHRONIZE. You may move between the two spreadsheets with the semi-colon (;). Thus, typing the semi-colon once moves you to the other spreadsheet; type it a second time to move back to the first. The CLEAR option removes the split screen returning you to the one screen.

The purpose of this exercise is to use the various commands that have been discussed to this point. Below is information that may be used to prepare a budget for Paula Baynett, for a thirteen week term at school. Following that, is a compressed printout of the completed budget. Your assignment is to prepare the worksheet to complete the budget.

The first step is to enter the labels of the various rows and columns. Then, enter the input information. Most of the labels for the output section of the budget may be copied from the input section. Once the formulas are in place for the first week, the formulas for the remaining weeks may be replicated from the first. Remember to use cell referencing whenever possible. The rule is to enter a number only once. Each time thereafter, use cell referencing.

NAME: Paula Baynett

ADDRESS: 3007 Campus Row
                Blacskburg, VA

SCHOOL: Virginia Tech   BEGINNING BALANCE $1,300

TERM: Fall   FIRST DAY AT SCHOOL ----->   08-Sep

                    CASH RECEIPTS:
SOURCE   AMOUNTS   PERIODICITY *
----------------   ---------   -------------
PARENTS $600   FIRST OF MONTH
PART-TIME JOB $40   WEEKLY
SCHOLARSHIPS $500   FIRST OF TERM
LOANS   AS NEEDED
INVESTMENTS $200   MONTHLY, AT FIRST OF MONTH
OTHER $300   END OF TERM

BUDGET ITEMS

WEEK BEGINNING

RECEIPTS:

	08-Sep	15-Sep	22-Sep	29-Sep	06-Oct	13-Oct	20-Oct	27-Oct	03-Nov	10-Nov	17-Nov	24-Nov	01-Dec
PARENTS	600				600				600				600
PART-TIME JOB	40	40	40	40	40	40	40	40	40	40	40	40	40
SCHOLARSHIPS	500												
LOANS													
INVESTMENTS	200				200				200				200
OTHER													
BEGINNING BALANCE	1300	870	740	610	440	810	680	550	380	1050	920	790	620
CASH AVAILABLE	2640	910	780	650	1280	850	720	590	1220	1090	960	830	1460

EXPENDITURES

	08-Sep	15-Sep	22-Sep	29-Sep	06-Oct	13-Oct	20-Oct	27-Oct	03-Nov	10-Nov	17-Nov	24-Nov	01-Dec
RENT	300				300								
FOOD	75	75	75	75	75	75	75	75	75	75	75	75	75
TUITION	1,000												
BOOKS	300												
OPERATION OF CAR AT SCHOOL	25	25	25	25	25	25	25	25	25	25	25	25	25
CAR TRIPS HOME				40				40				40	
ENTERTAINMENT	30	30	30	30	30	30	30	30	30	30	30	30	30
CLOTHING	7	7	7	7	7	7	7	7	7	7	7	7	7
OTHER	33	33	33	33	33	33	33	33	33	33	33	33	33
CASH AVAILABLE END OF MONTH	$870	$740	$610	$440	$810	$680	$550	$380	$1,050	$920	$790	$620	$1,290

EXERCISE 8-2 UPDATE STUDENT'S GPA

The purpose of this exercise is to practice using the LOAD PART and SAVE PART commands. You will be using the following files from your course diskette: GPA, which you completed in Exercise 4-4 and UPDAGPA, from your Course diskette. In addition, you are given four semester grade reports for I. M. Accountant--one of which is from Exercise 4-4. Below, the summary report for the four term period is reproduced. The purpose of this exercise is to prepare this summary report by using the LOAD PART and SAVE PART commands. The following steps are required.

Step 1   Retrieve the file GPA from Exercise 7-4. If you used a different name, adjust accordingly.

Step 2   Identify the range of the spreadsheet that contains the FALL 3 grade report, that is the range of the worksheet in which the courses, grades, and GPA are summarized. Write the range address on a note pad for future use. Use the SAVE command to save the file using the filename FALL3.

Step 3   Retrieve the file UPDAGPA. With the cursor at cell A41, use the LOAD PART command to combine the range which you recorded in step 2, containing the grade report from the file FALL3 into UPDAGPA. Save the file UPDAGPA.

Step 4   Using the old file GPA, change the courses and grades to reflect the SPRING4 report listed below, and save the file using the filename SPRING4. Note the range of SPRING4 that contains the grade report. It should be the same as in step 2. Use the LOAD PART command to combine SPRING4 grades into UPDAGPA, beginning one page (20 rows) below FALL3 grades.

Step 5   Repeat Step 4 for the FALL4 and SPRING5 reports. Note, it will be more efficient to prepare the two revised and renamed GPA files before using LOAD PART.

Step 6   Use SAVE PART to extract the single row for each report, that is FALL3, SPRING4, etc., that contains the summary information. Use

temporary filenames like F3, S4, etc. to
receive the extracted information.

Step 7   Use LOAD PART to combine the summary
          information for each term in the file UPDAGPA
          at the appropriate location. Note, in this
          case you will LOAD the entire file, e.g. the
          temporary file F3, etc.

Step 8   Print the summary report using the OUTPUT
          command.

          NAME: I. M. Accountant   UNIVERSITY: Masse College

       ADDRESS: 342 South Street   COLLEGE: Business
                South Boston, MA
                                          MAJOR: Accounting
        GRADES: A = 4.0   D = 1.0
                B = 3.0   F = 0.0
                C = 2.0

                              SUMMARY

CUMULATIVE GPA   2.42

TERM   CREDIT HRS QUALITY POINTS TERM GPA

FALL, YR 3   18   42   2.33
SPRING, YR 4   18   48   2.67
FALL, YR 4   18   39   2.17
SPRING, YR 5   18   45   2.50

GRADE REPORTS FOR EXERCISE 8-2

TERM: Fall, YR 3

COURSES	CREDIT HR	GRADE	QUALITY PTS.	COMMENT
ACCOUNTING 3111	3	3	9	NA
ACCOUNTING 3211	3	2	6	NA
ECONOMICS 3111	3	1	3	ERR
FINANCE 3111	3	3	9	NA
MARKETING 3111	3	4	12	NA
CHILD DEVELOPMENT 1	3	1	3	ERR
	--		---	
TOTALS	18		42	2.333

TERM: SPRING, YR 4

COURSES	CREDIT HR	GRADE	QUALITY PTS.	COMMENT
ACCOUNTING 3112	3	3	9	NA
ACCOUNTING 3212	3	4	12	NA
ECONOMICS 3112	3	2	6	NA
MANAGEMENT 3001	3	4	12	NA
ACCOUNTING 4000	3	2	6	NA
CLASSICAL MUSIC 1	3	1	3	ERR
	--		--	
TOTALS	18		48	2.667

TERM: Fall, YR 4

COURSES	CREDIT HR	GRADE	QUALITY PTS.	COMMENT
ACCOUNTING 4220	3	3	9	NA
ACCOUNTING 4500	3	4	12	NA
BUSINESS LAW 4000	3	1	3	ERR
BUSINESS POLICY 4000	3	2	6	NA
LIFE AFTER 40	3	2	6	NA
FIRST AID 2	3	1	3	ERR
	--		--	
TOTALS	18		39	2.167

TERM: SPRING, YR 5

COURSES	CREDIT HR	GRADE	QUALITY PTS.	COMMENT
ACCOUNTING 4111	3	2	6	NA
ACCOUNTING 4200	3	3	9	NA
FINANCE 4011	3	3	9	NA
FINANCE 4200	3	2	6	NA
ACCOUNTING 4700	3	4	12	NA
	--		--	
TOTALS	18		42	2.333

EXERCISE 8-3   TRAVEL REIMBURSEMENT FORM

The purpose of this exercise is to create a simple form that is used with the GLOBAL TAB command. A common form is a travel reimbursement request form. Retrieve the file EX83 from you course diskette. This file contains the labels and formulas to prepare the TRAVEL REIMBURSEMENT FORM reproduced below. To see how the GLOBAL TAB command works, first protect the worksheet with the PROTECT command. Next unprotect only those cells that requires input from the user with the UNPROTECT command. Finally, use the GLOBAL TAB command to enter the information given below.

TRAVEL REIMBURSEMENT FORM

The purpose of this worksheet is to demonstrate the use of the GLOBAL TAB command. The worksheet prepares a TRAVEL REIMBURSEMENT REQUEST form. The Form begins one page down, at cell A21. To input the required information, select the GLOBAL TAB command. The cursor will move only to those cells that have been unprotected with the UNPROTECT command.

REQUEST FOR REIMBURSEMENT OF TRAVEL COSTS

NAME Indiana Jones   DEPARTMENT A&S.
ADDRESS Dept of Archeology DATE   9-4-84
     Univ. of Louisville
     Louisville, KY

PURPOSE OF TRAVEL Retrieve art of covenant

TRANSPORTATION-coach rate, unless unavailable		500
LOCAL TRANSPORTATION (Bus, Rail, Cab)		50
AUTO-Miles @$0.20	100	
-Parking	20	
-Tolls	10	50
OTHER-Explain Purchase of Whip		50
LODGING		800
MEALS		200
TOTAL		1,650
DISALLOWED AS EXCESSIVE		1,100
AMOUNT TO BE PAID		550.

SIGNATURE OF TRAVELLER _____

AUTHORIZED BY   _____

ADVANCED APPLICATIONS
OF SuperCalc3

CHAPTER 9

The preceding chapters have covered the basic commands
that are used in SuperCalc3. The purpose of this chapter is
to go beyond the basics to examine the advanced features of
SuperCalc3. In essence it is these features that
distinguish SuperCalc3 from the earlier versions.

ARRANGE and // DATA MANAGEMENT COMMANDS

The SuperCalc3 ARRANGE and DATA MANAGEMENT commands
make up the database management capabilities of SuperCalc3.
These commands provide limited abilities to sort data and to
query data as done with typical data base management
software. As will be evident after the discussion of dBASE
II and III in Chapter 11, the SuperCalc3 database management
commands comprise a limited database management program.
Full discussion of what a data base is, the purpose of a
database management system, and the parts of a data base is
deferred to the discussion of dBASE II and III. However,
SuperCalc3 does perform several operations that are very
useful tools in spreadsheet analysis. We begin with the
ARRANGE command, the command used to sort portions of the
spreadsheet.

ARRANGE

The ARRANGE command allows the user to sort a ROW or COLUMN of data, within a specified range of the spreadsheet, in either ASCENDING or DESCENDING order. The ROW or COLUMN specified determines the order of the sorted range. Thus, if a ROW sort on row 2 from columns A to G is specified, all information in columns A to G, from row 1 to row 254, is sorted in the order of the data in ROW 2. You also have the option of resolving ties in the primary row or column by specifying a SECONDARY ROW or COLUMN; however, if a row is selected for the primary sort key, then a row, not a column, must be selected for the secondary sort. The data in the secondary key may be sorted in either ascending or descending order. While you have an option of adjusting or not adjusting any formulas in the range sorted, SuperCalc3 suggests that you NOT ADJUST the formulas. After the data is rearranged, the adjusted formulas may no longer be accurate. The resulting information may, in fact, be useless. Thus, by selecting NOT ADJUST, you avoid many problems.

To use the ARRANGE command, the first step is to select the ARRANGE command. The first option is to arrange a ROW or a COLUMN. Your selection will determine the specific data sorted, i.e. the sort key. The remaining data in the range associated with the key row or column, just follows along. Thus, the order of the sort is determined by your selection. You must select ROW or COLUMN. If you type the enter key after selecting ROW or COLUMN, you have selected the default settings. Thus, you sort the current row or column, i.e. your sort key is the row or column where the cursor is currently located. Furthermore, the sort is in ascending order, the entire spreadsheet is sorted, and no formulas are adjusted. Alternatively, you may continue selecting from the available options. Thus, you may specify the row number or column letter to serve as the sort key. The next option specifies the range of the spreadsheet that is sorted. Thus if you selected a ROW sort, you may specify the column range over which you wish to sort; if you selected a COLUMN sort, you may specify the row range over which to sort. The next option selects the order of the sort, ASCENDING or DESCENDING, followed by the choice to ADJUST or NO ADJUST the formulas. Typing the enter key at this point performs the sort. Alternatively, you may specify a SECONDARY row or column with the related order of the sort, ascending or descending. By default the formulas are not adjusted.

Unanticipated problems may occur during the ARRANGE command. Thus, as a precaution, it is recommended that you make a back-up copy of your spreadsheet BEFORE you use the ARRANGE command. One accountant, who shall remain nameless, sorted a series of checks according to the amount of the check. However, he erroneously selected to sort only the column containing the amounts. The amounts were sorted, but completely mismatched with the payees, dates, and check numbers. The only way to recover the data was to renter all the amounts. Beware of misspecifying the range to be sorted. Another useful precaution is to enter a column of sequential numbers starting with 1, so that you will be able to return the data to its original order should the need arise. One last precaution, recall that in a ROW sort, every row in the column range is sorted; in a COLUMN sort, every row is sorted. Thus, be careful that you do not sort an area of the spreadsheet by mistake. Be aware of the contents of cells in the area of the spreadsheet that is not displayed on the screen.

EXERCISE 9-1 -- THE ARRANGE COMMAND

Load the file CHECKSOR from your course diskette. CHECKSOR is a file with twenty checks payable to a variety of payees and accounts. Use these checks numbers to explore the limits of ARRANGE.

REQUIRED:

1. Sort the checks by account number and print out the results.

2. Sort the checks by payee and print the results.

3. Sort the checks by date, in ascending order and by amounts in descending order, as the secondary key. Print the final results.

// DATA MANAGEMENT

The // DATA MANAGEMENT command allows you to search a data base, and either FIND or EXTRACT the records that match the criteria which you specify in another part of the spreadsheet. If extracted, the matching records are written in the OUTPUT RANGE. The criteria can be as simple as all checks written on Account 101, or as complex as the checks written on Account 101 to a person whose last name begins with S and the amount is more than $500, but less than $1,000 (i.e. the item must meet one criteria to be a match). The criteria may be specified as an "EITHER OR" criteria or as an "AND" criteria i.e. the desired item must meet two or more criteria to be a match. Each row of data is referred to as a record; each column in the row as a field.

// DATA MANAGEMENT requires three types of ranges to be specified before it may be used. The first range is the INPUT range. This range contains the database. Every cell that is included in the data must be in the INPUT range, including the field names (the columnar labels.) The range is specified by entering the cell address of the beginning and ending point of the INPUT RANGE.

CRITERION RANGE

The second range is the CRITERION range. The concept of a CRITERION range seems to be the most difficult to understand. The file CHECKSOR, referred to in Exercise 9-1, contains several criterion ranges. It is suggested that they be studied closely. The CRITERION range is a range within the worksheet. The range must be at least two rows wide, but may be many rows more than two. The first row of the CRITERION range is normally an exact copy of the field names or columnar labels from the INPUT RANGE. To obtain an exact copy, it is suggested that the COPY command be used. The second and succeeding rows, contain the criteria that must be matched. Be careful that you do not accidently enter a blank space in the cell. If you do, one of your criteria is to find a blank in that field. Since the blank does not appear on the screen, it is difficult to discover the error.

Criteria are specified in true/false form. Thus, if you are searching for checks written on Account 101, the criterion may be expressed as D4=101, where D4 is the cell address of the top cell in the input range under the field name "account". Those checks that are written on account 101 are identified as matching the criteria. The // DATA MANAGEMENT command checks each cell in the INPUT range beginning with the first cell in the column or field identified and continuing down that column until it reaches the end of the INPUT range. In the cell containing the criteria, the value 1 is displayed if the criterion is true, or the value 0 is displayed if the criterion is false. The logical functions, AND, OR, and NOT, as well as >, <, >=, <=, or <> (i.e. not equal to) operate as part of a criterion. If a value within a range is desired, the criteria may be expressed as AND(C4>500,C4<1000), that is the value in cell address C4 is greater than 500 and less than 1,000. In the // DATA command, labels may be used as criterion just as values. However, text matches must be exact, thus Smith is does not match SMITH or smith. Also, SuperCalc3 allows certain wild card characters to be used. The criterion, S* will identify any word beginning with S, and J?ne will match Jane or June.

An AND criterion, the item being evaluated must meet all criteria, is specified by all entering the criteria on the same row. An "either or" criterion, the item being evaluated must meet either of the criteria, is specified by entering the criterion on succeeding (but separate) rows. Thus, an EITHER OR criterion range would be at least three rows: row 1, the field names or columnar labels; row 2, the first criterion; the row 3, the second criterion; and so on if additional criterion is specified. In the normal case, two criterion will identify the desired record.

OUTPUT RANGE

The third range to be specified is the OUTPUT range. The OUTPUT range is a portion of the spreadsheet reserved for the receipt of records EXTRACTED from the INPUT range. The OUTPUT range should begin with an exact copy of the columnar labels or field names in order to preserve the same fields in the OUTPUT range as in the INPUT range. If a different order is desired, the field names may be reordered. Again the COPY command may be used for an exact match. The OUTPUT range should be large enough to receive all possible extracted records. If the range is not large enough an error message is displayed. If the OUTPUT range has items already entered in it, they are overwritten by the EXTRACT operation.

FIND COMMAND

The FIND operation evaluates the records in the INPUT range according to the criteria that is in the CRITERION range, and reports any match in highlighted, reverse video on the screen. To move to the second matching record, type the down arrow key. To move to the third, type the down arrow key again, and so on until the last matching record is reached. When the last matching record is found, SuperCalc3 will not move down any further. To return to the top of the matching list, type the up arrow key. If you wish to move to other fields in the INPUT range that are related to the matching field, you may type the left or right arrow keys. Typing the enter key exits you from the // DATA MANAGEMENT command. If you wish to remain at one of the matching locations, you may select the REMAIN command. The REMAIN command may be used in conjuction with FIND to find a record and then edit or update that record. If you terminate a //DATA command with the enter key, you are returned to the cell location where you were before you started the // DATA command.

EXTRACT COMMAND

The EXTRACT command finds all items that match the criteria in the CRITERION range and writes them to the OUTPUT range. At this point, the extracted items are simply additional entries in the worksheet and may be so manipulated. The normal procedure is to print these matching items. The spreadsheet is not normally saved with items in the OUTPUT range. If the EXTRACT command is repeated, the new matches replace the previous results.

To change the criteria in the CRITERION range for a second EXTRACT operation, you may select the CRITERION command followed by the REMAIN command. You will remain at the criterion range and at that time may change the criteria. You must actually type the criteria in the CRITERION range. The SELECT command is similar to the EXTRACT command with the difference being that you may select which matching items you want to be written to the OUTPUT range.

Load the file CHECKSOR from your course diskette. This is the same file that was used to work with the ARRANGE command in Exercise 9-1. The settings for the //DATA MANAGEMENT command have been previously set. Review these settings by walking through the command. First select // DATA MANAGEMENT command from the command menu. Next, select INPUT. At this point you are prompted to enter the Input range. The current range (now) is correct, so review it first, and then enter it by pressing the enter key. Next, select CRITERION. You are prompted to enter the CRITERION range. Again, this has been done for you. Review the range that has been entered, and press the enter key to move back to the menu. Select OUTPUT to review the previously entered OUTPUT range. Press the enter key to return to the menu; select FIND. Note that the items that meet the criteria in the criterion range are highlighted in reverse video. Press the enter key to exit the command.

The criteria currently in the criterion range, asks for checks written on account 101. After you have reviewed these settings, use the REMAIN command to exit the CRITERION command at the CRITERION range. Change the criteria in the CRITERION range to find those checks written on account 102. Redo // DATA MANAGEMENT EXTRACT to list the checks written on account 102. Print the OUTPUT range. If you have a problem, recheck the ranges. Failing to specify the ranges is the most likely error. If you go astray, ZAP the spreadsheet, LOAD the file CHECKSOR, and review the settings. Once you have mastered // DATA MANAGEMENT, you have a very useful tool to aid in spreadsheet analysis.

The VIEW command is used to create one of seven types of graphs. The command utilizes many default options so that the preparation of a simple graph is very quick. Furthermore, the printing of the graph requires only that you press Function key 9, the PLOT key. You may view the current graph by pressing Function key 10, the VIEW key. By changing the default options, you can alter the size, the print font, the type of graph, headings, and labels for any or all of the graphs. Also, you may associate a graph number with a graph which allows you to recall any of nine graphs that may be saved with the spreadsheet. To display the graph, select the VIEW command, select the DATA option, specify the range in the spreadsheet where the data is to be found, and press Function key 10, the VIEW key, to view the graph. The default options produce a graph that is acceptable for most purposes. However, you may change the default options to design the graph you desire. The VIEW options are discussed below. In addition, the GLOBAL command provides several optional configurations of hardware, colors, fonts, and other options. The default options are acceptable for most accounting uses, thus, you are referred to the manual for a detailed discussion of these options. One that should be mentioned here is the GLOBAL GRAPHICS LAYOUT GRAPH SIZE command. With this command you may vary the size of your graph among a full page, half page, quarter page, or any size you select. Thus, the graph may be printed to the size necessary to fit the space you have available. The default size is a full page.

CHOOSING A GRAPH NUMBER

The first option of the VIEW command is to choose the graph, by number to be modified. The option is selected by typing #, the number sign. SuperCalc3 always assumes that you are modifying the current graph, that is, the last graph that you selected. If you are specifying the first graph in the spreadsheet, the number 1 is associated with the graph. If you start to modify what you hope is the second graph, you have to select graph number 2, or you in fact modify graph 1. When the spreadsheet is SAVED, the graph specifications and the related numbers are saved with it.

THE CURRENT GRAPH STATUS

To display the graph settings of the current graph while in the VIEW command press the question mark, ?. The graph number and type, the headings, the location of the variables and other labels, and other options that have been selected for the current graph are displayed. Recall that the current graph is the one specified with the # option. If you are just entering the first graph in the spreadsheet, most of the settings will be empty.

DATA, THE LOCATION OF THE VARIABLES

The DATA option specifies the location of the data that is to be graphed. SuperCalc3 allows ten ranges of data to be graphed, each identified by a letter from A to J. The range, identified with a letter, is entered by giving the upper left hand corner cell address, a colon, and the cell address of the lower right hand corner of the range. Each DATA variable is specified in response to a prompt. You must be careful to correctly identify the data variable letter, A to J, and the data ranges in the spreadsheet. If the data is in tabular form, the DATA VARIABLES range may be specified as one large range that includes the upper left hand corner of the first set of data, and the lower right hand corner of the last set of data. SuperCalc3 assumes that the first column of the range is variable A, the second is variable B, and so on until the limit of ten variables is reached. If there are no DATA VARIABLES specified, then you can not display a graph. A graph of nothing is nothing.

GRAPH TYPES

The seven types of graphs that may be selected are PIE, BAR, STACKED-BAR, LINE, AREA (or stacked line), HI-LO and X Y (or scatter plot) graph. The selection of the type of graph depends upon the type of problem The most useful types of graphs to display accounting information are the PIE, BAR, STACKED-BAR, and LINE. Figure 9-1 displays an example of a BAR graph plotted with SuperCalc3. To specify the type of graph, simply select G followed by the first letter of the graph type.

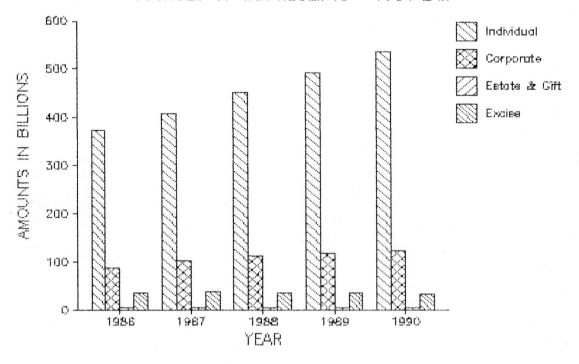

FIGURE 9-1   EXAMPLE OF A BAR GRAPH

LABELS--TIME, VARIABLE, POINT AND HEADINGS

The TIME-LABEL option allows you to specify the range of the spreadsheet that contains labels for the variables plotted on the X-axis. Since the X-axis of a graph frequently represents time, days, years, months, etc., SuperCalc3 refers to the labels as TIME-LABELS. The VARIABLE LABELS are also sometimes referred to as "legends". The VARIABLE LABELS option specifies the cells in the spreadsheet that contain the names of the variables. Thus, you are specifying the spreadsheet range where you have previously entered the names or labels of each of the variables. The POINT LABELS option allows you to assign a label or name to the individual plotted points. However, if you have more than five points plotted on a graph, the labels tend to run together and provide little information. POINT LABELS are designed for plots of a small number of points. The HEADINGS option includes a title or main heading, a subtitle or sub-heading, and headings for the X-axis and Y-axis. By default the headings are printed with the BLOCK font. The FONT may be changed with the GLOBAL GRAPHICS command. The X-AXIS heading is placed just below the X-axis; the Y-AXIS heading is placed to the left of the Y-axis.

OTHER OPTIONS

The OTHER options of the VIEW command deal with additional formatting options, location of the graph, and the quality of the final output. The default options are normally acceptable to most users. The EXPLOSION option is quite useful in creating PIE graphs. The EXPLOSION option allows you to specify by number the variable that you want to stand apart from the other variables, i.e. that explodes from the rest. Up to eight variables may be exploded.

EXERCISE 9-3 -- PREPARING A GRAPH

Load the file named "GRAPHS" from your course diskette. The data in the spreadsheet is the estimated Federal taxes to be paid under the 1985 tax law for the years 1986 through 1990 by type of taxpayer. This data served as the basis for the Bar graph in Figure 9-1. For this exercise you are to use the data in the file GRAPHS to prepare each of the other six types of graphs. You have to identify the DATA ranges. Give each graph a different number. Plot each graph. The default graph settings print full page graphs, which is acceptable. If you prefer, you may change the size of the graph with the GLOBAL GRAPHICS LAYOUT command. Save the spreadsheet with the graphs specified.

The OUTPUT command provides a full range of options that allow you to get the most from your printer. The limits on the use of the SuperCalc3 OUTPUT command are a function of the type of printer you have and the amount of creativity you possess. The printer options with the OUTPUT command are selected from the SETUP option. The options include page length, page width, double space, setup codes, and auto feed. The default margins are left, 4; right, 136; top, 2; and bottom, 2. Thus, the default printing width is 132 characters. The default page-length is 66 lines, the normal length for 8 1/2 by 11 paper. For printing, the default margins are acceptable, though if the output range exceeds 72 characters, the 73rd to 132d characters wraps around and is printed under the first 72. Normally, you do not want this. Thus, you should limit the width of the output range to only 72 characters at a time. The margins may be changed to accommodate wider or longer paper. Most wide paper used with microcomputers is 14 inches wide. The default margin setting for regular size type is acceptable when using the wide paper. In summary, the margins may be used as they are when the output range is restricted.

The PAGE-LENGTH has to be reset if you are not using the standard 11 inch paper. The default setting is 66 lines per page, which is designed for standard size paper. If you have shorter paper available, you should count the lines on the paper, reset the LENGTH of the page, print a page, and perhaps reset the length. Trial and error is one of the best ways to learn the OUTPUT options.

The DOUBLE SPACE and AUTO FEED options are toggle switches, i.e. they are either on or off. DOUBLE SPACE allows you to print the page double spaced. The default and normal selection is OFF. The AUTO FEED toggle allows you to use single sheets of paper with your printer. The default setting is OFF. With the OFF setting you are required to press the space bar after each page is printed. If you set the AUTO FEED ON, the printer does not stop after each page. If you are about to print a multi-page report using a printer with continuous paper and a tractor feed, it is advisable to set AUTO FEED ON.

SuperCalc3 allows the full use of the printer's type fonts through the use of SETUP codes. Use of SETUP codes requires knowledge of the specific printer that you are using. The printer's manual provides a listing of ASCII Control codes and Character Fonts. Similarly, in Appendix J to the SuperCalc3 manual, a listing of ASCII control codes is printed for use in entering the SETUP codes. SuperCalc3 uses the actual control sequences, not the HEX values for those sequences.

The control sequences are entered in response to the prompt from the OUTPUT SETUP SETUP command. The SETUP codes are transferred to the printer. Before the transfer may be made, the printer must be on-line. The specific codes vary with the type of printer. The ESPON RX-80 printer uses the control sequence ESC 69 to turn on the emphasized mode, which produces a darker, crisper type than the regular print. To enter this code, the SuperCalc3 sequence is CTRL [E, that is the key combination Control key and square bracket key, which represents ASCII name ESC, followed by the capital letter E. To turn on the Compressed Mode, the sequence is the key combination Control O. To turn the compressed mode back off, enter Control R, or alternatively, turning the printer off and back on again resets the printer to the default settings. A code that is useful in printing titles of reports is Control N, which turns on the Expanded Mode for the length of the line. The result is large type that looks good for a title.

After the SETUP codes are entered, select PRINT, and your print commands are executed. It takes some trial and error to learn to use these codes well. The capabilities are great and worth the efforts. It is the print codes that sets the appearance of your report apart from others.

EXERCISE 9-4 -- OUTPUT SETUP CONTROL CODES

Using the OUTPUT CODES discussed above, print out the following labels. For your reference the SETUP CODES are listed.

EXAMPLE 1 EMPHASIZED MODE, entered as follows: Ctrl [E

This is the emphasized mode; use the setup code Ctrl [as ESC and E to set the emphasized mode on. Note the results.

EXAMPLE 2 EXPANDED MODE Ctrl N

The EXPANDED MODE is for titles. However, only the first line of the OUTPUT range is printed in the expanded mode. The following lines revert to normal size print. Print the following company name.

Virginia Peanut Company

EXAMPLE 3 COMPRESSED MODE Ctrl O

The compressed mode allows 135 characters on regular size paper. It is useful to print large spreadsheets on regular size paper. You have to clear previous settings before you use compressed print. The easiest way is to turn the printer off and back on. This resets the printer to the default settings.

SuperCalc3 provides a series of date functions that handle the computation of time. The date functions are based upon the number of days since March 1, 1900, with 3-1-1900 assigned the number 1. The dates are displayed in the format day/month/year. For example February 11, 1986 would be displayed 2/11/86. Although displayed in numbers, the date is not a numeric entry. It is a special date value. Internally, the date is treated as an integer between 1 and 73,049. Thus, you may add, subtract, or perform other mathematical operations. To reference the date, you must use one of SuperCalc3 Date Reference Functions, discussed below. Examples of its use are to calculate the date that a 90-day note is due-- simply add 90 to today's date. Similarly, to obtain a listing of the dates of every Friday in the first quarter, enter the first Friday and add 7 to it for the desired period. The date functions are very flexible.

The date functions are divided into two types, Date Entry functions and Date Reference Functions. Dates are entered into a spreadsheet with one of the following three Date Entry Functions: TODAY; DATE or DAT(MM,DD,YY); or DVAL(value). TODAY is the system's date which should be the current day's date. Once it is entered, the spreadsheet always displays the current day's date. In this way you may keep track of the date the report is prepared. DATE is the workhorse of the date functions. It is also inconvenient to enter. The form is DATE(day,month,year). The year may be entered with or without the century number. Thus, 1985 may be entered as 85 or 1985. The DVAL(value) converts the integer value given into a date that is displayed. For example, DVAL(1) displays 3/ 1/00.

The Date Reference functions display the day of the month, DAY(Date Value); the month of the year, MON(Date Value); the year number, YEAR(Date Value); the number of the day of the week where 1 is Sunday to 7 for Saturday, WDAY(Date Value); and the modified Julian Date of the date value, JDATE(Date Value). In each case the Date Value is the result of a Date Entry Function, for example DATE. The Date Reference Functions may be included in formulas as values. For example, if you are preparing a schedule of the age of accounts receivable, those over thirty days old may be determined by an IF statement. Assume that the date of the receivable is January 6, 1986, and today's date is February 11, 1986, the IF statement would be

IF(DATE(1,6,86)-TODAY)>30,("OVER   DUE"),("CURRENT")).   The
result is the text value OVER DUE if the receivable is more
than 30 days old, or the text value CURRENT, if it is not
over thirty days old.

Another useful combination of functions is to combine
the WDAY date function with the LOOKUP function.   The result
identifies the day of the week as a text value.

THE LOOKUP FUNCTION

The LOOKUP FUNCTION is used to extract information from
a table, for example to compute income tax liability.   The
tax rates must be looked up in a table and then included in
a tax computation that results in the tax liability.   The
function is of the form LOOKUP(value, col/row range) where
the value is looked up in the range, i.e. the range in the
worksheet where the table is found.   If the range is a
column range, the number or textual value in the column to
the right is displayed.   If the range is a row range, the
value in the first row down is displayed.   The LOOKUP
function searches the column or row range until it finds a
value that is greater then the value being looked up.   Then,
it goes to the next column or next row, to find the desired
number or text value.   Since, SuperCalc3 is looking for a
greater value, the first value in the range must be lower
than any possible value that could be looked up; the last
value in the range must be larger than any possible value
expected to be looked up.   Refer to Figure 9-3 for an
example of both a ROW and a COLUMN LOOKUP function.

210

FIGURE 9-2   EXAMPLE OF LOOKUP FUNCTION

```
    |   A   ||   B   ||   C   ||   D   ||   E   |
 1| -10,000      .00      100      200
 2|       0      .20      400     1000
 3|   2,000      .40
 4|   5,000      .60
 5|   8,000      .80
 6| 100,000     1.00
 7|
 8|   3,200
 9|     100
10|
11|lookup(a8,a1:a6)       .40      COLUMN LOOKUP
12|
13|lookup(A9,a1:d1)       400      ROW LOOKUP
14|
15|
```

EXERCISE 9-5 -- DATE ARITHMETIC and LOOKUP FUNCTIONS

PART A

The Hardluck Company reports to you the following accounts
receivable. The company's policy is to age the accounts
into three classes: current, 30 days or less; past due,
more than 30 but less than 90 days; and hopeless, those more
than 90 days old. REQUIRED: Prepare a schedule of aging of
accounts receivable. Prepare the schedule as of January 1,
1986. One approach is to use IF statements to spread the
amounts into the three categories of accounts receivable.
Then, the columns may be SUMmed for the total of each
category.

DATE	CUSTOMER'S NAME	AMOUNT
December 2, 1985	George Bailey	$ 200.00
November 8, 1985	Clarence	500.00
August 10, 1985	Mr. Potter	1,400.00
February 2, 1985	Harry Bailey	500.00

PART B

The Chicken Parts-R-Parts Corporation reports taxable income
of $89,000 in 1985; $105,000 in 1986; and $48,000 in 1987.
Throughout the entire period, the tax rates stayed the same.
The rates for all these years are .15 on the first $25,000;
.18 on the second $25,000; .30 on the third $25,000; .40 on
the fourth $25,000; and .46 on any amount over $100,000.

REQUIRED: Compute the tax liability for each year using a
LOOKUP table.

The EXECUTE command allows you to program SuperCalc3. EXECUTE, selected by typing / X, reads a file on the default disk with a filetype .XQT, and executes the command string that its finds in the file. Each and every keystroke that is required to be entered from the keyboard must be in the .XQT file. Figure 9-3 lists an EXECUTE file that loads files into the current spreadsheet. The purpose of the execute file is to automate repetitive tasks. One of the most frequent repetitive tasks is use of the OUTPUT command to print a report from the spreadsheet. If the setup codes are entered to obtain a special print, such as compressed or emphasized, the use of an execute file makes that process easier and quicker. Another frequent use is to complete a form, for example a travel reimbursement form. The spreadsheet may be set up to receive data in designated cells. Then an execute file may be written that moves the cursor to only those cells. Including an ampersand (&) in the execute file causes the EXECUTE file to pause for user input from the keyboard. Typing the ampersand from the keyboard, resumes the execute file. The execute file may be terminated by entering either a CONTROL C or CONTROL BREAK key combination.

FIGURE 9-3   EXAMPLE OF AN EXECUTE FILE

In the following example of an EXECUTE file, the characters to the left of the line are entered to perform the functions explained to the right of the line.

```
                        |
                        | The purpose of this command is to LOAD
/lb:updatgpa,a          | the file UPDATGPA from the B disk
=a41                    | drive.  Next, the cursor is moved to
/lb:fall3,a41:h60       | A41.  At this point part of the file
=a61                    | FALL3 is loaded into UPDATGPA.
/lb:spring4,a41:h60|      Similarly for the other files.
=a81                    | The part loaded from each file is the
/lb:fall4,a41:h60       | grade report.
=a101                   |
/lb:spring5,a41:h60|
=a21                    | The cursor is returned to A21 and the
/gb                     | borders are removed for printing.
/odall,p                | This command prints the file and then
/qy                     | QUITS SuperCalc3 and returns to DOS.
```

The use of execute files may prove to be a frustrating experience. Frequently, they do not work the first time; just like programming with any language. The key is to remember that every keystroke that you type from the keyboard while using the commands must be entered in the execute file. If a series of selections is to be made, they are separated by commas. When a blank space is encountered on the line the enter key is assumed to have been entered. The execute file moves to the next line at that time.

The SuperCalc3 manual suggests that you first enter the keystrokes in a .CAL file so that they may be edited and refined. Once you are ready to use the file, use the OUTPUT command to write it to the disk but with a filetype of .XQT. If you do not specify .XQT, a .PRN filetype is automatically entered. When the keystrokes are entered in the CAL file, they must be entered as text or labels, thus, each line should start with a double quote (").

To enter OUTPUT SETUP Codes in an EXECUTE file you have to use word processing software, like WordStar. The problem is that the print setup codes require a key combination that includes the CONTROL key. If you are entering the SETUP from the keyboard, there is no problem. But you may not enter the Control key in a .CAL file, thus, you must use a word processor. In WordStar you have to type Control P before you enter the print setup. Once completed, the execute file will substantially eases the task of using the Output command.

EXERCISE 9-6   EXECUTE FILE

Enter the Execute file that is listed in Figure 9-3. If the ranges that you used in the files UPDATGPA, FALL3, SPRING4, FALL4, and SPRING5 are not the same as entered in Figure 9-3, adjust accordingly.

To use the execute file that has been named EX96, enter the following commands.

/ X B:EX96

APPLICATIONS OF ELECTRONIC SPREADSHEETS

CHAPTER 10

Electronic spreadsheets are designed to quickly make complex calculations that are repetitive in nature. Typically these computations are referred to as "What-if" type questions. The accountant is asking, "What will be the results if ...?" With an electronic spreadsheet, accountants are able to present the expected result of a proposed transaction based upon the results of several simulations of the possible variables. Furthermore, the next time a similar transaction occurs, a spreadsheet prepared for a different yet similar transaction, may be quickly modified to analyze the current transaction. The result is a more complete analysis than otherwise possible in the time available to prepare the analysis.

It is the ability to easily modify an existing spreadsheet and to perform complex computations very quickly that gives the electronic spreadsheet the what-if power. As a result of this what-if analysis, business decisions may be more completely analyzed that ever before. In additional, the entire area of graphical analysis, heretofore basically ignored by accountants, is available with the graphical abilities of electronic spreadsheets.

In addition to their use in analysis of business decisions, electronic spreadsheets are being used by accountants as their personal notepads. The spreadsheet format with its rows and columns, is useful for many simple listing operations. For example, a listing of telephone numbers, a listing of stock portfolios, a listing of current interest rates on short-term loans, a listing of birthdays of those business and personal associates that you wish to remember, and so on. The advantage of the use of electronic spreadsheets for listings such as these lies not with the spreadsheet, but with the nature of electronic files. While it is difficult at times, you must remember that the personal computer is really a computer. Accordingly, all the space advantages, the accessibility of information stored in electronic media, and the ability of printing an error free copy that comes with a "real computer" is available with the personal computer. The electronic spreadsheet allows access to these powers, but does not require a wide array of software. Many accountants are actually using the electronic spreadsheet as a word processor, entering labels that extend the full width of the page. While, certainly not as efficient as a word processor, the spreadsheet does get the job done when used as a word processor for short memos.

The limits are boundless. With trial, error, and creativity, accountants are finding avenues for use of spreadsheets never before considered. The purpose of this chapter is to give you some examples of uses of electronic spreadsheets. The examples also serve as learning experiences that give you more practice in the use of the spreadsheet software discussed in Chapters 4-9. Either Lotus 1-2-3, or SuperCalc3 may be used to solve these exercises.

LIST OF APPLICATIONS

Following is a listing of accounting applications of electronic spreadsheets used by a large company. The list is not presented as all inclusive, but as illustrative of the scope of applications currently being used by accountants.

LIST OF APPLICATION
OF ELECTRONIC SPREADSHEETS

Inventory valuation including currency conversion.

Investment model: treasury bond futures.

Investment model: tax shelter on depreciable property.

Job order cost accounting.

LIFO: project effect on taxable income given various price and inventory quantities.

LIFO: Conversion, determine effect on income.

LIFO: double extension of inventory.

Lease projection: Safe Harbor Lease analyses.

Lease/buy analysis.

Lease/buy analysis: compare net present value under different assumptions.

Compare costs under different pension plan benefit formulae.

Budget for audit plan

IRS model of business valuation.

Compensation studies: schedule of deferred compensation for key employees.

Compensation studies: stock computation.

Interfaces with Fast Tax Corporate Tax Worksheet.

Depreciation calculations: different lives, book vs. tax.

Divestiture analysis: model different divestiture arrangements.

ACRS depreciation.

Twelve month case flow projection with cash balance deficit carrying over month-to-month.

Depreciation: book/tax differences, current ACRS tables, straight line and double declining balance.

EPS computations: antidilutive issues, common stock equivalents, primary and dilutive computation.

Financial model: five year projections.

Operating Budgets
    by Departments
    by Nature of Cost (Fixed or Variable)

Training Budgets

Staff Scheduling

Property Records

EXERCISES

The following exercises are presented as problems relating to financial accounting and management accounting. The problems progress from the relative simple to the relative complexed. In some cases, you are given a print-out of the solution and asked to enter all the labels and formulas necessary to obtain that print-out. In other cases the decision is yours as to how to proceed in the design and set-up of the spreadsheet. The third approach taken, is to give you a partially completed spreadsheet, with many labels already entered, and ask that you complete it. The goal is to help you take that leap out of the pencil and paper age to the age of the use of the personal computer as a tool to do your job as an accountant.

EXERCISE 10-1 ADJUSTED TRIAL BALANCE

Retrieve or Load the file "ADJENT" from your course diskette. The file contains an unadjusted working trial balance for the Hiwassee Company. In the area below the trial balance, proforma financial statements--the Balance Sheet and the Income Statement--are listed.

REQUIRED: The following adjusting entries are to be posted to the unadjusted trial balance and the adjusted trial balance computed. The Balance Sheet and the Income Statement are to be updated to reflect the adjustments made.

ADJUSTING ENTRIES FOR HIWASSEE COMPANY

GENERAL JOURNAL FOR POSTING ADJUSTING ENTRIES

J/E #	DATE	ACCOUNT DESCRIPTION	ACCOUNT NUMBER	DEBITS	CREDITS
1	12-31	ALLOWANCE FOR UNCOLL	135	520	
		ACCOUNTS RECEIVABLE	130		520
		WRITE-OFF BAD DEBT,D.V.SAFTNER			
2		BAD DEBT EXPENSE	31	875	
		ALLOWANCE FOR UNCOLL	135		875
		RECORD BAD DEBTS EXPENSE			
3		INVENTORY, 12-31	140	28900	
		INCOME SUMMARY	999		28900
		INCOME SUMMARY	999	28000	
		INVENTORY	140		28000
		TO RECORD ENDING INVENTORY			
4		PREPAYMENTS	150	50	
		INSURANCE EXPENSE	42	300	
		RENT EXPENSE	40		250
		MISCELLANEOUS EXPENSE	50		100
		TO ADJUST PREPAID EXPENSES			

5	DEPRECIATION EXPENSE	46	600	
	ACCUMULATED DEPRECIATION	165		600

TO RECORD DEPRECIATION FOR THE YEAR

6	SALARIES EXPENSE	30	818	
	ACCRUED SALARIES PAYABLE	211		818

TO RECORD ACCRUED SALARIES

7	INTEREST EXPENSE	60	40	
	ACCRUED INTEREST PAYABLE	215		40

TO RECORD ACCRUED INTEREST

8	INTEREST RECEIVABLE	131	33	
	INTEREST REVENUE	12		33

TO RECORD ACCRUAL OF INTEREST REVENUE

9	FEDERAL INCOME TAXES	90	669	
	INCOME TAX PAYABLE	219		669

TO RECORD FEDERAL INCOME TAX LIABILITY

EXERCISE 10-2   PROOF OF CASH

The following partial template is on your course diskette saved with the name "EX102". The assignment is to retrieve or load the file EX102, and complete the proof of cash using the information both in the file and listed below. The partial template is reproduced below to give you an example of how the template will appear when displayed on your monitor.

The purpose of this template is to prepare a Proof of cash schedule as may be prepared for audit or internal control purposes.

The schedule begins at cell A21, one page down. Column A is used to enter the labels of the reconciling items. Columns C and D are used to enter the cash receipts and cash disbursements for the period. Columns B and E are used for the beginning and ending reconciliations.

The following additional information is available for your use.

Deposits in transit, December 31, 1985	$24,000
Deposits in transit, December 31, 1986	$31,000
Outstanding checks, December 31, 1985	$125,000
Outstanding checks, December 31, 1986	$89,000
Unrecorded bank charges, December 31, 1986	$2,100

LONGWOOD TREE SERVICE
PROOF OF CASH FOR DECEMBER 31, 1986
FARMVILLE NATIONAL BANK

	BALANCE 12-31-1985	RECEIPTS	DISBURSEMENTS	BALANCE 12-31-1986
Per bank	$589,000	$2,456,980	$2,312,456	$733,524
Deposits in transit				
Outstanding checks				
Reconciling items				
Per books				$673,424

223

EXERCISE 10-3 PROOF OF CASH

The following information is provided for your use in preparing a Proof of Cash for the Volunteer Company for February, 1986.

	PER BANK
Balance, January 31, 1986	$96,000
Cash receipts, February	$432,000
Cash disbursements, February, 1986	$512,000
Balance, February 28, 1986	$16,000
Deposits in transit, January, 31, 1986	$4,500
Deposits in transit, February 28, 1986	$6,000
Outstanding checks, January 31, 1986	$52,000
Outstanding checks, February 28, 1986	$64,000
Unrecorded bank charges, February 28, 1986	$400
Unrecorded interest income, January 31, 1986	$678
Unrecorded interest income, February 28, 1986	$723
Note collected by bank, February 21, 1986 Not recorded by company	$895
Check returned by bank, NSF, February 28, 1986	$245
Deposit erroneously recorded in company's account by bank	$3,200

EXERCISE 10-4 DISCOUNTING A NOTE RECEIVABLE

On July 30, 1986, the Y Gant Shirt Company discounted a $10,000 90-day note receivable that was due on September 30, 1986. The face amount interest rate is 12%; but the bank charged a 15% rate for this note. The note was received on June 30, 1986.

Determine the proceeds from discounting the note and the interest revenue related thereto.

The following column headings are provided for your use.

DISCOUNTING WITH RECOURSE

FACE AMOUNT	INTEREST TO MATURITY	AMOUNT AT MATURITY	BANK CHARGES (DISCOUNT)	PROCEEDS FROM DISCOUNTING

EXERCISE 10-5   AMORTIZATION OF DISCOUNT
ON NOTE RECEIVABLE

```
|     A    ||    B     ||    C    ||    D     || E   |
 1|EXERCISE 10-5  AMORTIZATION OF DISCOUNT ON NOTE
 2|               RECEIVABLE
 3|The purpose of this template is to prepare an
 4|amortization table for Discount on Notes Receivable.
 5|Below the table, adjusting entries are listed for each
 6|year of the note.
 7|The table assumes a full year, i.e. the note is dated
 8|December 31, for each period.  To modify to consider
 9|part years, the interest amount must be multiplied by
10|the appropriate fraction in order to adjust for the
11|interest difference.
12|***************     INPUT AREA      ******************
13|
14|Principal amount of note                 $100,000
15|Term of note, in years                      5
16|Nominal yearly rate                         6%
17|Effective yearly rate                      14%
18|
19|*****************************************************************
20|
21|COMPUTATION OF PRESENT VALUE OF NOTE RECEIVABLE
22|                                    Nominal      Present
23|                                    Amount        Value
24|
25|Principal amount of note            $100,000     $51,937
26|
27|Yearly interest rate                    6%          14%
28|Term of note, in years                  5            5
29|Yearly interest amount              $6,000       $7,271
30|Total interest over term          $30,000      $20,598
31|
32|Present value of note                           $72,535
33|
34|Discount on note receivable                     $27,465
35|
36|Period       Cash      Eff     Discount     Disc/    Net Book
37|          Interest Int          Amort      Notes      Value
38|                                            27,465    72,535
39|      1      6,000   10,155     4,155      23,310    76,690
40|      2      6,000   10,737     4,737      18,573    81,427
41|      3      6,000   11,400     5,400      13,173    86,827
42|      4      6,000   12,156     6,156       7,018    92,982
43|      5      6,000   13,018     7,018           0   100,000
44|
```

226

```
45|
46|Adjusting entries
47|
48|Year 1        Cash                                    6,000
49|              Discount on note receivable             4,155
50|                      Interest revenue                        10,155
51|
52|Year 2        Cash                                    6,000
53|              Discount on note receivable             4,737
54|                      Interest revenue                        10,737
55|
56|Year 3        Cash                                    6,000
57|              Discount on note receivable             5,400
58|                      Interest revenue                        11,400
59|
60|Year 4        Cash                                    6,000
61|              Discount on note receivable             6,156
62|                      Interest revenue                        12,156
63|
64|Year 5        Cash                                    6,000
65|              Discount on note receivable             7,018
66|                      Interest revenue                        13,018
67|
68|              Cash                           100,000
69|                      Note receivable                        100,000
```

EXERCISE 10-6   AMORTIZATION OF NOTE RECEIVABLE

The Barnett Company sold four barns to the Hokie Turkey Farms. In full payment for the barns, Hokie received a note for $150,000, with the principal payable in four years and interest payable yearly at a nominal rate of six per cent. The effective rate of interest for this type of note is fifteen per cent.

The note is dated May 1, 1985.

REQUIRED: Prepare a amortization table for the note receivable and a schedule of entries for each payment and for the adjusting entries at December 31, of each year.

EXERCISE 10-7   COMPUTATION OF INVENTORY ON THE LIFO, FIFO, AND WEIGHTED AVERAGE METHODS.

Load the file EX107 from your course diskette. The file contains a schedule of purchases and a schedule of sales for EXIT COMPUTERS RIGHT, a computer store in the theater district. You are to prepare a spreadsheet template to compute the inventory on the LIFO, FIFO, and WEIGHTED AVERAGE basis. It is suggested that you use the sorting commands and the maximum and minimum functions in the design of your spreadsheet.

EXERCISE 10-8 ANALYSIS OF ACCOUNTS RECEIVABLE

The Harmonica Company reports the following accounts receivable as of June 30, 1986. Prepare an Aging of Accounts Receivable schedule as of June 30, 1986. The accounts should be classified as Current, less than thirty days; Past due, more than 29 but less than 91; and Delinquent, if more than 90 days old. The addition to the Allowance for Doubtful Accounts is computed as follows: 1% of the current accounts; 5% of the past due accounts; and 20% of the delinquent accounts.

REQUIRED: Prepare the aging schedule and compute the addition to the allowance account.

DATE	CUSTOMER	AMOUNT
June 1,1986	William J. Smith	$120.00
June 10, 1986	Arnold G. Heathe	340.00
April 4, 1986	Joseph J. Bottom	500.00
January 5, 1986	Donald V. Saftner	1,050.00
February 11, 1986	James O. Hicks	3,876.00
March 5, 1986	Charlotte R. Reagan	567.00
April 28, 1986	Paul D. Sloane	873.00
March 25, 1986	Mary Ruth Lewis	956.00
February 27, 1986	Ann T. Baker	784.00
December 3, 1985	Tom V. Hall	1,345.00

EXERCISE 10-9 DEPRECIATION SCHEDULE

The Hapless Tool Company purchased the following assets
during the current year. Your assignment is to compute a
schedule comparing the amount of depreciation for the first
five years of the assets lives. Your schedule is to compute
depreciation under the straight-line, sum-of-years' digits,
double-declining balance method, and the ACRS tax method.
For tax purposes the assets are all classified as five-year
property. The ACRS percentages are 15% the first year; 22%,
the second; 21%, the third, fourth, and fifth year. Assume
the full Investment tax credit is taken if applicable. In
the table below, ITC stands for investment tax credit.

After completing the schedule, extract (or save) the part of
the file that contains the yearly amounts of depreciation
for each method of depreciation. Prepare a pie graph for
each method. Also, prepare a line graph that graphs the
amounts of depreciation for each method of depreciation by
year.

The assets are listed below.

PURCHASE DATE	TYPE OF ASSET	AMOUNT	LIFE	ITC Y OR N
1-1-86	EQUIPMENT	$5,000	5 YRS.	Y
1-1-86	MACHINE	145,000	8 YRS.	Y
7-1-86	OFFICE FURNITURE	8,000	5 YRS.	Y
9-1-86	PERSONAL COMPUTER	7,000	5 YRS.	Y

EXERCISE 10-10   AMORTIZATION OF BOND DISCOUNT

The Topside Corporation issued $1,000,000 in serial bonds. The nominal or face interest rate is 10%, payable semi-annually; the effective rate of interest is 12%. The bonds are to be retired at the rate of $100,000 per year beginning two years from date of issue. The date of issue is April 1, 1986.

REQUIRED: Prepare an amortization schedule to compute the interest expense and the balance of Bonds Payable for each year as of December 31. The columnar headings below are suggested. The initial carrying amount of the bond must be computed. Lastly, prepare journal entries to record the semi-annual payment of interest and the annual payment of principle.

DATE	CREDIT CASH	INTEREST EXPENSE	BOND DISCOUNT	BOND PAYABLE	CARRYING AMOUNT OF BOND

EXERCISE 10-11   PRICE LEVEL ADJUSTED
FINANCIAL STATEMENTS

Below, the balance sheet and income statement for the TEN COMPANY are reproduced. Following the statements, additional information about inflation in the United States is reported.

REQUIRED:

1. Prepare financial statements adjusted for changes in price-level.

2. Prepare a line graph of the CPI in the United States for the 10 year period, 1976 to 1985.

The balance sheet begins at cell A22.

The income statement begins at cell A52.
The additional information begins at cell A76.

TEN CORPORATION
BALANCE SHEET
DECEMBER 31, 1986 and 1985

	1986	1985
ASSETS		
Cash and receivables	$2,500	$2,100
Inventories	1,500	1,900
Investment in affiliated companies	2,200	2,000
Plant, property and equipment	10,000	7,800
Total assets	$16,200	$13,800
LIABILITIES and STOCKHOLDERS' EQUITY		
Accounts payable	$4,150	$3,500
Federal taxes payable	400	980
Long-term debt	4,200	3,500
Deferred federal income taxes	1,500	1,000
Total liabilities	$10,250	$8,980
Paid-in capital	3,000	2,900
Retained earnings	2,950	1,920
Total stockholders' equity	5,950	4,820
Total equities	$16,200	$13,800

TEN CORPORATION
INCOME STATEMENT
YEAR ENDED DECEMBER 31, 1986 and 1985

	1986	1985
REVENUES		
Net sales and operating revenues	$15,150	$12,950
Costs and expenses		
Cost of sales	7,650	7,000
Operating expenses	3,750	2,900
Selling general and administrative	1,500	1,250
Depreciation	850	650
Income before taxes	$1,400	$1,150
Federal income taxes	500	400
Net income	$900	$750

ADDITIONAL INFORMATION
Inflation in the United States

YEAR	CPI	YEAR	CPI
1967	100	1977	181
1968	104	1978	195
1969	109	1979	217
1970	116	1980	246
1971	121	1981	272
1972	125	1982	294
1973	133	1983	314
1974	147	1984	330
1975	161	1985	360
1976	170	1986	387

Assume that asset are purchased first day of year and that liabilities are incurred at the end of the year. The following table lists the year of acquisition for the assets.

ASSET	YEAR OF ACQUISITION
Cash and receivables	CURRENT YEAR, 1986 or 85
Inventories	CURRENT YEAR
Investment in affiliated companies	1975
Plant, Property and equipment	1980

Liabilities	
Accounts payable	CURRENT YEAR
Federal taxes payable	CURRENT YEAR
Long-term debt	1980
Deferred federal income taxes	1983

EXERCISE 10-12   ANALYSIS OF MARKETABLE SECURITIES

Retrieve or Load the file EX1012 from your course diskette.
The file contains a listing of marketable securities. Below
the listing, you are asked to compute certain information
useful in analyzing the marketable securities.
Specifically, you are asked to compute the effective rate of
return, to list those investments earning less than an
effective return of 10%, and to list those stocks that have
appreciated less than 8% per year. It is suggested that you
use the DATA or DATA MANAGEMENT commands to complete this
template.

EXERCISE 10-13   COMPUTATION OF PENSION EXPENSE

The determination of pension expense is composed of two
parts, the current pension expense relating to current
services rendered, and the amortization of past service
pension liability, i.e. the pension expense relating to past
services. It is not uncommon for past service pension costs
to be funded over a different time period than the period of
amortization of the past service costs.

REQUIRED: Prepare a template that will amortize the past
service costs. Compute the pension accrual for each year.
The following information is for you use.

Current pension costs amount to $50,000 each year. On
January 1, 1986, the date the pension plan is adopted, the
present value of future pension benefits relating to past
service amounted to $300,000. Door Company has decided to
amortize the past service cost over 15 years. The pension
trust assets are expected to earn an average return of 8%.
The past service costs will be funded over a ten year
period.

The following columnar headings are for your use.

YEAR, AMORTIZATION ANNUAL AMOUNT, INTEREST ADJUSTMENT,
PENSION EXPENSE, FUNDING CASH CREDIT, BALANCE SHEET DEFERRED
DEBIT OR CREDIT.

EXERCISE 10-14   AMORTIZATION OF INVESTMENT IN LEASE

The BIM Computing Corporation regularly engages in the business of leasing computers to businesses. One such transaction involves the lease of large mainframe computer to the State University. The fair market value of the computer is $3,000,000. The lease payments are per month over an eight year period. The normal market rate of interest for this type of property is 12%, on an annual basis. Additional costs of servicing the computer and taxes on the computer are $30,000 per year, incurred ratably throughout the year. The useful life of the computer is eight years.

REQUIRED: Determine the income to be reported each month from the capital lease. In determining your answer prepare a template to compute the monthly amortization of the lease investment. The following headings are suggested: DATE, ANNUAL LEASE PAYMENT, EXECUTORY COSTS, INTEREST ON THE NET INVESTMENT, NET INVESTMENT RECOVERY, NET INVESTMENT.

PART B. Using the same information above, assume that State University may borrow funds at a rate of 6%. It has been determined that the university should account for the lease as a capitalized lease.

REQUIRED: Modify the above template to compute the amortization of the lease obligation and the related expenses for State University, the lessee.

EXERCISE 10-15   ANALYTICAL REVIEW PROCEDURES

Retrieve or Load the file named EX1015 from your course diskette. The file contains balance sheet and income statement for the Hiwassee Limited Company for a four year period. Also, it contains instructions on the computation of certain ratios that have proven useful to auditors in performing an analytical review of an audit client. However, the formulas to compute the ratios have been erased.

REQUIRED: Complete the template by entering the formulas for the ratios that are listed. After completed, print the ratios. Also, prepare a line graph of the ratios that reflect the liquidity of the firms assets. Print the graph.

EXERCISE 10-16   ANALYSIS OF A REAL ESTATE INVESTMENT

Retrieve or Load the file named EX1016. The file contains certain information regarding an investment in an apartment house. The investment is to be made through a partnership. The investor is contemplating purchasing 25% of the partnership. Complete the schedule in the template. Determine the internal rate of return for the investment in the partnership.

EXERCISE 10-17   HIGH-LOW COST ANALYSIS

The producers of Buford Beer have incurred maintenance costs at various levels of activity as indicated below. In order to estimate the manufacturing overhead cost for maintenance of the brewing equipment, Buford Beer must segregate the variable and fixed components of the maintenance costs. The maintenance costs and related activity level are:

Hours of operation	Maintenance costs incurred
450	$1,900
350	1,500
395	1,680
200	900
275	1,200

REQUIRED:

A.   Prepare a template using the high-low method of cost analysis to estimate the average variable maintenance cost per unit and the fixed component of maintenance costs.

B.   Use the formula developed in part A to determine the budgeted maintenance overhead for an operating level of 325 hours of operation.

C.   Buford Beer has established a rule for investigating costs whereby costs that fall outside a zone in which 2/3 of the costs are expected to fall should be investigated. The statisticians have pointed out that actual costs may be expected to fall within the range of the budgeted costs plus or minus one standard deviation two-thirds of the time. If the actual maintenance costs are $1,275 when 325 hours of operation is maintained, should Buford Beer investigate the reason for the variance from budgeted maintenance costs.

Concrete Products, Inc. operates under the job order cost accounting system. At the beginning of the current year the company reported the following balances in the inventory accounts:

Raw materials	$6,000
Work-in-process	12,400
Finished goods	20,000

During the current year, the following transactions were completed:

1. Raw materials were acquired for $20,000 cash.
2. Raw materials were requisitioned for jobs in process of $12,000, and for manufacturing overhead, $6,000.
3. Factory payrolls were incurred and paid, production workers, $24,000; janitorial and plant maintenance workers, $6,000.
4. Additional manufacturing overhead costs incurred of $$18,000.
5. Manufacturing overhead applied at a rate of 110% of direct labor costs for all jobs.
6. Two jobs are in ending inventory of work-in-process. Job 345 has been charged with 10 direct labor hours, and $500 of materials. Job 350 has been charged with 2 direct labor hours and $100 of materials.
7. The ending inventory of Finished goods was $14,000.

REQUIRED: Retrieve or Load the file named EX1018 from your course diskette. Modify the template to determine the Cost of goods manufactured, the balance in ending inventory of work-in-process, and the over or under applied Manufacturing overhead in the period for the Concrete Products, Inc.

EXERCISE 10-19   PROCESS COST ACCOUNTING

The ABC Corporation has two processes, mixing and packaging. The packaging department incurred direct material costs of $30,000, and direct labor costs of $50,000. During the period, 20,000 units of product were completed and transferred to finished goods. The beginning inventory of work-in-process for the packaging department consisted of 2,000 units that were 100% complete as to materials and 50% complete as to labor and overhead. The total costs were $18,000, of which $6,000 was transferred-in costs from the mixing department, $3,000 was raw materials, and $6,000 direct labor. Manufacturing overhead is applied at a rate of 50% of direct labor costs. The ending inventory of work-in-process for the packaging department consisted of 3,000 units, 70% complete as to materials and 30% complete as to labor and overhead. During the period, 21,000 units were transferred into the packaging department from the mixing department at a total cost of $63,000.

REQUIRED:

A.   Prepare a template that will compute a cost of production report for the packaging department of the ABC Corporation. for the current period. Use the weighted average method of determining unit costs.

B.   Modify the template developed in part A to compute the cost of production report using the FIFO method of determining the unit costs.

C.   Prepare a pie graph to display the cost components of the cost per unit of the packaging department for the current period using the weighted average method of determining the unit costs.

EXERCISE 10-20   MASTER BUDGET

The XYZ Company manufactures two products, APBs and SASs, for sale to dealers. In order to simplify the situation, it is assumed that the master budget is being prepared immediately after the close of the year 19X3. The following information is presented for XYZ Company.

Product requirements

	APB	SAS
Material A	2 lbs.	4 lbs.
Material S	4 lbs.	2 lbs.
Direct labor	4 hrs.	6 hrs.

Inventory and labor cost data
Material A, $2 per lb.
Material S, $4 per lb.
Direct labor, $4 per hr.

Trial balance on 12/31/X3

Cash	$ 36,400
Accounts receivable	8,600
Material A (4,000 @ $2)	8,000
Material S (2,500 @ $4)	10,000
APB (200 x $44)	8,800
SAS (400 x $52)	20,800
Land	20,000
Building and equipment	60,000
Allowance for depreciation	<20,000>
Accounts payable	<24,000>
Taxes payable	<16,000>
Capital stock	<80,000>
Retained earnings	<32,600>

Desired inventory on 12/31/X4

Material A	5,000 units
Material B	4,000 units
APB	250 units
SAS	500 units

The company has appointed a budget director who operates under the direction of a budget committee. Information is sent to the committee, which acts on it and forwards decisions to the budget director for incorporation into the budget.

Additional information is provided on sales, manufacturing expense, selling and administrative expense, and expected cash flows as follows.

Sales budget

Product	Units	Unit Price	Expected Revenues
APB	3,000	$50	$150,000
SAS	6,000	65	390,000
			$540,000

Manufacturing-expense budget*

Supervision and inspection	$ 30,000
Factory depreciation	22,000
Taxes	3,520
Insurance	600
Repairs and maintenance	12,000
Supplies	15,000
Heat and light	2,480
Energy	12,000
	$ 97,600

*Actual overhead is allocated to products produced based on direct-labor hours used.

Selling and administrative-expense budget

Salaries	$ 42,000
Sales commissions	10,800
Advertising and promotion	12,000
Depreciation	1,200
Office supplies	500
Taxes	100
Insurance	100
Miscellaneous	200
	$ 66,900

The company expects to finance its operations through internally generated funds. Consequently, outside financing is undertaken only when cash flows from revenues fall short of immediate needs. Expected cash flows are shown below by quarter:

| | Quarter | | | |
	1	2	3	4
Sales collections	$120,000	$126,000	$142,000	$151,000
Expenditures				
Materials	36,050	40,000	42,000	45,400
Direct labor	46,000	50,000	49,800	49,400
Other expenses	15,200	29,250	41,000	55,580
Income taxes	16,000			

REQUIRED:

Prepare a master budget for the XYZ Company that includes a projected income statement and balance sheet.

EXERCISE 10-21 STANDARD COST VARIANCES

The actual cost data for the Upward Company is given below:

Beginning inventory, work-in-process	$ 0
Beginning inventory, raw materials	0
Raw materials purchased and used (20,200 units)	45,150
Direct labor (9,000 hours)	58,500
Variable overhead, actual	85,000
Fixed overhead, actual	62,000
Total units manufactured,	9,100 units

Standard cost data is as follows:

Standard cost per unit of raw material	$2.00
Standard units of raw material per unit of finished product	2 units
Standard cost of direct labor per hour	$6.00
Standard time to produce one unit	1 hour
Normal capacity, direct labor hours	10,000 hours
Budgeted variable overhead at normal capacity	$75,000
Budgeted fixed overhead	$60,000

REQUIRED: Retrieve the file named EX1021 from your course diskette. Use this partially completed template to compute the material, labor, and overhead variances.

EXERCISE 10-22   STANDARD COST VARIANCES

The Green Company has installed a standard cost system and a flexible overhead budget. Standard costs have been recently developed for its only product and are as follows:

Direct material, 2 pounds at $15/pound	$30
Direct labor, 6 hours per unit at $6/hr.	36
Variable overhead, 6 hours per unit at $1	6
Fixed overhead per unit	9

Total stand cost per unit	$81
	=====

Normal capacity is 12,000 standard direct labor hours per month. Fixed overhead is expected to be $18,000 per month.

The actual costs for a month in which 2,000 units were produced are as follows:

Direct materials purchased, 5000 pounds	$73,000
Direct material used in production,	4,100 pounds
Direct labor hours, actual 10,000 hours	61,000
Variable overhead	9,100
Fixed overhead	18,800

REQUIRED: Develop a template to compute the standard cost variances for material, labor, and overhead.

EXERCISE 10-23   DIRECT COSTING INCOME STATEMENT

The Taylor Rental Company produced at normal capacity in 1986. The sales and production data are given below:

Number of units sold	90,000
Unit selling price	$ 15
Number of units manufactured	100,000
Variable manufacturing cost per unit	$ 7
Fixed manufacturing cost per unit	$ 3
General and Selling expenses--Fixed	$100,000
General and Selling --Variable	$ 50,000

REQUIRED: Prepare a template that will compute a summary income statement based upon absorption costing, based upon direct or variable costing, and a schedule reconciling the the pre-tax income under the two methods, i.e. reconciling absorption and direct costing.

EXERCISE 10-24   BREAK-EVEN ANALYSIS

The Frisco Bottling Company reports the following cost analysis for its normal operations in the production of 1,000,000 units.

Costs	Variable costs	Fixed costs
Direct materials	$ 3,000,000	0
Direct labor	3,000,000	0
Factory overhead	800,000	$ 500,000
Marketing expense	700,000	300,000
Administrative expense	500,000	200,000

The selling price is $10 per unit. Frisco's income tax rate is 30%.

REQUIRED: Prepare a template that will provide the answers for the following questions. The template should be general enough to handle a variety of cost-volume-profit problems.

A.   Compute the break-even point in sales dollars.

B.   Compute the break-even point in units of product.

C.   If fixed costs are increased by $100,000 what is the effect on break-even point in terms of sales.

D.   A new machine can be leased at a cost of $200,000 per year that will allow a reduction in direct labor costs of $50,000 per year. What will be the effect on break-even point in terms of sales if the new machine is purchased.

The Wise Company uses machine tools that it has been manufacturing for its own use. The company currently has excess capacity and expects the excess to continue. Currently, there is no alternative use for the plant area being used to manufacture the tools.

A salesman of machine tools, who has been attempting to sell his machine tools to Wise for two years, has prepared the following analysis in cooperation with company personnel.

	Cost of next year's supply of tools if	
	Manufactured	Purchased
Cost of purchasing tools		$210,000
Cost of parts and materials	$100,000	
Cost of direct labor	40,000	
Cost of indirect labor	50,000	
Variable overhead	10,000	
Fixed overhead:		
Depreciation	28,000	
Other fixed overhead	12,000	
Total cost	$240,000	$210,000

Additional information:

1. The depreciation is on equipment especially purchased for making these machine tools. This special equipment may be sold for $1,000, its scrap value.

2. The purchased machine tools will have no operational advantage over the tools made by the plant.

REQUIRED: Prepare a template to analyze whether the Wise Company should purchase or make its own machine tools. The template should be as general as possible to facilitate its use in the future.

EXERCISE 10-26   CAPITAL BUDGETING

Bert's Hamburger Emporium, "The Best Burgers in Town", is considering investing $90,000 in an automatic burgermaker. The burgermaker is expected to produce $50,000 annual cash inflows (gross) each year of its five year useful life. Cash outflows during each of these years are expected to be $10,000 per year for out-of-pocket maintenance expense. The burgermaker will have a resale value of $15,000 at the end of five years. For book purposes, the machine will be depreciated on the straight-line basis; for tax purposes, ACRS five-year property will be used. (The percentages are 15%, 22%, 21%, 21%, and 21%.) The marginal income tax rate is 40%; the average income tax rate is 25%.

If the new burgermaker is purchased, old equipment with an adjusted basis of $5,000, will be scrapped for nothing. Thus, Bert will realize a tax deductible loss of $5,000. Additional working capital in the amount of $10,000 will be required throughout the period.

The lowest acceptable rate of return that Bert will consider is 15%.

REQUIRED: Prepare a generalized template to compute the following information useful in capital budgeting.

A.   Compute the yearly net cash inflows or outflows.

B.   Determine the payback period. (Hint, compute the unrecovered investment for each period.)

C.   Determine the internal rate of return of the investment.

D.   Compute the net present value of the investment.

E.   Write a short memo to advise Bert on the purchase of the Burgermaker.

EXERCISE 10-27   CAPITAL BUDGETING

The Peel Electric Company is considering an investment in a new labor saving insulating machine. The president, Ms Emma Peel, has set 15% as the after-tax return required on investments of this type. The president has supplied the following information:

1.   The cost of the new insulation machine is $50,000.

2.   ACRS depreciation is taken for all machinery. The ACRS rates are 15% for year 1, 22% for year 2, 21% for the remaining three years. The new machine will have a salvage value at the end of five years of $10,000. Depreciation on the old machine will be $2,000 per year for the next 5 years. At that time, the old machine will have no value.

3.   Peel Electric Company has a marginal tax rate of 45%.

4.   The new machine will generate a $12,000 savings in labor cost over its five-year life.

5.   The old machine can be sold for $6,000. The original cost of the old machine was $24,000. Accumulated depreciation for book purposes amounted to $12,000. Tax depreciation to date on the old machine is $14,000.

6.   The old machine will require repairs of $2,000 at the of the third year if it is continuously operated.

REQUIRED: Prepare a template to analyze whether or not the Peel Electric Company should purchase the new machine.

EXERCISE 10-28   CAPITAL BUDGETING FOR SANTA

Santa Claus is considering acquiring a new sleigh. The
available information is listed below. You are asked to
prepare an analysis of the decision to replace the old
sleigh with a new computerized sleigh. Santa's cost of
capital is 13.45%.

ADDITIONAL INFORMATION:

1. The new sleigh costs $10,000, cash on delivery.
2. The annual operating costs of the NEW sleigh are $3,000
    per year for the first three years; $5,000 per year in
    the 4th and 5th year.
3. The annual operating costs of the OLD sleigh are $8,000
    per year.
4. The current market value of the OLD sleigh is $1,000;
    its adjusted basis and book value is $1,000; and its
    salvage value in five years will be zero.
5. The expected salvage value of the NEW sleigh at the end
    of Year 5 is zero.
6. For tax purposes, ACRS five-year class is used for
    determining depreciation. The percentages are 15%, 22%,
    21%, 21%, and 21%. For book purposes, straight-line
    depreciation is used.
7. The NEW sleigh is wider than the old, thus, it will
    require a larger garage for storage. The remodeling may
    be done for $2,000. The addition will be expensed for
    tax purposes (under Section 179). The salvage value of
    the garage at the end of five years will be zero.

REQUIRED: Prepare   a   template   to   analyze   Santa's
            contemplated purchase of a NEW sleigh. Determine
            the net present value of the purchase. Note,
            there will be no effect on Rudolph or any of the
            other reindeers.

EXERCISE 10-29   ECONOMIC ORDER QUANTITY

The Killinger Company has a steady demand of 40,000 units a year for its product. The carrying cost is estimated to equal $2 per year and the order cost is fixed at $100 per order. The firm purchases in lots of 2,000 units at a cost of $3 a unit. If Killinger is willing to increase its order size to 4,000 units, the vendor will reduce its price to $2.98 per unit.

REQUIRED:

A. Prepare a template to compute the economic order quantity at a price of $3 and at a price of $2.98 per unit.

B. At what price would Killinger adopt an order size of 4,000 units.

EXERCISE 10-30   LINEAR REGRESSION

The L & W Company is reviewing its budget formula for its overhead costs. To aid in the review, the information contained in the file named EX1030 on your course diskette has been gathered. Using the information in the file (overhead costs at various levels of direct labor hours and machine hours) develop a revised budget formula. In developing your formula, identify a simple linear regression equation that will best estimate the overhead costs.

PART III: DATABASE MANAGEMENT SYSTEMS

FUNDAMENTALS OF dBASE

CHAPTER 11

INTRODUCTION

WHY USE A DATABASE MANAGEMENT SYSTEM?

All of us store information, such as names and phone numbers of acquaintances, checks we have written, bills that need to be paid, or appointments that we must keep. Pencil and paper is a cheap, convenient, and very flexible way of handling small amounts of information. For the examples above most of us use address books, check books, folders, and appointment calendars. These pencil and paper techniques work well with small volumes of data.

Unfortunately paper and pencil techniques quickly become unwieldy when larger amounts of data are encountered. Even small businesses can have significant volumes of data in accounts receivable, accounts payable, general ledger, payroll and inventory control systems and will find it cost beneficial to computerize their operations. Database management systems, such as dBase, allow even relatively large bodies of data to be manipulated easily. Retrieving individual records or sorting the entire file require little human effort.

DBASE VERSUS ELECTRONIC SPREADSHEETS

dBase is an elementary relational database management system. The term "relational" refers to the storage of data

FIGURE 11-1   LIQUOR INVENTORY EXAMPLE

NUM	TYPE	BRAND	OZS	QTY	COST	PRICE
110	BOURBON	EL CHEAPO	16	5	1.15	1.70
120	BOURBON	THE WILD WEST	16	22	1.94	3.18
130	BOURBON	THE WILD WEST	32	21	3.82	6.04
140	BOURBON	THE WILD WEST	64	5	7.11	10.83
150	BOURBON	THE TAME EAST	64	3	7.53	11.51
210	VODKA	PRUSSIAN	16	75	1.65	3.23
220	VODKA	PRUSSIAN	32	35	4.10	6.65
230	VODKA	PRUSSIAN	128	9	9.23	13.34
310	SCOTCH	OLD COUNTRY	32	88	3.06	5.44
320	SCOTCH	OLD COUNTRY	64	23	6.23	9.54
330	SCOTCH	OLD COUNTRY	128	7	11.06	16.37
410	WHISKEY	SOUTHERN RYE	64	44	5.75	8.83
420	WHISKEY	OLD WYOMING	16	44	2.14	3.74
430	WHISKEY	OLD WYOMING	64	19	5.93	9.00
440	WHISKEY	THE NEW SOUTH	128	4	8.77	12.52

in two dimensional tables such as Figure 11-1. Each column represents some characteristic that is common to all the records or rows. Each row contains information on various characteristics for a particular entity such as an item of inventory in Figure 11-1.

Electronic spreadsheets such as Lotus 1-2-3 and SuperCalc3 store information in two dimensional matrices of cells that superficially resemble the tables of a relational database. There is no requirement, however, in a spreadsheet that a particular column be used for a single characteristic. Nor is there any requirement that the entries in a row pertain to a single entity. Theoretically, it would be possible for cell A1 to bear no conceptual relationship to cells A2 or B1. Cell A1 might be the product of numbers found in cells C30 and Z50. This allows a spreadsheet to be used for some very fancy and powerful analysis of data. It can also make a spreadsheet difficult to understand.

Relational databases are somewhat more constrained. Each row and column has a particular and consistent meaning that reduces the range of analysis that is possible. Relational databases easily handle data analysis that requires repetitive calculations on each record of the database or on some defined subset of the database. Many business data processing tasks such as accounts receivable, accounts payable, general ledger, payroll, and inventory control require just such a repetitive analysis. dBase and the spreadsheet packages differ in the nature of the analysis that they conveniently allow.

dBase and the spreadsheet packages also differ in the way they are implemented. The spreadsheet packages load the entire spreadsheet into primary storage. With all the information in primary storage, the recalculation of the spreadsheet can be performed very quickly. Primary storage does, however, constrain the size of the spreadsheet that can be implemented. dBase makes greater use of secondary storage. Only part of the file may be brought into memory at any one time. This allows dBase to handle larger bodies of data, but it also slows down the analysis. If the portion of the database that is needed is not in primary storage, it must be read in from secondary storage which slows down the processing. Summarizing what has been said so far: spreadsheet packages are able to do a relatively complex analysis of small bodies of data, while database packages such as dBase are able to do a simpler repetitive analysis of relatively large bodies of data.

Another difference between dBase and the spreadsheet packages is the format of the data presentation. dBase only brings data onto the screen when it is instructed to do so. Spreadsheets have their data on the screen all of the time. Some people feel that they understand the application better if they can see the data all the time, other people prefer to only look at the data in the form they request when they request it.

dBase and spreadsheets are two different tools. Their ranges of application are different but they do overlap. If you have a simple analysis of a small body of data then either tool might reasonably be used. It would probably be a matter of picking the tool with which you had the most experience and felt most comfortable. Many business problems do not involve simple analysis of small bodies of data. It is in this realm that dBase and spreadsheet packages may be thought of as complementary tools rather than as competitors.

As an example of the use of dBase and spreadsheets as complementary tools, consider a general ledger system. A typical journal would be too large to fit into primary storage as a worksheet. dBase could be used to store journal entries and post them to a general ledger. Once the journal has been summarized into ledger form, either dBase or a spreadsheet package could be used to produce financial statements. A complex "what if" analysis of the summarized data could be more easily performed by the spreadsheet. This example is typical of the use of the two packages as complementary tools. One can let dBase store and summarize a large body of data, pass the results to a spreadsheet where the analysis of the data is completed.

DBASE COMMANDS

dBase consists of over 75 distinct commands. This number of commands can be confusing to the beginner. To make learning dBase easier, only the most common and useful commands will be introduced in the following discussion. Related commands are introduced together with a discussion of their relative merits. Frequent hands on experience allows you to practice what you have learned. It is hoped that as you read the dBase material, you will work through the examples on a computer. By receiving constant feedback on what you have learned, the experience of learning dBase should be both productive and pleasurable.

The dBase discussion starts with an introductory section that demonstrates some of the power of this database management package. After the introductory section, related commands are discussed together. A single command may be entered in a number of different ways, but some rules must be followed. The documentation on the system for a command typically includes a presentation of the syntax or general form of the command. By examining the syntax, the full possibilities of a command may be discovered.

To understand the syntax some rules and customs must be learned. Consider the following syntax statement for the list command.

LIST [<scope>][<field list>][FOR/WHILE <condition>][OFF]

At this time do not try to understand the list command or the various options but rather the rules that are used in defining the syntax. dBase commands begin with a verb, in this case LIST, that is required. Any phrases found between the square brackets (i.e. [ ]) are optional. Any phrase between the angle brackets (i.e. < >) and written in small letters is the general name for the item. The user should substitute a specific occurrence of the item. The slash (i.e. /) indicates an either/or situation where the user must choose between the options. Neither the brackets nor the slash are keyed in when entering the command. Anything in capital letters must be entered exactly as it appears if it is entered at all. The only exception to this is that the first four letters of any capitalized word may be used as an abbreviation.

DBASE II VERSUS DBASE III

dBase III is an enhanced version of dBase II. There never was a dBase I. Most of the dBase language is exactly the same in both dBase II and dBase III. It is this central core that is emphasized in this text. Some of the enhancements of dBase III are of little value to the novice user who typically works with small files. These enhancements include an increase in the number of fields per record (from 32 to 128) and the number of records per file (from 65 thousand to 1 billion). Faster sorts are also not noticeable with small files. Some commands, such as REPORT, are important commands and have been changed significantly in their operation. In such a case the use of the command with dBase II is explained separately from its use with dBase III. One improvement in dBase III is that headings are placed over the columns of data when the database is listed. Since this improvement makes the displays easier to understand, the headings are used in this text.

*　*　*　*　*　*　*　*　*　*　*　*　*　*　*

EXERCISE 11-1

Why are computers used in modern businesses? Don't restrict
yourself to the answers given above.

EXERCISE 11-2

What are the differences between database packages and
electronic spreadsheets?

EXERCISE 11-3

Explain the use of the special symbols in a dBase syntax
statement (i.e. [ ], < >, /).

USING DBASE THE FIRST TIME

The purpose of this section is to give you a quick overview of the operation of dBase. No attempt is made to give a detailed explanation of each command, that is done later. If this is the first time you are using a computer, please be assured that there is no way to damage the computer through the keyboard. Relax and enjoy this learning experience.

ENTER DBASE

Place the DOS system disk into drive A, place your course diskette in drive B and then turn the machine on. After keying in the date and time you should receive an A> prompt. Press the CAPS LOCK key. If dBase is on a separate diskette place it into drive A at this time. At the A> prompt key in:

                        DBASE

and press the return key. This should take you into dBase and leave the cursor by a period prompt. The period prompt is required to enter a dBase command. In the sections that follow, the command is placed on a line by itself. After keying in the command you must press the return key to tell dBase that you have finished keying in the command.

POINT AT DATABASE

Tell dBase that the course disk is in drive B with the following SET command:

                  SET DEFAULT TO B

You will know that dBase accepted the command when it does not give an error message and responds with another period prompt. In this section you will be using a liquor inventory database file that has already been set up for you. Its name is LIQINV. Tell dBase which file to use with the following command:

                     USE LIQINV

DETAILED LISTING

To find out what the file contains enter the LIST command:

LIST

Compare your results to Figure 11-1, which appears early in this chapter. The first column on the screen is the sequential record number. This information is not stored in the record itself nor is it shown in Figure 11-1 but rather is attached to the line by dBase when the listing is made. The second column on the screen is the stock number and that is followed by the type of liquor, brand, number of ounces, number of bottles on hand, the cost per bottle, and finally by the selling price per bottle. In producing a listing of the file, the LIST command gives all the detail.

SUMMARIZED LISTING

With the REPORT command it is possible to prepare a report form that produces a summarized report. A report form that summarizes the liquor inventory by type has been prepared and its name is LIQTYPE. Enter the following REPORT command:

REPORT FORM LIQTYPE

Compare your results to Figure 11-2. To stop the report from scrolling off the top of the screen, remember that CTRL-NUMLOCK temporarily pauses the operation of the computer. Pressing any character key (the space bar is convenient) resumes the functioning of the computer. Note that in preparing the report, dBase calculates the total cost (i.e. quantity * cost) and retail value (i.e. quantity * price) for each item and then summarizes by type of liquor.

FIGURE 11-2   LIQUOR INVENTORY SUMMARY REPORT

Page No.   1
09/30/85

LIQUOR INVENTORY TOTALS BY TYPE

	QUANTITY	TOTAL COST	RETAIL VALUE
** BOURBON ** Subtotal **			
	56	186.79	293.98
** VODKA ** Subtotal **			
	119	350.32	595.06
** SCOTCH ** Subtotal **			
	118	489.99	812.73
** WHISKEY ** Subtotal **			
	99	425.91	668.20
*** Total ***			
	392	1453.01	2369.97

EDIT A RECORD

The edit command allows one to change the contents of the database. Let us assume that we have just received a shipment of 12 more bottles of whiskey. Referring to the listing (you may want to repeat the LIST command at this point) it may be seen that whiskey is record number 12. Enter the following command:

EDIT 12

and then using the down arrow key on the right side of the keyboard (on the same key as the numeral "2") move the cursor down to the quantity field (i.e. QTY). Change the 32 to a 44 by keying 44 on top of the 32. To save the change you just made, do a CTRL-W, which means holding the control key down while pressing the "W" key. The CTRL-W returns you to the period prompt. You may want to repeat both the LIST and the REPORT FORM LIQTYPE commands at this time to see the change made to the whiskey inventory.

LEAVE DBASE

To leave dBase and force any recent changes out onto the disk, enter the following command:

QUIT

It is important that you enter the QUIT command before turning off the machine. Without the QUIT command any recent changes to the database might be in primary storage only and not saved to the disk permanently. As soon as the power is turned off, primary storage loses its contents so you must make sure the changes to the database have been placed on the disk by entering the QUIT command.

In this section you have seen some of the power of dBase. You can look at the contents of the database with the LIST command. Summarized reports of the database can be prepared easily with the REPORT command. You also found that changes can be made to the database with the EDIT command.

* * * * * * * * * * * * * * *

EXERCISE 11-4

How was each of the following commands used in the above section:
(a) DBASE
(b) SET DEFAULT
(c) USE
(d) LIST
(e) REPORT
(f) EDIT
(g) QUIT

SETTING UP THE DATABASE

In this section you will create a new database.* It will be a simplified payroll file which is used often in the subsequent sections. Remember that in a relational database a file resembles a two dimensional table. Most tables have a title or name. Most tables also have columns of information with column titles at the top of each column. In setting up a table you must also decide how wide each column is to be.

CREATE COMMAND

Setting up a dBase file is very similar to setting up a table on paper. You must decide what to call the table, what columns of information are required, and how wide they should be. An additional step in setting up a dBase file is deciding whether you want each column of data to contain numbers and letters or strictly numbers. The two major types of fields that make up the columns are character (i.e. numbers and letters) and numeric (i.e. numbers only). Peoples' names would naturally be character fields while quantity fields would just as naturally be numeric fields. A field such as zip code could reasonably be declared either character or numeric. Although it contains only numbers, you probably never want to perform arithmetic operations on the field. The stock number in the liquor inventory example was declared to be a character field even though it only contains numbers.

To set up a dBase file enter the CREATE command:

CREATE

When dBase asks for the name of the new file respond with PAYROLL. The name of a dBase file may contain up to eight letters, digits, and underscores. It must begin with a letter and contain no embedded blanks. It is automatically given a file name extension of DBF, which is an abbreviation for data base file.

----

* If you left dBase after working on the previous section then enter DBASE from the DOS A> prompt and then enter SET DEFAULT TO B from the dBase period prompt.

dBase then asks for information about each column of data. You must enter the field name, type (C for character or N for numeric), and width. If you declare a field to be numeric, you must also tell dBase how many decimal places (i.e. positions to the right of the decimal point) you want stored for the numeric field. Note: If you make a mistake in setting up the database, do not be concerned. Later in this section you will be shown how to correct any errors. dBase II and III differ in how they request column information from you. See the appropriate paragraph below.

dBase II: When entering the column information into dBase II you must separate each piece of information with a comma and press the return key after each field is described. For instance DEPARTMENT,C,2 means that the field name is DEPARTMENT, it is a character field, and it is two positions wide. Enter the following lines into dBase:

```
DEPARTMENT,C,2
EMPNO,C,4
LNAME,C,15
FNAME,C,15
POSITION,C,3
SALARY,N,9,2
```

When you are done with the above, press the return key again. When dBase asks "INPUT DATA NOW?", respond with an N for no. Now tell dBase II that you want to use this file by entering:

USE PAYROLL

dBase III: When entering the column information into dBase III, you are given separate data entry fields for each piece of information. After entering the field name DEPARTMENT the cursor automatically goes to the type data entry field since you filled the name field. Next enter the type by keying the letter C for character. Then enter the width by keying 2 and pressing the return key. Enter the following fields of information into dBase:

Field Name	Type	Width	Dec
DEPARTMENT	C	2	
EMPNO	C	4	
LNAME	C	15	
FNAME	C	15	
POSITION	C	3	
SALARY	N	9	2

When you complete the above, press the enter key. dBase requests that you press the enter key again to confirm that you are done. dBase then asks if you wish to "Input data records now? (Y/N)." Respond with N for no.

LIST STRUCTURE COMMAND

You have just completed setting up the structure of the database file PAYROLL. To see the structure enter:

LIST STRUCTURE

and dBase responds with the following:

Structure for database : B:PAYROLL.dbf
Number of data records :   0
Date of last update   : 09/30/85

Field	Field name	Type	Width	Dec
1	DEPARTMENT	Character	2	
2	EMPNO	Character	4	
3	LNAME	Character	15	
4	FNAME	Character	15	
5	POSITION	Character	3	
6	SALARY	Numeric	9	2
** Total **			49	

In dBase II the type is indicated by a C or N. In the above structure, EMPNO is short for employee number, LNAME is short for last name, and FNAME may be used to store the first name and middle initial of the employee.

MODIFY STRUCTURE COMMAND

If you make an error in setting up the structure, you can correct it in one of two ways. If the error is extensive, the easiest way to correct the problem is to delete the file (see the section on "Working with files") and start over with the CREATE command. The other way is to modify the existing structure. For the sake of practicing this later technique let us assume that it is decided that the users of the payroll database would prefer to use the abbreviation DEPT rather than the whole name DEPARTMENT. To make this change, key in the following command:

MODIFY STRUCTURE

If you are using dBase II answer Y for yes in response to the question "Modify erases all data records . . . proceed? (Y/N)" since there is no data in the file yet.

Change the field name DEPARTMENT to DEPT by just retyping the line. Correct any errors that you may have made. When you are done, use a CTRL-W to save the changes. You may want to use the LIST STRUCTURE command again to assure yourself that the change was made to the structure.

Special care must be taken when there is data in the file and you want to modify the structure. Changes may be classified as : 1) Changing the name of a field or fields or 2) Changing anything else such as adding fields, deleting fields, or changing the length of a field. You should not attempt to make changes that fall into both classes above at the same time. If you have data in the database, making more than one class of change at a time results in lost data. If you wish to rename a field and make some other change, then make the name change with one MODIFY STRUCTURE command and the other change with a separate MODIFY STRUCTURE command. If you are a dBase II user you must take additional precautions (see problem 33 at the end of chapter 12).

In this section you have set up the database PAYROLL. You looked at the structure with LIST STRUCTURE and changed the structure with MODIFY STRUCTURE.*

----

* If you are going to leave dBase at this time, remember to enter the QUIT command before turning the machine off.

* * * * * * * * * * * * * * *

EXERCISE 11-5

List the structure of the LIQINV file.

EXERCISE 11-6

Create a file that has fields for the names and addresses of
your friends and acquaintances and then modify the structure
to allow room for a phone number.

APPEND COMMAND

Now that you have set up the structure for the database, it is time to add some data.* The APPEND command is used to add data to the end of a database. In order to receive information on the APPEND command enter the following HELP command:

HELP APPEND

In response to the HELP command, dBase displays the syntax of the command for which help was requested (i.e. APPEND in this case). It also gives a short description of the command. The HELP command is a quick and easy way to get information about dBase commands. It is particularly useful when you enter a command and get a syntax error. Simply type in the word HELP followed by the name of the command with which you are having trouble. In dBase III press the ESC key to return to the period prompt after a HELP command.

In this section you add records to the database using both the APPEND and the APPEND FROM commands. First try the APPEND command:

APPEND

You are immediately given a blank data entry screen. Do not enter anything further at this time. Some sample data will be given to you after a discussion of the APPEND command.

The number of the record that is being constructed is shown at the top of the screen. Since this file was just created it should be empty and therefore the record being added is number one. After keying in a particular field, the cursor will automatically go to the next field if you fill the current field. If you do not fill the current

----

* If you left dBase after working on the previous section, then enter DBASE from the DOS A> prompt and then enter SET DEFAULT TO B from the dBase period prompt. In any case you probably need to enter USE PAYROLL from the dBase period prompt. A USE command is necessary anytime you wish to work with a file and you have previously QUIT dBase or USEd another file.

field, then press the return key to move to the next field. When you exit the last field of a record, the record is added to the database, the input screen is cleared, the record counter is incremented by one and the cursor is placed at the beginning of the first input field.

If you realize you have made an error before exiting the last field in a particular record, then use the up arrow key to move the cursor to the field with the error and change it. If you exit the last field of a record and then realize that you made an error, do not be concerned. The next section shows how to modify the contents of a record and the last section of this chapter shows how to remove the entire record.

After entering the last field of the last record press the return key again without keying anything, not even blanks, into the next input screen. This returns you to the period prompt. If you accidently press the return key and get a period prompt before you are finished adding records, then simply enter the APPEND command again.

At this time add the following four records to the database using the APPEND command. To remain consistent with the book, make sure you have pressed CAPS LOCK so that entering the information in all capital letters is easy.

DEPT	17	17	17	17
EMPNO	6010	5698	3312	2315
LNAME	FIRST	AIDER	SHARALIKE	LEAVES
FNAME	I. M.	RAY D.	SHARON	T.
POSITION	211	569	531	231
SALARY	5947.84	1794.92	2123.87	4943.19

After you add the four records, LIST the file

LIST

and compare your records to the following list:

DEPT	EMPNO	LNAME	FNAME	POSITION	SALARY
17	6010	FIRST	I. M.	211	5947.84
17	5698	AIDER	RAY D.	569	1794.92
17	3312	SHARALIKE	SHARON	531	2123.87
17	2315	LEAVES	T.	231	4943.19

Note that the four records can be shown in a vertical or horizontal format as shown in the above two samples. In general, the horizontal format (as produced by the LIST command) is used in the following discussion.

APPEND FROM COMMAND

The APPEND FROM command allows records to be added to the database file in use from another file. On your course diskette there is a file called XPAYROLL that contains extra records for the PAYROLL file. To add these extra payroll records to the file and list the entire file enter the following two commands:

```
APPEND FROM XPAYROLL
LIST
```

Your file should now contain 19 records and appear as in Figure 11-3.

FIGURE 11-3 PAYROLL FILE

DEPT	EMPNO	LNAME	FNAME	POSITION	SALARY
17	6010	FIRST	I. M.	211	5947.84
17	5698	AIDER	RAY D.	569	1794.92
17	3312	SHARALIKE	SHARON	531	2123.87
17	2315	LEAVES	T.	231	4943.19
23	6677	BREAKER	J. L.	967	2167.34
23	1034	SETTERA	ED	145	2592.11
23	7433	TRESS	MATT	743	2882.54
23	3486	CABOODLE	KIT ANNE	348	3023.80
31	5533	THYME	JUSTIN	967	3740.98
31	1044	HIGHWATER	HELEN	143	3787.41
31	4569	ERDBUNS	BUD	612	3814.08
31	8754	MAID	TAYLOR	211	3800.25
40	6110	DOVER	BEN	875	3989.92
40	6458	LIFE	ALMA	145	4078.83
45	2348	WANNAKRACKER	POLLY	334	5102.24
45	5443	AYRE	CLAIRE D.	875	5175.34
45	5435	ZOFF	HANS	143	5550.72
58	6128	DESTINKSHUN	MARCO	612	7106.58
58	1987	LAST	I. M.	143	2667.19

The APPEND command adds records to the end of the database. It is also possible to add records at the beginning or in the middle of the file with the INSERT command. To find out more about the INSERT command enter the following request for help:

HELP INSERT

Note that the help message mentions a current record. Before using the insert command it is necessary to understand the record pointer and to understand the use of the GO command. It is the record pointer that determines which record is the current record.

Whenever you first USE a database file a pointer is established within the dBase software and it is initialized pointing at the first record in the file. After a command is executed, the record pointer is left pointing at the last record processed or sometimes just beyond that record. For instance the LIST command leaves the record pointer at the end of the file. The GO command can be used to intentionally reposition the record pointer. Enter the following HELP command to find out more about the GO command:

HELP GO

Assume that you want to add Ben's wife to the payroll file in department 40. List the file and note that the payroll file is in order by department.

LIST

To keep the file in order by department, you must position the record pointer to department 40 before doing the INSERT. Lets keep Eileen close to her husband Ben (record 13) so enter the following commands:

GO 13
INSERT

Now add Eileen to the file using the following information:

DEPT	EMPNO	LNAME	FNAME	POSITION	SALARY
40	9132	DOVER	EILEEN	113	4117.65

List the file and note that Eileen was added after Ben.

                              LIST

     If you had wanted to add Eileen ahead of Ben you could
have used INSERT BEFORE instead of INSERT. If you had
wanted to add Eileen before the first record in the file you
could have used GO TOP followed by INSERT BEFORE. Note that
GO TOP is equivalent to GO 1. The command GO BOTTOM takes
the record pointer to the end of the file. The command
INSERT BLANK puts a blank or empty record into the file. It
is particularly useful within dBase programs. The blank
record is added to the file and then the program can place
information into the blank record.

     In this section you have added records to the file
using the APPEND, APPEND FROM, and INSERT commands. In
order to use the INSERT command you have also learned the GO
command.*

     *   *   *   *   *   *   *   *   *   *   *   *   *   *   *

EXERCISE 11-7

Add the following records to the liquor inventory keeping
the file in order by stock number:

NUM	TYPE	BRAND	OZS	QTY	COST	PRICE
160	BOURBON	APPALACHIAN	64	12	7.98	12.48
510	MOONSHINE	ROTGUT	256	200	1.00	4.00

----

* If you are going to leave dBase at this time, remember to
  enter the QUIT command before turning the machine off.

MODIFYING THE CONTENTS OF A DATABASE

In this section you learn how to modify the contents of an existing database.* There are three commands that are particularly useful in this regard: EDIT, BROWSE, and REPLACE. The EDIT command brings one record at a time up on the screen and allows the operator to make changes to it. The BROWSE command fills the screen with records and permits the operator to change any of them. When issuing the REPLACE command, the operator tells dBase what changes are required and dBase then makes those changes without any further interaction with the operator.

EDIT COMMAND

In order to practice the EDIT command let us assume that Ms. Leaves marries Mr. Tottler and she decides to change her last name to match his. To receive further information about the EDIT command enter:

HELP EDIT

In order to use the edit command efficiently, you must know the number of the record you want to change. The LIST command can supply you with that information:

LIST

Note that Ms. Leaves has a record number of four. Next enter:

EDIT 4

Use the down arrow key to mover the cursor to the last name field and key TOTTLER over LEAVES. To exit the edit mode do a CTRL-W. Now list the file to see the change:

LIST

----

* If you left dBase after working on the previous section, then enter DBASE from the DOS A> prompt and then enter SET DEFAULT TO B from the dBase period prompt. In any case you probably need to enter USE PAYROLL from the dBase period prompt. A USE command is necessary anytime you wish to work with a file and you have previously QUIT dBase or USEd another file.

BROWSE COMMAND

The BROWSE command allows changes to be made to several records on one screen. Enter the following HELP command:

HELP BROWSE

The BROWSE command includes a FIELDS option that allows you to work with a subset of the fields in the database. This option is discussed further and demonstrated in the "Retrieving Data" section.

Before using the BROWSE command it is desirable to position the record pointer.

GO TOP

This step is not necessary, however, because it is possible to move around in the file while in the BROWSE mode. Table 11-1 lists the various keystrokes that allow easy movement of the cursor and editing of data when using the BROWSE command. Many of these keystrokes (e.g. inserting and deleting characters) also work with other commands such as EDIT and APPEND.

To practice the BROWSE command assume that ever since Eileen and Ben have been working in the same department they have been fighting a lot and finally get a divorce. He requests and gets a transfer to department 31. She decides to resume using her maiden name, Back. Enter the BROWSE command and by using Table 11-1 change Ben's department to 31 and Eileen's last name to Back.

BROWSE

To exit the BROWSE command do a CTRL-W. List the file to see the changes.

LIST

TABLE 11-1 NORMAL OPERATION OF KEYS

(Experiment with a copy of your file
when using a key for the first time.)

ACTION   KEY(S)

MOVE CURSOR

Previous field   Up arrow, CTRL-E
Next field   Down arrow, CTRL-X
One position to left   Left arrow, CTRL-S
One position to right   Right arrow, CTRL-D
Move up >=1 line   PGUP
Move down >=1 line   PGDN
Write then display prev.   CTRL-R
Write then display next   CTRL-C
Scroll right in BROWSE   CTRL-B
Scroll left in BROWSE   CTRL-Z

CHANGE MODE

Quit without saving   CTRL-Q, ESC*
Write then exit   CTRL-W, CTRL-END*
Delete character   CTRL-G, DEL*
Insert mode on/off   CTRL-V, INS*
Insert blank line   CTRL-N
Delete line   CTRL-T
Mark for delete/recall   CTRL-U
Remove line/column   CTRL-U*
Clear field to blanks   CTRL-Y

                            * dBase III only

REPLACE COMMAND

The REPLACE command allows you to make changes to all the records in the database with a single line of input. To illustrate the power of this command assume that Mr. Destinkshun, the president of the company, decides to give everyone a 10% raise. First list the file and note the salaries of a couple individuals.

LIST

Then enter the following command which is explained in detail below:

REPLACE ALL SALARY WITH SALARY*1.1

Now relist the file and notice the 10% raise that everyone, including Mr. Destinkshun, has received.

LIST

The REPLACE command is very flexible. The syntax for the REPLACE command illustrates the fact quite well:

```
REPLACE    [<scope>] <field> WITH <exp>
           [,<field> WITH <exp> . . .]
           [FOR/WHILE <condition>]
```

In our use of the REPLACE command to give everyone a 10% raise, we said "REPLACE ALL SALARY WITH SALARY*1.1". In that example "ALL" was the scope. If the scope had been omitted (i.e. "REPLACE SALARY WITH SALARY*1.1") only the salary on the current record would have been changed. Other possible scopes are "RECORD n" where "n" is a valid record number and "NEXT m" where the current record and the following m-1 records would be effected. Note that the scope allows changes to be made to a contiguous subset of the database.

In our example "REPLACE ALL SALARY WITH SALARY*1.1", SALARY was the name of the field being changed. It was replaced with the value of the expression "SALARY*1.1" where the "*" is used to indicate multiplication. Part of the above syntax statement (i.e. "[,<field> WITH <exp> . . .]") indicates that multiple fields could have been changed at the same time.

Finally the syntax statement ends with "[FOR/WHILE <condition>]". This conditional statement allows changes to be made to a possibly noncontiguous subset of the database. For instance if the phrase "FOR EMPNO<'2000'" had been added to our previous REPLACE statement then only those people whose employee number was less than 2000 would have received the 10% raise. The "<condition>" statement implies that two things are compared. If the comparison is true than the command is executed on that record.

When using a literal expression such as 2000, surround it with quotes if it is being used as a character string or compared to a character variable. If it is used as a number or compared to a numeric variable, do not surround it with quotes. dBase is sensitive concerning which quotes you use. Above and to the left of the right shift key there is a key that contains a single quote (when unshifted) and a double quote (when shifted). You may use either of these quotes just as long as you do not mix them (e.g. if you start a literal with a single quote then end the literal with a single quote). Do not use the single quote that is above and to the right of the right shift key.

To illustrate further the use of the REPLACE command and its flexible form consider the following statement:

REPLACE RECORD 19 POSITION WITH '001'

The above statement changes Mr. Destinkshun's position number to 001 which seems appropriate for the president of the company.

Next assume that Mr. Destinkshun has decided to give a $1,000 raise to everyone who works with dBase (i.e. POSITION 211). He realizes how valuable such people are to his company. He also decides to give them a more charismatic position number. Both sets of changes can be accomplished with the following statement where the semicolon allows long statements to be continued on the next line.*

REPLACE ALL SALARY WITH SALARY+1000,;
POSITION WITH '007' FOR POSITION='211'

----

* If you are going to leave dBase at this time, remember to enter the QUIT command before turning the machine off.

* * * * * * * * * * * * * * *

EXERCISE 11-8

You have just received 12 bottles of stock number 150. Modify your liquor inventory file to recognize the shipment.

EXERCISE 11-9

Using the BROWSE command, CTRL-G, and PGDN modify all brand names of Prussian to Russian. It is becoming difficult to buy good Prussian vodka.

EXERCISE 11-10

Your supplier has just announced a 5% increase in his selling price. Add this amount to both the cost and price. Make both changes with a single REPLACE command.

REMOVING RECORDS FROM DATABASE

In the previous two sections you added records to the database and then modified the contents.* One must also be able to remove records from the database. In dBase this is a two step process. First one flags those records that are to be removed by using the DELETE command. The PACK command is used to remove the flagged records from the database. If a record is flagged and then you decide not to remove the record, the flag can be removed with the RECALL command. By using the following two HELP commands it may be seen that both DELETE and RECALL allow the use of scope and conditional statements:

```
HELP DELETE
HELP RECALL
```

DELETE COMMAND

To demonstrate the use of these commands assume that Mr. Breaker calls from police headquarters and says that he is unavoidably detained. Also assume that you believe that Mr. Breaker is the only welder (POSITION = 967). The following would be a reasonable way to flag Mr. Breaker for removal from the payroll file:

```
DELETE ALL FOR POSITION = '967'
```

After DELETING records and before PACKING them you should list the file to make sure that only those records you want to remove are flagged:

```
LIST
```

----

* If you left dBase after working on the previous section, then enter DBASE from the DOS A> prompt and then enter SET DEFAULT TO B from the dBase period prompt. In any case you probably need to enter USE PAYROLL from the dBase period prompt. A USE command is necessary anytime you wish to work with a file and you have previously QUIT dBase or USEd another file.

RECALL COMMAND

Notice the asterisks by the record number of Mr. Breaker and Mr. Thyme. Both of these men are flagged for removal. The following statement will unflag Mr. Thyme so that he is not removed from the file:

RECALL ALL FOR LNAME = 'THYME'

List the file and note that Mr. Thyme is no longer flagged for removal:

LIST

PACK COMMAND

With the upcoming PACK it could be said that he was saved just in time. Once you are sure only the correct record is marked for deletion, PACK the file:

PACK

Then list the file and note the absence of Mr. Breaker. If he should be rehired his record would have to be added again, there is no way to RECALL it after a PACK. List your file and compare it to Figure 11-4.

LIST

If there are any differences, use the EDIT, BROWSE, REPLACE, APPEND, INSERT, DELETE, and PACK commands to eliminate the differences.*

*   *   *   *   *   *   *   *   *   *   *   *   *   *   *

EXERCISE 11-11

An employee points out that moonshine is illegal. You certainly don't want to do anything that is wrong, so remove all moonshine from the shelves and dispose of it properly. Update the liquor inventory file to recognize that you no longer carry moonshine by removing the record completely.

----

* If you are going to leave dBase at this time, remember to enter the QUIT command before turning the machine off.

FIGURE 11-4 PAYROLL FILE AFTER PACK

DEPT	EMPNO	LNAME	FNAME	POSITION	SALARY
17	6010	FIRST	I. M.	007	7542.62
17	5698	AIDER	RAY D.	569	1974.41
17	3312	SHARALIKE	SHARON	531	2336.26
17	2315	TOTTLER	T.	231	5437.51
23	1034	SETTERA	ED	145	2851.32
23	7433	TRESS	MATT	743	3170.79
23	3486	CABOODLE	KIT ANNE	348	3326.18
31	5533	THYME	JUSTIN	967	4115.08
31	1044	HIGHWATER	HELEN	143	4166.15
31	4569	ERDBUNS	BUD	612	4195.49
31	8754	MAID	TAYLOR	007	5180.28
31	6110	DOVER	BEN	875	4388.91
40	9132	BACK	EILEEN	113	4529.41
40	6458	LIFE	ALMA	145	4486.71
45	2348	WANNAKRACKER	POLLY	334	5612.46
45	5443	AYRE	CLAIRE D.	875	5692.87
45	5435	ZOFF	HANS	143	6105.79
58	6128	DESTINKSHUN	MARCO	001	7817.24
58	1987	LAST	I. M.	143	2933.91

1. What are the advantages of using database management systems?

2. Compare and contrast dBase and spreadsheet packages.

3. List the advantages of dBase III over dBase II.

4. How is the command INSERT BLANK used in dBase programs?

5. Explain the steps used to remove records from a database.

6. Enter the command HELP (just the word HELP, nothing else) and write a brief description of what dBase does.

7. Someone throws a party, and buys one bottle of each stock number. Reduce the liquor inventory records accordingly.

8. Add information on at least ten friends and acquaintances to the database you set up in Exercise 11-3.

9. Display the structure and list the following database files:
    (a) PERSON
    (b) RAISE
    (c) AR

10. Create a database called POSSESS to record an inventory of your personal possessions. Add fields for name, serial number, model, date purchased and purchase price. Such a record could be handy in case something is lost or stolen.

11. Create a database file called GRADES. Include fields for semester (or quarter), year, department, course number, number of credits, numeric grade, and grade point. Enter into the computer all of the courses you have taken at your current institution. It is unnecessary to key in the grade point, an easy means for initializing that field is discussed in chapter 12.

12. Create a database called CHECKS by examining the fields defined in your own checkbook. Enter the transactions you have made since the last bank reconciliation.

13. If you have a printer attached to your computer, try the following and report your results:
    (a) Do a CTRL-P and then LIST the file. Another CTRL-P turns off the printing.
    (b) USE the LIQINV file and then enter: REPORT FORM LIQTYPE TO PRINT

ADDITIONAL WORK WITH dBASE

CHAPTER 12

INTRODUCTION

In the previous chapter there were sections on creating a dBase database and modifying its structure. The chapter also covered adding, modifying, and canceling records. This chapter begins with sections on retrieving data and generating reports from the database created in the previous chapter. Another section covers copying, erasing, and renaming files. Then sorting and locating records are covered. The advanced dBase material that follows includes the SET command, which allows you to tailor various dBase options to fit your needs, and functions, which are powerful subroutines built into dBase. The chapter concludes with a discussion of summarizing files and transfering them to other systems.

RETRIEVING DATA FROM THE DATABASE

Throughout the previous chapter you have used the LIST command to retrieve data from the database. In this section the LIST command and its close relative DISPLAY are shown to be flexible commands for producing tabular listings. The COUNT and SUM commands are also covered. They are used to produce summary statistics. In this section they are also used to introduce memory variables that are places in primary memory to store intermediate results independent of the database files.*

LIST COMMAND

Examine the LIST help statement:

HELP LIST

As you have already seen, the LIST command produces a tabular display of the records in the database. By using the scope and conditional statements it is possible to look at a subset of the records. Enter the following commands:

```
LIST FOR DEPT='31'
LIST FOR SALARY>5000
LIST FOR DEPT='31' .AND. SALARY>5000
```

The conditional statement helps make the LIST command a flexible data retrieval tool. Note that conditional statements may be connected by the use of .AND. that allows the records to list that satisfy both conditional statements. If you wish to see those records that satisfy either condition use the .OR. connector:

```
LIST FOR DEPT='31' .OR. SALARY>5000
```

By using the field list it is possible to look at a subset of the fields and to rearrange the order the fields are presented.

```
LIST FNAME, LNAME, SALARY
```

Use the OFF option to remove the record number from the listing.

```
LIST FNAME, LNAME, SALARY OFF
```

----

* If you left dBase after working on the previous section, then enter DBASE from the DOS A> prompt and then enter SET DEFAULT TO B from the dBase period prompt. In any case enter USE PAYROLL from the dBase period prompt.

DISPLAY COMMAND

The DISPLAY command is closely related to the LIST command.

HELP DISPLAY

Other than the names of the commands, the syntax statements for the two commands are identical. There are two significant differences between the commands, however. The scope of the DISPLAY command defaults to the current record.

GO TOP
DISPLAY

The LIST command defaults to a scope of ALL. In order to see the entire file with the DISPLAY command enter:

DISPLAY ALL

If a conditional statement is used with the DISPLAY statement then the scope defaults to ALL. The following two statements are equivalent:

DISPLAY FOR DEPT='31'
DISPLAY ALL FOR DEPT='31'

The other major difference between LIST and DISPLAY is that if the file contains enough records, the DISPLAY command pauses after each screenful of information. Depressing the space bar (or any character key) causes the presentation to continue.

COUNT AND SUM COMMANDS

The COUNT and SUM commands generate summary statistics.

HELP COUNT
HELP SUM

The count command reports the number of records that satisfy any specified condition:

COUNT FOR DEPT='31'
COUNT FOR SALARY>5000

If no condition is specified then the COUNT command responds with the number of records in the database.

COUNT

The SUM command adds the contents of the specified field (must be numeric) of all records that satisfy any specified condition. Key in the following commands and note the results:

SUM SALARY FOR DEPT='31'
SUM SALARY

MEMORY VARIABLES

Both the COUNT and SUM commands have an option that allows the result of the command to be stored in a memory variable. Memory variables may be thought of as a temporary note pad where intermediate results can be stored. The contents of the note pad are lost when you leave dBase. Memory variables are particularly useful in programming, which is covered in the next chapter. Enter the following commands:

COUNT TO EMPCNT
SUM SALARY TO SALSUM

To see the results of the previous two commands enter:

LIST MEMORY

The LIST MEMORY command displays the employee count found in the memory variable EMPCNT and the salary sum found in the memory variable SALSUM. It is also possible to initialize memory variables with the STORE command.

HELP STORE

It is possible to have character as well as numeric memory variables.

STORE 'NICK O. TEENE' TO NAME
STORE 1234 TO NUMBER
LIST MEMORY

It is also possible to use the STORE command to store the results of arithmetic expressions:

```
STORE SALSUM/EMPCNT TO AVRSAL
LIST MEMORY
```

AVRSAL now contains the average salary of all the employees.
Note that dBase III users could find the average salary more
directly by using the AVERAGE command.*

    *   *   *   *   *   *   *   *   *   *   *   *   *   *   *

EXERCISE 12-1

What is the average cost of the liquor inventory? Display
those records whose cost exceeds the average.

----

* If you are going to leave dBase at this time, remember to
   enter the QUIT command before turning the machine off.

REPORT COMMAND

dBase has the ability to generate some very nicely formatted reports.* Creating the report is a two step process. First you must enter into a conversation with dBase in which it requests information from you concerning the layout of the report. dBase stores the results of the conversation in a report form file that has a filename extension of FRM. Then whenever you want a report generated with the given format you use the REPORT command.

HELP REPORT

The report command extracts data from the database (DBF) file in use and puts it into the format specified in the report form (FRM) file. The report form can be modified in response to the detection of errors or changing business requirements. To see an example of the REPORT command enter:

REPORT FORM EMPROLE

This command uses a report form stored in EMPROLE.FRM to generate an employee role from the PAYROLL.DBF file. Remember that CTRL-NUMLOCK pauses the execution of the computer so that the top part of the report does not scroll off the screen. If you add the option PLAIN then the report does not include the date and page number in the heading.

REPORT FORM EMPROLE PLAIN

The TO PRINT option sends the report to the printer. Be careful to only use it with a printer attached or else the computer will lock up and need to be rebooted. It is possible to use a scope and/or conditional statement with the REPORT command.

REPORT FORM EMPROLE FOR DEPT='31'

----

* If you left dBase after working on the previous section, then enter DBASE from the DOS A> prompt and then enter SET DEFAULT TO B from the dBase period prompt. In any case enter USE PAYROLL from the dBase period prompt.

The use of the REPORT command to generate reports from existing report forms has been illustrated above. dBase II and III differ significantly in how they create and modify the report form file. Because of this difference, the maintenance of the FRM file is discussed in two separate sections below.

DBASE II: REPORT MAINTENANCE

In dBase II the REPORT command is also used to create a report form file. To modify the report form file, the MODIFY COMMAND command is used.

HELP MODIFY COMMAND

To illustrate the use of these commands, the REPORT command is used to create the report form file DEPTSAL.FRM for the departmental salary report found in Figure 12-1. Next MODIFY COMMAND is used to modify DEPTSAL.FRM to correct any errors. Then the summarized departmental salary report found in Figure 12-2 is created using the REPORT command.

First enter the command:

REPORT FORM DEPTSAL

dBase II responds by asking a series of questions that should be answered as shown below. The reasons for some of the answers follow the listing of the conversation.

```
ENTER OPTIONS, M=LEFT MARGIN, L=LINES/PAGE, W=PAGE WIDTH W=55
PAGE HEADING? (Y/N) Y
ENTER PAGE HEADING: MONTHLY DEPARTMENTAL SALARIES
DOUBLE SPACE REPORT? (Y/N) N
ARE TOTALS REQUIRED? (Y/N) Y
SUBTOTALS IN REPORT? (Y/N) Y
ENTER SUBTOTALS FIELD: DEPT
SUMMARY REPORT ONLY? (Y/N) N
EJECT PAGE AFTER SUBTOTALS? (Y/N) N
ENTER SUBTOTAL HEADING: DEPARTMENT
COL      WIDTH,CONTENTS
001      5,EMPNO
ENTER HEADING: EMP #
002      15,LNAME
ENTER HEADING: LAST NAME
003      15,FNAME
ENTER HEADING: FIRST NAME
004      9,SALARY
```

ENTER HEADING: SALARY
ARE TOTALS REQUIRED? (Y/N) Y
005

When asked for the fifth field, respond by pressing the return key.

The first answer allows the page layout of the report to be changed. The entry W=55 changes the page width to 55 print positions. The answer DEPT to the question "ENTER SUBTOTALS FIELD:" tells dBase II to give subtotals for each department. Compare your report to Figure 12-1. If you need to see the report again enter:

REPORT FORM DEPTSAL

If you made any errors in keying in the answers, they may be corrected by using the MODIFY COMMAND command. First compare the answers you gave in the above conversation to the answers that appear below. Then enter the command

MODIFY COMMAND DEPTSAL.FRM

and compare your answers on the screen to the answers that appear below. Use the techniques of Table 11-1 to make any necessary changes to your answers.

```
W=55
Y
MONTHLY DEPARTMENTAL SALARIES
N
Y
Y
DEPT
N
N
DEPARTMENT
5,EMPNO
EMP #
15,LNAME
LAST NAME
15,FNAME
FIRST NAME
9,SALARY
SALARY
Y
```

Use a CTRL-W to exit the MODIFY COMMAND command. To run the
report again enter:

REPORT FORM DEPTSAL

The use of the MODIFY COMMAND command to modify report
forms is error prone and therefore should probably only be
used for simple changes. For extensive changes such as
modifying report form DEPTSAL to generate the summarized
report of Figure 12-2 it is better to just start over. If
you wish to use the same report form name for the modified
report then refer to the section "Working with files" and
delete the FRM file. In this case, use the new name
SDEPTSAL, which is an abbreviation for summarized
departmental salaries.

REPORT FORM SDEPTSAL

Answer dBase II's questions in the following way:

```
ENTER OPTIONS, M=LEFT MARGIN, L=LINES/PAGE, W=PAGE WIDTH W=35
PAGE HEADING? (Y/N) Y
ENTER PAGE HEADING: SUMMARIZED MONTHLY;DEPARTMENTAL SALARIES
DOUBLE SPACE REPORT? (Y/N) N
ARE TOTALS REQUIRED? (Y/N) Y
SUBTOTALS IN REPORT? (Y/N) Y
ENTER SUBTOTALS FIELD: DEPT
SUMMARY REPORT ONLY? (Y/N) Y
EJECT PAGE AFTER SUBTOTALS? (Y/N) N
ENTER SUBTOTAL HEADING: DEPARTMENT
COL      WIDTH,CONTENTS
001      30,SALARY
ENTER HEADING: >SALARY
ARE TOTALS REQUIRED? (Y/N) Y
002
```

The semicolon in the page heading causes the heading to
appear on two lines. The greater than sign (i.e. ">") in
front of the heading SALARY makes the heading right
justified over the right justified column of salaries.
After entering the following command, compare your report to
Figure 12-2*:

REPORT FORM SDEPTSAL

----

* If you are going to leave dBase at this time, remember to
  enter the QUIT command before turning the machine off.

FIGURE 12-1 DETAILED REPORT

Page No.   1
09/30/85

MONTHLY DEPARTMENTAL SALARIES

EMP #	LAST NAME	FIRST NAME	SALARY
** DEPARTMENT 17			
6010	FIRST	I. M.	7542.62
5698	AIDER	RAY D.	1974.41
3312	SHARALIKE	SHARON	2336.26
2315	TOTTLER	T.	5437.51
** Subtotal **			
			17290.80
** DEPARTMENT 23			
1034	SETTERA	ED	2851.32
7433	TRESS	MATT	3170.79
3486	CABOODLE	KIT ANNE	3326.18
** Subtotal **			
			9348.29
** DEPARTMENT 31			
5533	THYME	JUSTIN	4115.08
1044	HIGHWATER	HELEN	4166.15
4569	ERDBUNS	BUD	4195.49
8754	MAID	TAYLOR	5180.28
6110	DOVER	BEN	4388.91
** Subtotal **			
			22045.91
** DEPARTMENT 40			
9132	BACK	EILEEN	4529.41
6458	LIFE	ALMA	4486.71
** Subtotal **			
			9016.12
** DEPARTMENT 45			
2348	WANNAKRACKER	POLLY	5612.46
5443	AYRE	CLAIRE D.	5692.87
5435	ZOFF	HANS	6105.79
** Subtotal **			
			17411.12

```
** DEPARTMENT 58
 6128  DESTINKSHUN      MARCO              7817.24
 1987  LAST             I. M.              2933.91
** Subtotal **
                                         10751.15

*** Total ***
                                         85863.39
```

FIGURE 12-2 SUMMARY REPORT

```
Page No.          1
09/30/85

        SUMMARIZED MONTHLY
        DEPARTMENTAL SALARIES

                             SALARY
** DEPARTMENT 17
** Subtotal **
                          17290.80

** DEPARTMENT 23
** Subtotal **
                           9348.29

** DEPARTMENT 31
** Subtotal **
                          22045.91

** DEPARTMENT 40
** Subtotal **
                           9016.12

** DEPARTMENT 45
** Subtotal **
                          17411.12

** DEPARTMENT 58
** Subtotal **
                          10751.15

*** Total ***
                          85863.39
```

In dBase III the CREATE REPORT command is used to create a report form file.

HELP CREATE REPORT

In dBase III the command MODIFY REPORT is equivalent to CREATE REPORT. Either command may also be used to edit the file once it has been created.

To illustrate the use of these commands, the CREATE REPORT command will be used to create the report form file DEPTSAL.FRM for the departmental salary report found in Figure 12-1. Then the MODIFY REPORT command will be used to modify DEPTSAL.FRM so that the summarized departmental salary report found in Figure 12-2 can be generated.

First enter the command:

CREATE REPORT DEPTSAL

dBase III gives you an input form that requests the page heading and some miscellaneous formatting information. Use the return key to move from one field to the next. Enter MONTHLY DEPARTMENTAL SALARIES as the page heading and then change the page width to 55. Leave the other fields unchanged. To move to the next screen press the PGDN key or use the return key to exit the last field on the screen.

The second screen of the dBase III CREATE REPORT command is the grouping screen, which allows two levels of subtotals to be placed in the report. For this example, only the first level subtotal is required. Key DEPT as the group/subtotal field (i.e. key DEPT where screen says "Group/subtotal on:") and key DEPARTMENT as the group/subtotal heading. Leave the other fields unchanged.

Another PGDN (or a return out of the last field of the grouping screen) takes you to the first of a series of screens that allow you to define the column contents and headings. Each column is defined on a separate screen. In the first column the field is EMPNO (i.e. key EMPNO on the first line where the screen says "Field contents") with a heading of EMP (i.e. key EMP on the first line where the screen says "Field header"). The second column is field LNAME with a heading of LAST NAME. The third column is FNAME with a heading of FIRST NAME. The fourth column is

SALARY with 2 decimal places. Figure 12-1 shows totals for the SALARY field so answer Y for yes to the "TOTAL?" question. The column heading is SALARY. Do a CTRL-END to exit the CREATE REPORT command and then compare your report to Figure 12-1.

REPORT FORM DEPTSAL

To correct any errors you made key

MODIFY REPORT DEPTSAL

By using the PGDN key proceed to the screens that have errors and correct them. To run the report again key:

REPORT FORM DEPTSAL

In dBase III to modify the report form DEPTSAL to produce the report found in Figure 12-2, key:

MODIFY REPORT DEPTSAL

Several things must be changed. On the first screen that appears, change the one line heading to a two line heading where the first line is SUMMARIZED MONTHLY and the second line is DEPARTMENTAL SALARIES. Change the page width to 35. Using the PGDN key skip to the grouping screen where the question "Summary report only?" should be answered with a Y for yes. Next proceed to the column contents screen with another PGDN. The first three columns should be deleted leaving only the SALARY column. To delete these columns start with the cursor in the EMPNO column definition screen. While holding the CTRL key down depress the U key three times. Each CTRL-U deletes a column from the report. Finally change the width of the SALARY column to 30. Use a CTRL-END to exit the MODIFY REPORT command. Compare your report to Figure 12-2.*

REPORT FORM DEPTSAL

----

* If you are going to leave dBase at this time, remember to enter the QUIT command before turning the machine off.

* * * * * * * * * * * * * * *

EXERCISE 12-2

Create a report that gives a detailed listing of the liquor
inventory with total cost and retail value per item shown.
Then modify the report so that only the stock number and
total cost per item are shown.

WORKING WITH FILES

It is possible to manipulate entire files in dBase. The commands in this section allow you to look at the directory, copy files, rename files, and delete files.*

LIST FILE COMMAND

To look at the directory you can use the LIST FILES command. Using the LIST FILES command by itself without any of its options results in a listing of the database files on the default drive.

LIST FILES

To see files other than just DBF files use the LIKE option and the "wild card" characters discussed in Chapter 2.

LIST FILES LIKE *.FRM

The above command lists all the report form files on the default drive. To see the directory of a nondefault drive use the ON option.

LIST FILES ON A LIKE *.*

The above command lists all the files on the A drive.

COPY COMMAND

It is possible and highly desirable to make frequent copies of database files using the COPY command.

HELP COPY

----

* While working with files you will occasionally receive an error message from dBase which states that the file is already open. If this happens try to close the file with a USE command (i.e. the verb USE alone without any file name following it). If you still get the error message then QUIT and reenter dBase.

To illustrate this command make a copy of the in use database PAYROLL with the following command (if you already have a database called TEMP then use another name in this command)*:

COPY TO TEMP

Using the LIST FILES command note that you now have a file TEMP that is a copy of your PAYROLL database.

LIST FILES

The COPY command allows the use of a scope, field list, and/or conditional statement. The use of the SDF/DELIMITED option is discussed below in the "Summarize and transfer files" section.

RENAME COMMAND

The RENAME command allows files to be renamed.

HELP RENAME

To illustrate the use of the RENAME command enter:

RENAME TEMP.DBF TO TMP.BAK

By listing the files you may see that the TEMP database file has been renamed TMP.BAK.

LIST FILES LIKE T*.*

DELETE FILE COMMAND

The DELETE FILE command erases files from the directory.

HELP DELETE FILE

----

* If you left dBase after working on the previous section, then enter DBASE from the DOS A> prompt and then enter SET DEFAULT TO B from the dBase period prompt. In any case enter USE PAYROLL from the dBase period prompt.

298

To illustrate the use of the DELETE FILE command enter:

DELETE FILE TMP.BAK

By listing the files you may see that the TMP.BAK file has been erased (i.e. no file with the name TMP.BAK exists).*

LIST FILE LIKE T*.*

* * * * * * * * * * * * * * *

EXERCISE 12-3

List the files on the course disk whose name begins with LIQ.

EXERCISE 12-4

Make a backup copy of the liquor inventory data base file and then list the backup file.

----

* If you are going to leave dBase at this time, remember to enter the QUIT command before turning the machine off.

REORDERING FILES

It is often desirable to change the order of a file.* There are two main ways in dBase to change the apparent order of a file: SORT and INDEX. The SORT command creates a new database file in the desired order. INDEX only changes the apparent order of the file by creating an index or set of pointers similar to the index that appears in the back of a book. After looking at each command in more detail, this section ends with a comparison of the two commands.

SORT COMMAND

The SORT command copies the in use database to another database and in the process changes the order of the file that is the copy.

HELP SORT

The SORT command does not alter the in use database. To see the results of the SORT command you must first USE the new file and then list it. To illustrate the SORT command assume that Mr. Destinkshun has requested a list of all employees sorted by last name.

SORT ON LNAME TO NAMESASC

The above command creates a new database file that has been arbitrarily called NAMESASC, an abbreviation for names in ascending order. To see the list in order by last name enter the following commands:

        USE NAMESASC
        LIST

To resume using the original PAYROLL file enter:

        USE PAYROLL

----

* If you left dBase after working on the previous section, then enter DBASE from the DOS A> prompt and then enter SET DEFAULT TO B from the dBase period prompt. In any case enter USE PAYROLL from the dBase period prompt.

To get a list of names in reverse alphabetical order enter the following commands:

```
SORT ON LNAME TO NAMESDSC DESCENDING
USE NAMESDSC
LIST
```

Use the LIST FILES command to see the two new files:

```
LIST FILES LIKE NAMES*.*
```

INDEX COMMAND

The index command creates an index file that has an extension of NDX.

```
HELP INDEX
```

The NDX file contains pointers into the database file just like an index to a book has page numbers that point into the contents of the book. After an index has been created, any use of the file is by way of the index file. The apparent order of the DBF is different but the actual order stays the same. If the NDX file is "disconnected" with a USE command then the DBF file may be seen to have been left unaltered. The NDX file can then be reconnected with another USE command.

To illustrate the use of the INDEX command assume once again that Mr. Destinkshun has requested an alphabetical list of the employees. Enter the following commands:

```
USE PAYROLL
INDEX ON LNAME TO NAMES
LIST
```

The INDEX command has changed the apparent order of the PAYROLL file. Notice that it was not necessary to USE a different file. You are still looking at the original PAYROLL file. The record numbers are still attached to the original record and so the record numbers appear to be out of order. The NAMES file that was created is an NDX file.

```
LIST FILES LIKE NAMES*.*
```

As further proof that the original DBF has remained unaltered enter the following USE command that "disconnects" the index:

```
                  USE PAYROLL
                  LIST
```

The index can be "reconnected" with the following USE command:

```
            USE PAYROLL INDEX NAMES
            LIST
```

To see if new records are also indexed enter the following command:

```
                  APPEND
```

and add the following record:

```
  DEPT EMPNO LNAME      FNAME        POSITION    SALARY
  58   9999  BEANS      FRANK N.     143         3333.00
```

Remember that a CTRL-W gets you out of the APPEND command. Note that as long as the INDEX file is in use that updates to the DBF file automatically update the NDX file at the same time.

```
                  LIST
```

Mr. Beans is in the correct alphabetical position.

SORT VERSUS INDEX

The SORT command is probably easier to understand than the INDEX command. Most people have sorted a list of some kind and, therefore, are comfortable working with SORT. Few people have indexed a file and, therefore, the INDEX command seems foreign to them. Upon closer examination, however, the INDEX command has certain distinct advantages.

One of the advantages of the INDEX command has not yet been covered. Random access to records is possible with an indexed file. In the next section the FIND command is discussed. With the FIND command it is possible to access individual records in an indexed file within seconds. This is possible even in large files. Without the ability to directly access the records, it could easily take many minutes to retrieve the information.

As was demonstrated above, when working with an indexed file, updates to the database automatically update the NDX file. If you are working with a DBF file and a related sorted DBF file, then each file must be kept updated separately. Updating one file does not automatically update the other. Other advantages of using the INDEX command are that it generally executes faster and the resulting NDX file usually takes up less room on a disk than another copy of the DBF file.

A sorted file, however, has the advantage that records are physically stored on the disk in their apparent order. In sequentially processing the file the read/write head moves little in getting from one record to the next. This results in faster processing when a significant percent of the file must be read in the apparent order.*

* * * * * * * * * * * * * * *

EXERCISE 12-5

Index the liquor inventory file by brand and then make a backup copy of the file. In what order is the backup file?

EXERCISE 12-6

Sort the liquor inventory file on type and then after using the new file run the report LIQTYPE.

----

* If you are going to leave dBase at this time, remember to enter the QUIT command before turning the machine off.

Each database file that is open (USE command issued) has a record pointer.* The record pointer determines which record is the current record. The actions of the INSERT, DISPLAY, and BROWSE commands are definitely influenced by the record pointer. Any command that has a scope (i.e. allows the use of the NEXT option) is potentially affected by the record pointer. The WHILE option in a conditional statement allows the associated command to process until a record is encountered that does not satisfy the condition. The command begins processing on the current record. The position of the record pointer, therefore, affects the action of a command that has a WHILE conditional statement.

Some commands such as LIST and SORT affect the positioning of the record pointer as a side affect of their primary task. The GO, SKIP, FIND, and LOCATE commands have as their primary function the positioning of the record pointer. The GO command is covered above in the "Adding records to database" section. The SKIP, FIND, and LOCATE commands are discussed in this section.

SKIP COMMAND

The SKIP command is similar to the GO command in that they both simply move the record pointer.

HELP SKIP

SKIP is different than GO in that the GO command dictates an absolute position for the record pointer (e.g. GO 5, GO BOTTOM) whereas the SKIP command moves the record pointer relative to its current position (e.g. SKIP 3, SKIP -5).

To illustrate the SKIP command first position the record pointer on record 5 and display it.

GO 5
DISPLAY

----

* If you left dBase after working on the previous section, then enter DBASE from the DOS A> prompt and then enter SET DEFAULT TO B from the dBase period prompt. In any case enter USE PAYROLL from the dBase period prompt.

A SKIP command with a positive value behind it moves the record pointer down in the file (i.e. record pointer is moved to a record with a higher record number).

                        SKIP 3
                        DISPLAY

A negative value behind the SKIP command moves the record pointer up in the file.

                        SKIP -6
                        DISPLAY

If the SKIP command is used without a value behind it, a positive one is assumed.

                        SKIP
                        DISPLAY

FIND COMMAND

     The FIND command positions the record pointer to the first record in the indexed order of the file that has leading characters that match the string being searched for.

                        HELP FIND

The FIND command takes advantage of the index to go directly to the record desired rather than searching sequentially through the entire file. The FIND command does require an indexed file and it can only search for a character string within the field on which the file is indexed.

     To illustrate the FIND command, assume that you want to be able to identify quickly those individuals holding a certain position within the company. In a file as small as the PAYROLL file, the quick and easy way would be to do a LIST of the file and then visually scan it for the desired position number. An alternative for a slightly longer file would be to do a LIST FOR POSITION=x command. Both of these techniques become slow for files of even moderate size. To make the FIND command a reasonable alternative you must imagine that the PAYROLL file is larger than it actually is.

     The first step in using the FIND command is to make sure you have an up to date index file that was created using the field upon which you wish to search.

INDEX ON POSITION TO POS

The actual use of the FIND command is easy.

FIND 001
DISPLAY

Remember that the FIND command only changes the position of
the record pointer. It is necessary to DISPLAY, BROWSE
EDIT, or something similar to actually see the record.

FIND 569
BROWSE

LOCATE AND CONTINUE COMMANDS

The LOCATE command is also used to search the database.

HELP LOCATE

The LOCATE command is more flexible than the FIND command in
that an indexed file does not need to exist and any field
can be searched. The search is sequential, however, which
means that for large files the LOCATE command may take a
long time to position the record pointer. After the first
record matching the condition has been found, subsequent
searches for the same condition can be initiated with the
CONTINUE command.

HELP CONTINUE

Let us repeat the same searches as were performed by
the FIND command. First disconnect the index file to assure
yourself that it is not needed.

USE PAYROLL

Next search for position 1.

LOCATE FOR POSITION='001'
DISPLAY
CONTINUE

Note that when no more records matching the condition are
found an end of file message is given. Next search for
position 569.

```
LOCATE FOR POSITION='569'
DISPLAY
CONTINUE
DISPLAY
CONTINUE
```

To see the flexibility of the LOCATE command, try the following:

```
LOCATE FOR DEPT>'40' .AND. SALARY>6000
DISPLAY
CONTINUE
DISPLAY
CONTINUE
```

Since the LIST and DISPLAY commands search no more slowly than the LOCATE, they are probably preferred when the only purpose is to see all records that match a certain condition.

```
LIST FOR DEPT>'40' .AND. SALARY>6000
```

LOCATE should be used when you wish to stop with the record pointer set after each match is found, perhaps to do an EDIT of the record.*

*   *   *   *   *   *   *   *   *   *   *   *   *   *   *

EXERCISE 12-7

Use the LOCATE command to set the record pointer for a display of the record whose brand is 'THE NEW SOUTH'. Then use the FIND command to set the record pointer for a display of the record.

----

* If you are going to leave dBase at this time, remember to
  enter the QUIT command before turning the machine off.

307

TAILORING DBASE TO YOU

dBase is a flexible piece of software.* There are many parameters that affect the way dBase behaves. These parameters may be changed so that dBase better suits your individual preferences. It is the SET command that allows these modifications. The SET command is not one but actually an entire group of commands. The other command covered in this section is DISPLAY STATUS. This command allows you to look at the current parameter settings.

DISPLAY STATUS COMMAND

DISPLAY STATUS shows you not only the current parameter settings but also lists information on the currently open databases and indexes.

DISPLAY STATUS

The output from the DISPLAY STATUS command consists of three main parts. The first part shows information about the currently open databases and indexes. To see the second and third parts it is necessary to depress the space bar or any character key. The second part of the display shows the general parameter settings. The third part shows the function key definitions.

Note that F6 is defined as LIST or DISPLAY STATUS. Pressing the F6 key redisplays the status just the same as if you had rekeyed the entire command. The F6 key's definition is the only one that needs to be memorized. Keying F6 brings up a menu of the definitions of the other function keys if you should forget them.

----

* If you left dBase after working on the previous section, then enter DBASE from the DOS A> prompt and then enter SET DEFAULT TO B from the dBase period prompt. In any case enter USE PAYROLL from the dBase period prompt.

SET COMMAND

The SET command may be used to change the definitions of the function keys. The following statements change the definition of F10 to REPORT FORM DEPTSAL.
In dBase II enter:

SET F10 TO 'REPORT FORM DEPTSAL'

In dBase III enter:

SET FUNCTION 10 TO 'REPORT FORM DEPTSAL'

Pressing the F6 key shows you that the menu of function keys has been changed. Test the change by pressing the F10 key. When defining a function key, a semicolon (i.e. ";") on the end of the command causes the command to be automatically entered when the function key is pressed. Without the semicolon you have a chance to modify the command and then you have to press the enter key yourself.

Once again press the F6 key and note the variety of parameters in the second part of the display. Notice in particular that there is a parameter called BELL, which is set ON. In the EDIT and APPEND commands each time you fill a field, the computer beeps at you. If you find that annoying, enter:

SET BELL OFF

Test the change by editing a record and filling a field completely. If you preferred having the beep then enter:

SET BELL ON

That returns dBase to its initial condition.

All of the parameters can be set in a similar manner. Actually you have been using this command for some time. Remember the SET DEFAULT TO B command that you enter each time you load dBase. Use the HELP SET command to learn more about the parameters. In dBase II enter:

HELP SET

In dBase III enter individual HELP SET commands such as:

HELP SET BELL

The SET command allows you to make dBase fit your personal preferences.*

                * * * * * * * * * * * * * * *

EXERCISE 12-8

Redefine the ninth and tenth function keys so that you can quickly switch between USEing LIQINV and PAYROLL.

                        ----

* If you are going to leave dBase at this time, remember to
  enter the QUIT command before turning the machine off.

USING FUNCTIONS

Functions are small routines in dBase. They must be used in conjunction with regular commands.*

TRIM FUNCTION

As an example consider the TRIM function. Entering TRIM by itself results in an error message.

TRIM

To understand the use of the TRIM function enter the following commands and note the results:

```
LIST FNAME+LNAME
LIST TRIM(FNAME)+LNAME
LIST TRIM(FNAME)+' '+LNAME
```

The TRIM function removes the trailing blanks from a character field. The first command above leaves a perhaps undesirable large blank area between the first and last name. The TRIM function in the second command removes all the trailing blanks from the first name that leaves it butted up against the last name. The third command puts one space back in, which gives an attractive listing.

INT FUNCTION

As another example consider the INT function. It truncates a real number to an integer.

```
LIST INT(SALARY),SALARY
```

LEN FUNCTION

The LEN function returns the length of a character field. Functions may be combined as in the following:

```
LIST LNAME,LEN(TRIM(LNAME))
```

----

* If you left dBase after working on the previous section, then enter DBASE from the DOS A> prompt and then enter SET DEFAULT TO B from the dBase period prompt. In any case enter USE PAYROLL from the dBase period prompt.

This listing shows the last name and the length of the trimmed last name. Use the HELP FUNCTION command to gain more information on functions.

HELP FUNCTION

In dBase III you must pick the number of the function you are interested in and enter it at the bottom of the screen. Also in dBase III you should use a PGUP to return to the HELP FUNCTION menu and an ESC to return to the period prompt.*

* * * * * * * * * * * * * *

EXERCISE 12-9

What are the lengths of the brand names in the LIQINV file? What are the lengths of the trimmed brand names in the LIQINV file? What is the average length of the trimmed brand names in the LIQINV file?

----

* If you are going to leave dBase at this time, remember to enter the QUIT command before turning the machine off.

It is possible to use dBase to capture, store, and retrieve relatively large bodies of data.* You may want to analyze that data using a spreadsheet package or a Basic program. Often times you don't need all the detailed information for the analysis. Summarized information is sufficient. In this section the TOTAL command is used to summarize the data and the COPY command is used to prepare files of data that can be read by the other systems.

TOTAL COMMAND

The TOTAL command creates another file with the same structure as the original. The new file has one record for each group of records in the original file that has the same key (i.e. a field in the file singled out for special attention). The original file must be sorted or indexed on the key field. The numeric fields in each record of the new file contain the sum of the corresponding fields in the group of records that were summarized to make up that record.

HELP TOTAL

To investigate the TOTAL command enter the following:

TOTAL ON DEPT TO TPAYROLL

In order to look at the new file it must be USEd and then LISTed.

USE TPAYROLL
LIST

Notice that there is one record for each department and that the salary is the total salary for that department. The employee number, name, and position in the summary record are taken from the first record found in the associated group of the original file. If we assume that the first record in the department is someone special such as the

----

* If you left dBase after working on the previous section, then enter DBASE from the DOS A> prompt and then enter SET DEFAULT TO B from the dBase period prompt. In any case enter USE PAYROLL from the dBase period prompt.

313

department head then it may make sense to have their information in the summary record. If we don't want the EMPNO, LNAME, FNAME, and POSITION fields in the summary record, they can be removed with the MODIFY STRUCTURE command.

COPY COMMAND

The COPY command was used above in the "Working with Files" section to create a DBF file. DBF files contain information about the structure of the file, which confuses other software packages when they attempt to read the file. The COPY command can also create non-DBF files by using the SDF and DELIMITED options. When using these options, the structure information is not included with the data being written to the output file. These non-DBF files can then be read by other software packages. This allows information to be passed from dBase to other software packages.

HELP COPY

Enter the following command:

COPY TO PAYROLL1 SDF

Unless you specify an extension, the new file has an extension of TXT. To see what this new file contains, use the MODIFY COMMAND command. The command is explained in the next chapter.

MODIFY COMMAND PAYROLL1.TXT

The file created with the SDF option has all the fields butted up against each other. The receiving program must know the length of each field so that it can separate them for further processing. Abort MODIFY COMMAND without saving any changes by doing a CTRL-Q.

Next enter the following command, which illustrates the use of the DELIMITED option:

COPY TO PAYROLL2 DELIMITED WITH "

Now look at the second file.

MODIFY COMMAND PAYROLL2.TXT

It has double quotes surrounding each character field and a comma between each field. Abort MODIFY COMMAND without saving any changes by doing a CTRL-Q.*

     *   *   *   *   *   *   *   *   *   *   *   *   *   *   *

EXERCISE 12-10

Summarize the liquor inventory file by type. Note that the only numeric field whose summarized value makes sense is the quantity field.

----

* If you are going to leave dBase at this time, remember to enter the QUIT command before turning the machine off.

1. Compare and contrast the LIST, DISPLAY, and BROWSE commands.

2. Explain memory variables. What dBase command is used to see the memory variables currently used?

3. List the dBase commands that are used to initialize memory variables. Describe how these commands work.

4. What do the following commands show you:
   (a) LIST FILES
   (b) LIST FILES LIKE *.*
   (c) LIST FILES ON A LIKE *.FRM

5. Compare the syntax of the COPY command and the RENAME command.

6. Describe the processes for removing records from a database file and for removing a file from the diskette.

7. Distinguish between the SORT command and the INDEX command. Discuss the advantages and disadvantages of each command.

8. What is the function of a record pointer? What dBase commands can be affected by the record pointer.

9. What process is required to use the FIND command?

10. List the dBase commands used to search the database. Explain how each of these commands works.

11. When are the LIST and DISPLAY commands preferred to the LOCATE command in searching a database file? When should the LOCATE command be used?

12. Explain the output from the DISPLAY STATUS command.

13. What are functions in dBase? How do they differ from regular commands in terms of usage?

14. Explain how the following functions work:
    (a) TRIM
    (b) INT
    (c) LEN

15. The TOTAL command can be used to get summarized data.
    (a) Explain how to use the TOTAL command?
    (b) Explain the differences in the output between the numeric fields and the character fields.

16. Describe the functions of the COPY command.

17. Compare and contrast the EDIT, BROWSE, CHANGE, and REPLACE commands. Under what circumstances should each be used?

18. Index the LIQINV file on PRICE and then LIST the result. What is the result if you index on -PRICE?

19. The plus sign can be used to concatenate two character fields. Try indexing the LIQINV file on TYPE+BRAND and describe the result. Try sorting the LIQINV file on TYPE+BRAND and describe the result.

20. INDEX the LIQINV file on TYPE+BRAND. Describe how you can FIND a record based on the values of two fields.

21. Use the file PERSON that is on your course diskette. This file has more fields in it than can fit on a single line at one time. Compare and contrast the way that DISPLAY and BROWSE solve this problem.

22. Using the PERSON file, describe the action of the CTRL-B and CTRL-Z key combinations when using the BROWSE command.

23. Create a file that has 26 fields, each named for a letter of the alphabet and one character long. How does EDIT behave when presented with a file that has more fields (i.e. 26) than there are lines on the monitor (i.e. 25)?

24. What is the average percent markup on the liquor inventory. Use as few statements as possible in solving the following:
    (a) Calculate a percent markup for each stock number and average these figures.
    (b) Do the same as (a) but weight the average by the quantity.
    (c) Calculate the total cost and total retail value and then use them to calculate the average percent markup.

25. What response does dBase give you when you attempt to LOCATE a nonexistant record such as a brand called "THE WILD EAST" in the LIQINV file? Do you get the same response when you try to FIND such a record?

26. It is sometimes difficult to understand a help message or a reference manual. Sometimes they just don't have the information you need. In such cases you need to experiment. To illustrate this point, consider the SET DELETED ON/OFF command. Try to learn as much as you can about this command from existing documentation. Then run an experiment on a database file that has a couple records marked for deletion. With DELETED ON how do common commands such as LIST, REPORT, COPY, LOCATE, and FIND act differently than when DELETED is set OFF. Store the results of your experiment in a table that has DELETED ON at the top of one column and DELETED OFF at the top of another. Establish a row for each command you test.

27. Using your favorite software (other than dBase) find out how to read into that software the summarized payroll information created in the last section of this chapter. Report your findings to the class.

28. If you created the GRADES file in problem 11 at the end of chapter 1 then use the REPLACE command to calculate and store the grade point for each course (i.e. number of credits * numeric grade). Next calculate your grade point average. Index the file on numeric grade and generate a report that has control breaks whenever the grade changes. Index the file on department and generate a report that has control breaks whenever department changes.

29. Pick a SET command that has not been discussed in this text. Investigate the command by using existing documentation and by "playing" with the computer. Report back to the class what you are able to find. Highlight any information that you found through experimentation that was not in the documentation.

30. Repeat the previous problem using a function instead of a SET command.

31. Produce a listing of those people in the PAYROLL file who have an initial stored in their FNAME field? (Hint: Normally an initial is followed by a period. In dBase

II the @ function and in dBase III the AT function can tell you if a period exists.)

32. USE the PERSON file and note that it contains a phone number. Assume that you spill something on a message that states that you had an important phone call and you should call back. Unfortunately the name and all but the last four digits of the phone number on the message have been obliterated by the spill. Assuming that the PERSON file is too large to scan manually, how would you determine who the message may have been from?

33. In dBase II, the MODIFY STRUCTURE command erases all data from the file.
    (a) Enter the following commands to add a backorder field to the liquor inventory database:

```
USE LIQINV
COPY TO TEMP
USE TEMP
MODIFY STRUCTURE
     At this point add a field BACKORDER,N,9,2
APPEND FROM LIQINV
DISPLAY STRUCTURE
DISPLAY ALL
     At this point check your work and repeat
     the above steps until you are satisfied.
COPY TO LIQINV
USE LIQINV
DELETE FILE TEMP
```

This series of commands could also be used to delete a field or change the length of a field.

    (b) To change the name of a field, a different series of statements is required. Use the following series of commands to change the name BACKORDER to BKORDER.

```
USE LIQINV
COPY TO TEMP1
USE TEMP1
COPY TO TEMP2 SDF
MODIFY STRUCTURE
     At this point change only the name of a
     field.
APPEND FROM TEMP2.TXT SDF
DISPLAY STRUCTURE
DISPLAY ALL
```

At this point check your work and repeat the the above steps until you are satisfied.
COPY TO LIQINV
USE LIQINV
DELETE FILE TEMP1
DELETE FILE TEMP2.TXT

34. Using the HELP facility and/or the dBase manual, investigate the CHANGE command. Modify the structure of the LIQINV file to include a backorder field. (If you are a dBase II user see problem 33.) Then use the CHANGE command to initialize the values in the new field (use your imagination in coming up with the appropriate backorder quantities).

dBASE PROGRAMMING

CHAPTER 13

INTRODUCTION

In dBase there are two basic modes of operation: an interactive mode, which is what you have been using, and a program mode, which is discussed in this chapter.* Writing programs requires an investment of your time up front but the return on your investment in terms of time saved and convenience of operation can be large. The investment of time takes two forms: learning a number of programming commands and then the actual writing of the programs.

Even if you haven't enjoyed programming in the past, you will probably enjoy your work with dBase. It is fairly easy and a lot of fun to create a simple menu driven system. A menu driven system allows you (or less well trained staff) to operate a dBase system without needing to know the dBase commands.

----

* If you left dBase after working on the previous section, then enter DBASE from the DOS A> prompt and then enter SET DEFAULT TO B from the dBase period prompt. In any case enter USE PAYROLL from the dBase period prompt.

A SIMPLE PROGRAM

Your investment need not be large. To illustrate that point, check the time on a clock or your watch. Within five minutes you should have written and executed a useful dBase program. First enter:

MODIFY COMMAND IT

This should present you with an essentially blank screen. On the first three lines enter the following (don't expect any response from dBase after each line):

SET DEFAULT TO B
USE PAYROLL
DISPLAY STATUS

You have just written a dBase program. To save it do a CTRL-W. Once you have a period prompt execute the program by entering:

DO IT

Now check the time again, probably less than five minutes have elapsed.

The program you wrote is called IT. You wrote the program on a simple dBase text editor called MODIFY COMMAND. This simple program consisted entirely of commands that you have used in the past. Normally you enter them in an interactive manner from the period prompt. Interactive means that you key in a command and press the return. dBase executes the command, gives you a period prompt and then the process repeats. In program mode you enter a series of commands once and then when you want them executed you enter a single DO command. Remember that any time you find yourself interactively entering a series of commands over and over, you can probably put them in a program and save yourself some time.

MODIFY COMMAND COMMAND

The MODIFY COMMAND command allows you to create and modify command files. These command files are also called programs.

HELP MODIFY COMMAND

Unless you specify an extension on the file name it is assumed to be PRG. The MODIFY COMMAND command is a simple text editor. The rules for operating it are listed in Table 11-1.

Some of the more useful commands with which you should become familiar are inserting a blank line (CTRL-N) and deleting a line (CTRL-T). To practice these commands enter:

MODIFY COMMAND IT

Move the cursor down one line using the down arrow key, then do a CTRL-N. Your file should now contain four lines with the second line being blank. Key the following into the second line:

SET BELL OFF

and then press the return. Now to practice deleting lines let us assume that you decide not to SET BELL OFF. Move the cursor up to the SET BELL OFF line with the up arrow key and do a CTRL-T.

MODIFY COMMAND is a simple text editor. If you are familiar with a more powerful text editor/word processor such as Wordstar, you can use it to create dBase programs. In using Wordstar for this purpose, be sure to use the nondocument mode.*

----

* If you are going to leave dBase at this time, remember to enter the QUIT command before turning the machine off.

* * * * * * * * * * * * * * *

Modify the program IT so that the ninth and tenth function keys are defined to allow quick changes between USEing the LIQINV database and PAYROLL database (see Exercise 12-8). QUIT dBase and then from the A> prompt enter:

DBASE B:IT

You are able to enter dBase and immediately execute a dBase program with a single command in DOS. You should note in the status listing that the default drive has been set to B, the in use file is PAYROLL and the last two function keys are redefined.

INDEXER PROGRAM

The INDEXER is a simple dBase program that indexes the database in use on whatever field you select and then displays the database in indexed order.* Try using it by entering:

DO INDEXER

and selecting a field from the field name list. In dBase III on the second and subsequent executions of INDEXER you will have to answer the question "TEMP.ndx already exists, overwrite it? (Y/N)" with a Y for yes.

Enter the following help commands to obtain an overview of the new commands to be found in INDEXER:

HELP NOTE
HELP ?
HELP ACCEPT

To study the INDEXER program refer to Figure 13-1 and enter:

MODIFY COMMAND INDEXER

FIGURE 13-1   INDEXER PROGRAM

```
NOTE This program produces a "sorted" list
?
DISPLAY STRUCTURE
?
ACCEPT 'WHICH FIELD SHOULD BE INDEXED? ' TO FIELDNAME
INDEX ON &FIELDNAME TO TEMP
?
DISPLAY ALL OFF
?
```

----

* If you left dBase after working on the previous section, then enter DBASE from the DOS A> prompt and then enter SET DEFAULT TO B from the dBase period prompt. In any case enter USE PAYROLL from the dBase period prompt.

NOTE COMMAND

The first line contains the command NOTE followed by an introductory comment. The NOTE command (or an asterisk) is used solely for documentation purposes, it does not affect the execution of the program. It is a good idea to put NOTE commands and an explanation in your program where someone reading your program might become confused.

? COMMAND

The ? command used by itself, as it is here, causes a blank line to be displayed on the screen. This helps to make the output appear less cluttered, which makes it easier to read. The DISPLAY STRUCTURE command was covered earlier in the "Setting up the database" section.

ACCEPT COMMAND

The ACCEPT command receives input from the operator after giving the operator the prompt "Which field should be indexed?". The operator's response is stored in the memory variable FIELDNAME

MACRO FUNCTION

Although you have already seen the INDEX command, the next line does contain a new function, the "&" or macro function. The macro function tells dBase to use the contents of the character memory variable that follows, rather than the name itself. We don't want dBase to index on FIELDNAME since there is no field called FIELDNAME. We want dBase to index on the field name that is stored in the variable FIELDNAME. That is exactly what "&" tells dBase to do.

IMPROVED INDEXER

INDEXER would be more flexible if it allowed the operator to choose the file as well as the field to be indexed. Move the cursor down to the first "?". Using CTRL-N add five blank lines. Then enter the following into the blank lines:

```
?
DISPLAY FILES
?
ACCEPT 'Which file should be indexed?' TO FILENAME
USE &FILENAME
```

Do a CTRL-W to exit and get a period prompt. Test the change by entering:*

DO INDEXER

*   *   *   *   *   *   *   *   *   *   *   *   *   *   *

EXERCISE 13-2

Increase INDEXER's flexibility even more by having it request a default drive and then set it.

----

* If you are going to leave dBase at this time, remember to
  enter the QUIT command before turning the machine off.

It is possible with dBase to write a series of programs that allow a user with little dBase training to operate a fairly sophisticated system.* To implement such a system it is customary to design a number of menus that allow the operator to make choices. A choice in one menu often takes the operator to a submenu where another choice may be made. Underlying these layers of menus are the programs that accept input, update the files and produce the reports.

In this section there is a simple menu driven program called MENU. It allows the operator to add, modify and cancel records. Enter the following command and experiment with the operation of the program. You may want to add a record, modify it, and then cancel it.

DO MENU

After you are done experimenting with the program, key a 0 (i.e. zero) to return to a period prompt. Enter the following help commands to obtain an overview of the new commands to be found in MENU:

HELP DO WHILE
HELP @
HELP READ
HELP DO CASE
HELP IF

If you are using dBase II enter:

HELP ERASE

If you are using dBase III enter:

HELP CLEAR

----

* If you left dBase after working on the previous section, then enter DBASE from the DOS A> prompt and then enter SET DEFAULT TO B from the dBase period prompt. In any case enter USE PAYROLL from the dBase period prompt.

To examine the MENU program look at Figure 13-2 if you are dBase II user and at Figure 13-3 if you are a dBase III user. Also enter:

MODIFY COMMAND MENU

FIGURE 13-2 DBASE II MENU PROGRAM

```
STORE '1' TO CHOICE
DO WHILE CHOICE # '0'
   ERASE
   @    5,20 SAY 'FILE MAINTENANCE MENU'
   @    7,20 SAY '0 = EXIT'
   @    8,20 SAY '1 = ADD RECORDS'
   @    9,20 SAY '2 = MODIFY RECORDS'
   @   10,20 SAY '3 = CANCEL A RECORD'
   @ $+2,20 SAY 'YOUR CHOICE IS NUMBER ' GET CHOICE
   READ
   ERASE
   DO CASE
      CASE CHOICE = '1'
         APPEND
      CASE CHOICE = '2'
         EDIT
      CASE CHOICE = '3'
         DO CANCEL
   ENDCASE
ENDDO
```

DO WHILE COMMAND

The first statement initializes the memory variable CHOICE with the value "1". The next line contains the DO WHILE command. It sets up a loop (i.e. series of statements that are executed repeatedly) that extends to the ENDDO at the end of the program. Everything between the DO WHILE and the ENDDO is indented to aid in identifying the range of the loop. The indentation is optional. The loop is repeated as long as the condition CHOICE#0 is true. The "#" is read "not equal to". In other words the loop is repeated until CHOICE=0.

FIGURE 13-3   DBASE III MENU PROGRAM

```
STORE '1' TO CHOICE
DO WHILE CHOICE # '0'
    CLEAR
    @    5,20 SAY 'FILE MAINTENANCE MENU'
    @    7,20 SAY '0 = EXIT'
    @    8,20 SAY '1 = ADD RECORDS'
    @    9,20 SAY '2 = MODIFY RECORDS'
    @   10,20 SAY '3 = CANCEL A RECORD'
    @ $+2,20 SAY 'YOUR CHOICE IS NUMBER ' GET CHOICE
    READ
    CLEAR
    DO CASE
        CASE CHOICE = '1'
            APPEND
        CASE CHOICE = '2'
            EDIT 1
        CASE CHOICE = '3'
            DO CANCEL
    ENDCASE
ENDDO
```

ERASE OR CLEAR COMMAND

The ERASE command in the dBase II program and the CLEAR command in the dBase III program clear the display so that, in this case, the menu can appear on an uncluttered screen. The above commands do not wipe out the database file or the programs. The effect is restricted to the screen.

@ SAY GET AND READ COMMANDS

The next six lines are responsible for putting the menu on the screen. The @ n,m part of the commands tells the cursor to go to the n'th row from the top and m'th column from the left. The SAY 'literal' part of the command is responsible for putting the literal on the screen beginning at the current position of the cursor. When composing the literals, realize that you are communicating with the operator. Use vocabulary that is familiar to that operator. dBase does not care what you place between the quotes.

Pay particular attention to the sixth @ command. The "$+2" part of the statement tells dBase to go down two lines from the last line displayed. In this particular case that would be equivalent to row 12. A "12" would not have been as flexible as "$+2", however, because now when you add additional choices to the menu, the "$+2" automatically adjusts downward whereas a "12" would need to be changed manually. At the end of the sixth @ command is the phrase GET CHOICE. This phrase sets up an area on the screen for the operator to key in a choice from the menu. The operator's response is stored in the memory variable CHOICE whenever the READ command (found on next line) is executed.

DO CASE COMMAND

The DO CASE line informs dBase that a series of CASE statements follow. This command ends with an ENDCASE statement. The optional indentation is once again used to show the range of the command. Each CASE statement is followed by a conditional statement. If the conditional statement is true than the line(s) that follow(s) it (up to the next CASE statement) is (are) executed and then control is passed to the line after the ENDCASE. If the conditional statement is false, the next CASE is tested. The CASE conditional statements correspond to the choices on the menu. At this time you should compare each menu choice to the dBase commands used to implement it.

SUBROUTINES

Note the DO CANCEL statement. This line illustrates the point that it is possible to call another program (making it a subroutine) from a program. The CANCEL program is shown in Figure 13-4.

FIGURE 13-4 CANCEL PROGRAM

```
ACCEPT 'ENTER RECORD # ' TO RECNUM
?
DISPLAY RECORD &RECNUM
?
ACCEPT 'CANCEL THIS RECORD? (Y/N) ' TO ANSWER
IF ANSWER='Y' .OR. ANSWER='y'
    DELETE RECORD &RECNUM
    PACK
ENDIF
```

IF COMMAND

The IF command allows a condition to be tested and when the condition is true, the statements between the IF command and the ENDIF are executed. In the CANCEL program the user has a chance after seeing the record to stop the cancellation. Only if the condition ANSWER='Y' .OR. ANSWER='y' is true does the record get DELETEd and PACKed.

AN IMPROVED MENU

At this point the menu allows the operator to add, modify and cancel records. It would be better if it also allowed at least a simple listing of the file. To make this change, the program must be modified in two places. An additional option should be added to the menu and a corresponding CASE statement should be added to actually implement the option.

Move the cursor down to the last @ SAY GET command and do a CTRL-N to add a blank line above it. On the blank line key:

```
@ 11,20 SAY '4 = LIST FILE'
```

Next move the cursor down to the ENDCASE statement and do three CTRL-N's. Put the following statements on the three blank lines:

```
CASE CHOICE = '4'
    DISPLAY ALL
    WAIT
```

The WAIT command pauses execution of the computer until the operator strikes a key. This keeps the end of the file listing from being removed by the next menu before the operator has a chance to examine it.

In this chapter you have seen that programs can be created and modified using the MODIFY COMMAND command. The DO command is used to execute the program. The commands introduced in the programs of this section that can also be used in the interactive mode include the "?", ERASE and CLEAR commands. The other commands are typically only used in programs. These include: NOTE, ACCEPT, DO WHILE, @ SAY

332

GET, READ, DO CASE, IF, and WAIT.*

    * * * * * * * * * * * * * * *

EXERCISE 13-3

Increase the functionablity of the MENU program even further
by adding "SELECT AND INDEX FILE" to the menu. Remember the
existance of the program INDEXER when implementing the new
choice.

----

* If you are going to leave dBase at this time, remember to
  enter the QUIT command before turning the machine off.

1. Explain two basic modes of operation in dBase. Discuss the advantages and disadvantages of the two modes.

2. The commands NOTE and ? are used to make your program easier to understand. Explain how these commands work.

3. Explain how you can insert a blank line when using MODIFY COMMAND. How can you delete a line?

4. Describe how the ACCEPT command is used.

5. What is the macro function?

6. Explain a loop in computer programming. How can you set up a loop in a dBase program? How can you stop the loop?

7. What dBase command can be used to clear the display on the screen?

8. Explain the commands used to place a literal on the screen.

9. Describe how you can set up an area on the screen for the operator to key in a choice from the menu? When is the operator"s response read by the program?

10. Explain how the DO CASE command works.

11. Describe the function of the WAIT command in a dBase program.

12. Write a program that produces a small management report showing the average percent markup on the liquor inventory file. (Hint: the "?" command can be used to output literals and the contents of memory variables.)

13. In dBase II write a program called MODSTRUC that safely modifies the structure of a file containing data. The program should ask the user two things: 1. whether he plans to rename a field or make some other change, 2. what file should be modified? (See problem 33 at the end of chapter 12.)

14. dBase does not contain an easy way to do subscripting. The macro function, however, does allow a form of subscripting. Execute the following program and explain the results.

```
STORE 1 TO XNUMERIC
DO WHILE XNUMERIC < 10
    STORE STR(XNUMERIC,1) TO XCHARACTER
    STORE XNUMERIC*XNUMERIC TO SQUARE&XCHARACTER
    STORE XNUMERIC+1 TO XNUMERIC
ENDDO
DISPLAY MEMORY
```

15. It is often desirable to scan an entire file under program control. The following general form can be used as a guide:

```
dBase II                        dBase III

USE filename                    USE filename
DO WHILE .NOT. EOF              DO WHILE .NOT. EOF()
        :                               :
    SKIP                            SKIP
ENDDO                           ENDDO
```

Use the general form above to write a program that reads the CHECKS file (created in problem 12 at end of chapter 11) and maintains the current balance field.

16. Write a menu driven system that maintains the GRADES file discussed in problem 11 at the end of chapter 11. You should be able to request various reports from the menu.

17. Write a menu driven system that maintains the POSSESS file created in problem 10 at the end of chapter 11. The system should produce at least two reports.

18. The program called JOINER uses the SELECT and JOIN commands to create a temporary file that includes information from both the PERSON and PAYROLL files. Investigate the commands SELECT and JOIN by using the help facility of dBase and/or by using a dBase manual. Execute the program JOINER and study its code. Modify the JOINER program so that it accepts the names of the files to be joined and any other necessary information

from the operator. After you are done, the operator should be able to use your program in place of remembering the syntax for the JOIN command.

19. The program called UPDATER uses the UPDATE command (and in dBase III the SELECT command) to transfer raise information from the RAISE file to the PAYROLL file. Investigate the command UPDATE (and in dBase III the SELECT command) by using the help facility of dBase and/or by using a dBase manual. Execute the program UPDATER and study its code. Modify the UPDATER program so that it accepts the names of files and any other necessary information from the operator. After you are done, the operator should be able to use your program in place of remembering the syntax for the UPDATE command.

20. Compare and contrast the JOIN and UPDATE commands. When should each be used?

21. Write a program that ages the accounts receivable information in the file AR.

22. Write a program that produces a frequency distribution by size of account for the file AR.

23. Write a program that produces a frequency distribution by employee position for the file PAYROLL.

24. Add the field(s) to the LIQINV file that is (are) needed to calculate the inventory turnover rate. Using your imagination put reasonable numbers in the field or fields. Next write a program that produces an inventory report in order by turnover rate.

PART IV: WORDPROCESSING

AN OVERVIEW OF WORDSTAR

CHAPTER 14

WordStar, developed by MicroPro, is the best selling and most popular word processing software package currently on the market. Since its introduction in 1978, WordStar and its various revisions has become the defacto standard against which others are compared. However, the Lotus Development Corp., developers of Lotus 1-2-3 and Symphony, and Ashton-Tate, developers of Framework, each have integrated packages that include word processing. In the future, it is very likely that business professionals will be using one of these integrated software packages for word processing. The purpose of this chapter is to introduce you to word processing on the personal computer. All word processing software have similar types of commands. The WordStar commands discussed here will be similar to those of any new software that may you may be using in the future. Thus, while WordStar is specifically being discussed, the knowledge that you gain will be transportable to your specific software.

WordStar is a screen-oriented, "what you see is what you get", word processing package with text displayed on the monitor substantially like the printed version. The only differences are a few special printing codes that appear on the screen but are not printed, i.e. they are only for WordStar's use in printing. The program is sufficiently flexible to be used with most printers, requiring only that you specify the particular brand of printer you are using.

WordStar is completely menu-driven requiring only that you learn the major commands necessary to access the appropriate sub-menus. Each main menu can be displayed on the top third of the screen using help level 3. The main menu is displayed immediately upon entering WordStar. (See Figure 14-1.) It provides single-key commands that allow you to open a new file, return to a previously saved file for editing, change the default disk drive (the "logged disk drive" in the words of WordStar), set the help level that will be displayed on the screen, or even run a separate program or application, without leaving WordStar. Also, the main menu contains several combination keys that allow you to print a file, format the text for special printing characters, save a file, or ask for help. The combination keys begin with depressing and holding down the control key (on the left side of the keyboard.) The second key is typed while still holding down the control key. After selecting the main command with key combinations, a subcommand is selected by pressing a single letter. Thus in the save and resume command Ctrl KS, Ctrl K selects the main commands, and S, the subcommand. Using WordStar's full capabilities require learning what the various main and sub menus do. However, the default settings are normally sufficient, thus even the beginner may easily use WordStar.

FIGURE 14-1 MAIN MENU

```
   A:WSSAMPLE  PAGE 1 LINE 1 COL 01
                 < < <     M A I N   M E N U     > > >
      --Cursor Movement--      : -Delete- :   -Miscellaneous-  : -Other  Menus-
  ^S char left ^D char right :^G  char  : ^I Tab    ^B Reform : (from Main only)
  ^A word left ^F word right :DEL chr lf: ^V INSERT ON/OFF    :^J Help  ^K Block
  ^E line  up  ^X line down  :^T word rt:^L Find/Replce again:^Q Quick ^P Print
      --Scrolling--          :^Y  line  :RETURN End paragraph:^O Onscreen
  ^Z line down ^W line up    :          : ^N Insert a RETURN :
  ^C screen up ^R screen down:          : ^U Stop a command  :
      L!----!----!----!----!----!----!----!----!----!------------------R
```

                                                                    .
                                                                    .
                                                                    .
                                                                    .
                                                                    .
                                                                    .
                                                                    .
                                                                    .
                                                                    .
                                                                    .

1HELP   2bldfac 3supsct 4subsct 5UNDLIN 6dblstk 7BEGBLK 8ENDBLK 9BEGFIL 10ENDFIL

LOADING WORDSTAR

WordStar is loaded by inserting the properly installed WordStar diskette in the A disk drive and typing WS. With an autoexec file, WordStar will be entered directly upon booting the system. The default disk drive is the A drive. The storage diskette is the one you use to save your text files and is kept in the B disk drive. For convenience, it is normally advisable to change the current "logged" disk drive from A to B. To accomplish this, simply type the letter L and answer as instructed by typing B: and the enter key. If the logged disk drive is not changed, you will have to enter the disk drive prefix (e.g., b:filename) each time a file is loaded or printed.

Like all DOS files, names of WordStar files on the IBM PC are limited to eight characters. File names should be selected to both fit into the eight character limit and to describe the contents of the file. In addition, a three letter filetype may be added to the file. The filetype may be used to group types of WordStar projets, e.g. LET for letter, MEM for MEMOS, etc.

SETTING THE MARGINS

The default margins provide for a 65 character line which is acceptable for most purposes. However, if you wish to expand or contract the text to different margins, you may do so. Use the OL (FUCTION KEY 3) and OR (FUNCTION KEY 4) commands to set the left or right margins. To use the function keys, simply move the cursor to the desired location for each margin and press FUNCTION KEY 3, F3, for the left margin and FUNCTION KEY 4, F4, for the right margin.

WordStar allows you to set the space between lines of text. The default setting depends upon which version of WordStar you are using. The later version uses double spacing. If triple spacing is desired, the user must so specify. The command to do so is OS, followed by specifying 1-9 line spacing--for example, 1 is single spacing and 2 is double spacing. If the line spacing is not specified at the beginning, the document will have to be reformed (discussed below) one paragraph at a time to obtain the desired line spacing.

MOVING AROUND IN A WORDSTAR DOCUMENT FILE

The IBM keyboard supports most of the common movements within a WordStar file. The four arrow keys at the right of the keyboard on the number pad move the cursor one character in the direction of the arrow. If the cursor is at the end of the line, the right arrow moves it to the beginning of the next line; if the cursor is at the beginning of the line, the left arrow key moves the cursor to the end of the previous line. If the cursor is at the end of a line, the up and down arrow keys move the cursor to the end of the previous or following line. Likewise, if the cursor is at the beginning of the line, the up and down arrow keys move the cursor to the beginning of the previous or following lines. The NUM LOCK key turns the number pad on or off. The number pad must be off in order for the arrow keys to move the cursor. WordStar does not indicate whether or not the number pad is on; thus, you are required to experiment to determine if the number pad is on or off.

The other keys on the IBM keyboard take the place of several of the more commonly used keystrokes. The HOME and END keys on the IBM keyboard, take the place of the QE and QX commands and will move the cursor to the top edge or lower edge of the text displayed on the screen. The backspace key operates just as the left arrow key, that is, it moves the cursor to the left, but it does NOT delete the character. The PAGE UP and PAGE DOWN keys move the cursor up and down the text one page, i.e 14 lines of text assuming a full help screen at the top of the screen. The INSERT key will turn on or off the insert mode. While the insert mode is on, typing will result in the character being inserted into the text. If INSERT is off, typing replaces the text previously entered. The DELETE key deletes the character to the LEFT of the cursor.

Several useful key combinations are available to help the user move throughout the text. These are used in conjunction with the control key marked "Ctrl" on the left side of the keyboard and commonly indicated by the caret. In this chapter, Ctrl will be used which the control key is to be pressed. Those useful in moving throughout the text are listed below.

Ctrl F   moves the cursor forward one word at a time

Ctrl A   moves the cursor backward (aft?) one word at a time.

Ctrl QS   moves the cursor to the left end of the line.

Ctrl QD   moves the cursor to the right end of the line.

Ctrl K 0-9, marks the text with numbers 0-9. These locations may be reached directly by typing Q number 0-9. This ability is useful in addressing long text or documents.

The keystroke combination Ctrl G will delete the character to the right of the cursor; Ctrl T, deletes the "word" to the right of the cursor; and Ctrl Y, deletes the entire current line, i.e. the location of the cursor.

Frequently, in using word processing, the user will need to insert a word or thought that extends the line beyond the screen area. While the paragraph may be reformed, as discussed below, it may also be split into two lines. To achieve the splitting, simply move the cursor to the desired split, set INSERT ON, by pressing the INS key, and strike the ENTER key. The text to the right of the cursor will be moved to the next line. The cursor will remain at its current location. To rejoin the spit line, press the DELETE key.

REFORMING A PARAGRAPH

WordStar right justifies each line in the text, i.e. each line is forced to line up at the right margin. Right justification results in spaces distributed throughout the text. If additional words or letters are added or others deleted, the right margin will no longer be right-justified. To reform the paragraph, or to re-establish the right justification, the paragraph is REFORMED by typing the command Ctrl B. Unfortunately, each paragraph must be reformed individually, one at a time.

FILE AND BLOCK OPERATIONS

Two of the most important features of word processing are represented by WordStar's FILE operations and BLOCK moves. FILE operations concern the interface of the current primary storage, RAM, with disk storage. WordStar files may be saved to disk storage and recalled at a later time to be printed or further edited. The commands relating to saving a file are listed below: Refer to the Block Menu in Figure 14-2.

Ctrl KD   Saves a file to disk storage but stays in WordStar in order to perform further operations in WordStar, e.g. print the just saved file.

Ctrl KX   Saves a file to disk storage and exits WordStar to the operating system, DOS. From DOS other programs may be loaded into primary memory.

Ctrl KS   Saves a file to disk storage but remains in the current file for further operation on the same file. The major use of this command is to save the file while it is still being worked on, always advisable given the potential for a power interruption and loss of RAM.

Ctrl KQ   Quits the files. Sometimes it is better to discard the editing that has been done and simply start over again. With this command, the current file is simply abandoned. If it has previously been saved, the saved file is not affected and may form the beginning of a new attempt.

FIGURE 14-2 BLOCK MENU

```
^K        A:WSSAMPLE  PAGE 1 LINE 1 COL 01
                      < < <    B L O C K   M E N U    > > >
-Saving Files- : -Block Operations- : -File Operations- :   -Other Menus-
S Save & resume : B  Begin  K  End   : R  Read  P  Print  :  (from Main only)
D Save--done    : H  Hide / Display  : O  Copy  E  Rename : ^J Help  ^K Block
X Save & exit   : C  Copy   Y  Delete: J  Delete          : ^Q Quick ^P Print
Q Abandon file  : V  Move   W  Write : -Disk  Operations- : ^O Onscreen
-Place Markers- : N  Column  now OFF :L Change logged disk! Space Bar returns
0-9 set/hide 0-9!                    :F Directory now OFF : you to Main Menu.
        L!----!----!----!----!----!----!----!----!----!-----------------R
                                                                      .
                                                                      .
                                                                      .
                                                                      .
                                                                      .
                                                                      .
                                                                      .
                                                                      .
1HELP    2bldfac 3supsct 4subsct 5UNDLIN 6dblstk 7BEGBLK 8ENDBLK 9BEGFIL 10ENDFIL
```

Other BLOCK commands are used to identify a block of text that is then moved or copied from one part of the text to another. By using this command, paragraphs, sentences, or even words may be moved throughout the text in order to edit the text to the desired form. The commands are used as follows:

FUNCTION KEY 7 is used to mark the beginning of the block that is to be moved or copied. Function key 7 is used in the place of Ctrl KB.

FUNCTION KEY 8 is used to mark the end of the block to be moved or copied. Function key 8 is used in the place of Ctrl KK.

The cursor is moved to the location within the text where you want the text moved or copied. With the cursor at the desired location, Ctrl KV is typed.

One of the more confusing aspects about the move operation is that either the markers appear on the screen or the screen darkens the area marked to be moved. While a command is available to "hide" these markers (Ctrl KH), they will nonetheless remain in the document. However, they will not be printed, thus, they are truly just for the use of WordStar and can be rightly ignored.

While the normal move or copy operation is performed on lines, WordStar Version 3.x will allow columns to be moved or copied. The command is Ctrl KN. This changes the block moving capabilities of WordStar to columns rather than lines.

IBM FUNCTION KEYS

The IBM PC, and PC compatibles, have ten function keys on the left side of the keyboard. These function keys have been programmed to perform some of the more common keystrokes. (Note, the function keys may be redefined during the installation of your WordStar if you desire.) The function keys are listed below and the default commands they represent are explained.

FUNCTION KEY 1 Ctrl JH Sets the level of HELP that will appear at the top of the screen. The default level is Level 3, which is a listing of all the major commands. The beginner will find this level very useful.

FUNCTION KEY 2	Ctrl OG	Paragraph Tab allows you to temporarily reset your left margin. Pressing Function Key 2 once sets the left margin to the first tab stop. Each successive pressing of F2 or Ctrl OG moves the ruler line one additional tab stop to the right.
FUNCTION KEY 3	Ctrl OL	Set the left margin. Move the cursor to the desired location for the left margin and type Function Key 3.
FUNCTION KEY 4	Ctrl OR	Set the right margin. Move the cursor to the desired location and type Function Key 4.
FUNCTION KEY 5	Ctrl PS	Marks the text for underlining or underscoring. While the S will appear on the screen it will not be printed. Again, it is only for WordStar's use to indicated where to begin and end with the underlining. Type Function Key 5 before and after the word or phrase you desire to have underlined.
FUNCTION KEY 6	Ctrl PB	Sets the printer to print in BOLD TYPE the word or character that follows. The mark must be placed before and after the item to be printed in bold type.
FUNCTION KEY 7	Ctrl KB	Mark the beginning point for a move or copy block operation. Simply type Function Key 7 before the part of the text you wish to move.
FUNCTION KEY 8	Ctrl KK	Marks the end of the portion of the text you wish to move or copy in a block operation. Simply type Function Key 8 at the end of the text to be moved or copied. Once the beginning and end has been specified, move the cursor to the

location that the text is to be moved or copied to and type KV to complete the move and KC to complete the copy.

FUNCTION KEY 9 Ctrl QC   Moves the cursor to the END of the file.

FUNCTION KEY 10 Ctrl QR   Moves the cursor to the TOP of the file.

PRINTING A WORDSTAR FILE

A WordStar file is only printed from disk storage. In order to print a file, the file must first be saved to disk storage. The file may be printed from the BLOCK commands or directly from the main menu with the PRINT command. The default options are generally sufficient for most print requirements.

Regardless of the approach to printing the file, WordStar will ask the following questions. Frequently, the default settings will be appropriate for printing the file. If this is the case, you may type the "ESCAPE" key, upper left-hand corner of the keyboard, and by-pass all of the questions.

1. "NAME OF FILE TO PRINT?" Again, it must be remembered that WordStar will print the file only from the disk storage. Therefore, if the user is working on a file, it must be saved before it is printed or none of the recent changes will be included in the printed copy.

2. "DISK FILE OUTPUT? Y/N" Normally your answer is No and this is the default answer. Thus, in most cases you will simply hit the enter or return key.

3. START AT PAGE NUMBER? The default number is one. To start at 1, simply type the return. Often, you will not want the first page of the text to be numbered, e.g. a letter or memo. The number on the first page may be suppressed by using the DOT command ".op", which must be entered at the top of the file to be printed. (Use of DOT commands is discussed further below.) Question 3, gives you an opportunity to begin printing at a page other than the first page. Thus, if you desired to print only pages 3 to 8 of a twelve page paper, you could elect to start printing at page 3 at this point. To stop at page 8, the next question must be answered 8.

4. "STOP AFTER PAGE NUMBER?" Normally, you will desire to stop at the last page of the document; thus, the default is the last page. This is entered by typing the RETURN. However, if you desired to only print a portion of the document, you may do so by typing the page number at which you wish to stop in answer to this question.

5. "USE FORM FEEDS? Y/N" If you are using single sheets of stationary, perhaps with letterhead, you must answer NO at this point. Form feeds are faster and should be used for all draft or file copies. If further processing is to be performed, e.g. photocopying, form feed paper may suffice for the final copy. The default setting is Yes.

6. "SUPPRESS PAGE FORMATTING? Y/N" Page formatting refers to the ruler line at the top of the WordStar screen which inserts appropriate page breaks. Normally, you would want page formatting, thus the default answer is no. That is, yes you do want page formatting. Typing the return will get you there.

7. "PAUSE FOR PAPER CHANGE BETWEEN PAGES? Y/N" The default setting is NO. If you are using form feed paper or have an automatic single sheet feeder, you will not want to pause between pages. However, if you are manually feeding single sheets to the printer, you will need to pause between pages; hence, answer YES.

8. "READY PRINTER, HIT RETURN." The printer must be on and the paper should be aligned to the top of the page. If the paper is not aligned, the page breaks will be out of alignment. The results do not look good.

DOT COMMANDS

Through the use of DOT commands, you have a variety of enhancements available, the most useful of which are listed below. Dot commands look unusual; but it must be remembered that they exist for WordStar to read, not for human eyes. The Dot commands must begin at the left margin with a period. The period is followed by letters that have special meanings to WordStar. Only DOT commands may be on the line. Frequently, these command will be placed at the top of the file. Some may be at the top of other pages.

DOT COMMAND	FUNCTION OF DOT COMMAND
.cw	CHARACTER WIDTH This command sets the character width, thus it allows you to set the size of type--12 characters per inch is the default size. To set the width of the character, type .cw# beginning in column one. To obtain 10 characters per inch, type .cw10.
.op	OMIT PAGE NUMBERS This command, entered at the top of page one followed by .pn2 at the top of page 2 will result in the page number being suppressed on only page one.
.pn #	Specifies the page number at which WordStar is to begin.
.pa	START NEW PAGE This command will move to the top of the next page regardless of the amount of room left on the page.
.he	PAGE HEADING With .HE you may enter a header that will be printed at the top of every page. Frequently the name of the company will be printed on every page, this Dot command will do it.
.fo	PAGE FOOTER Similar to Header, except at bottom of page.
#	Use to enter page number. It will print the current page number. May be added to a Header or Footer.

Figure 14-3 lists the other menus that are available with WordStar. The key to their use is to press the control key and the MENU Letter (K for Block, O for On Screen, Q for Quick, P for Print) followed by the letter of the feature that you desire. For example to underscore a word with WordStar type Ctrl PS before and after the word. On the screen it will appear as Ctrl S word Ctrl S, but it will print with word underlined.

Recall the general guide to using the personal computer is to not be afraid to try anything new. The productivity gains are worth the risk. Of course the collorary to this rule is to back-up your work before you try something new, just in case.

FIGURE 14-3 OTHER WORDSTAR MENUS

```
^P        A:WSSAMPLE  PAGE 1 LINE 1 COL 01
                  < < <   P R I N T   M E N U   > > >
     ------ Special  Effects ------- ! -Printing  Changes- ! -Other  Menus-
     (begin and end) !  (one time each) ! A Alternate pitch  ! (from Main only)
  B Bold D Double ! H Overprint char  ! N Standard pitch   !^J Help  ^K Block
  S Underscore    ! O Non-break space ! C Printing pause   !^Q Quick ^P Print
  X Strikeout     ! F Phantom space   ! Y Other ribbon color!^O Onscreen
  V Subscript     ! G Phantom rubout  !  --User  Patches-- !Space Bar returns
  T Superscript   ! RET Overprint line ! Q(1) W(2) E(3) R(4) !you to Main Menu.
         L!----!----!----!----!----!----!----!----!----!------------------R
                                                                          .
                                                                          .
                                                                          .
                                                                          .
                                                                          .
                                                                          .

1HELP    2bldfac 3supsct 4subsct 5UNDLIN 6dblstk 7BEGBLK 8ENDBLK 9BEGFIL 10ENDFIL


^Q        A:WSSAMPLE  PAGE 1 LINE 1 COL 01
                  < < <   Q U I C K   M E N U   > > >
     ---Cursor Movement---  ! -Delete- ! --Miscellaneous-- ! --Other  Menus--
  S left side  D right side !Y line  rt!F Find text in file ! (from Main only)
  E top scrn   X bottom scrn!DEL lin 1f!A Find & Replace    !^J Help  ^K Block
  R top file   C end file   !          !L Find Misspelling  !^Q Quick ^P Print
  B top block  K end block  !          !Q Repeat command or !^O Onscreen
  0-9 marker   Z down  W up !          !  key  until  space !Space Bar returns
  P previous   V last Find or Block    !  bar  or other key !you to Main Menu.
         L!----!----!----!----!----!----!----!----!----!------------------R
                                                                          .
                                                                          .
                                                                          .
                                                                          .
                                                                          .
                                                                          .

1HELP    2bldfac 3supsct 4subsct 5UNDLIN 6dblstk 7BEGBLK 8ENDBLK 9BEGFIL 10ENDFIL


^O        A:WSSAMPLE  PAGE 1 LINE 1 COL 01
                  < < <   O N S C R E E N   M E N U   > > >
     -Margins & Tabs-  ! -Line  Functions- ! --More Toggles-- ! -Other  Menus-
  L Set left margin !C Center text    !J Justify   now OFF ! (from Main only)
  R Set right margin!S Set line spacing !V Vari-Tabs now ON !^J Help  ^K Block
  X Release margins !                  !H Hyph-help now OFF !^Q Quick ^P Print
  I Set  N Clear tab!   ---Toggles---  !E Soft hyph now OFF !^O Onscreen
  G Paragraph tab   !W Wrd wrap now ON !D Prnt disp now ON !Space Bar returns
  F Ruler from line !T Rlr line now ON !P Pge break now ON !you to Main Menu.
         L!----!----!----!----!----!----!----!----!----!------------------R
                                                                          .
                                                                          .
                                                                          .
                                                                          .
                                                                          .
                                                                          .

1HELP    2bldfac 3supsct 4subsct 5UNDLIN 6dblstk 7BEGBLK 8ENDBLK 9BEGFIL 10ENDFIL
```

Load WordStar by typing ws at the DOS prompt. Change the logged disk drive from the default drive of A, to drive B by pressing L followed by B: in response to the request. From the Main Menu, select D (by pressing D), that is, open a document file. In response to the question, What is the filename of the file to be edited?, enter WSEX1.

The file WSEX1 contains a copy of Lincoln's famous Gettysburg Address. However, some errors have been made (Colonel Beaugard type it I believe.) Please correct the errors. If you need to look it up, shame on you.

Add one of the following sayings as prompted at the bottom of the Gettysburg Address.

"A beard creates lice, not brains."   Ammianus

"A learned person is not learned in everything; but the capable person is capable in everything, even in what he is ignorant of."   Montaigne

"No one knows what he can do till he tries"

                                        Publilius Syrus